WHITE DEATH

Russia's War on Finland, 1939–40

WHITE DEATH

Russia's War on Finland, 1939–40

Robert Edwards

WEIDENFELD & NICOLSON

First published in Great Britain in 2006
by Weidenfeld & Nicolson

1 3 5 7 9 10 8 6 4 2

A CIP catalogue record for this book
is available from the British Library.

ISBN-13 978 0 297 84630 2
ISBN-10 0 297 84630 2

Printed in Great Britain by Clays Ltd, St Ives plc

Weidenfeld & Nicolson
The Orion Publishing Group Ltd
Orion House, 5 Upper Saint Martin's Lane, London,
WC2H 9EA

www.orionbooks.co.uk

Contents

List of Maps

List of Photographs

Mannerheim as Chairman of the Defence Council, 1937.

King Gustav of Sweden (left), Erkko and President Kallio at the Stockholm Conference, 1939 (IWM).

Väinö Tanner, Paasikivi and Baron Yrjo Koskinen depart for Moscow, October 1939 (IWM).

A 'Lotta' unit preparing food at a Finnish reservist camp, October 1939 (IWM).

A passenger bus takes a direct hit, Helsinki, December 1939 (Photo Pressens Bild, Stockholm).

A Red Baltic Fleet bomber, one of many downed over the Isthmus. It would be recycled very soon (IWM).

Life on the Mannerheim Line (IWM).

Morning prayers (IWM).

The northern front at Salla, where Wallenius had, early in the war, distinguished himself (IWM).

The terrain at Tolvajärvi.

The monochrome landscape of the Winter War.

A Finnish machine-gun crew on the Karelian Isthmus, January 1940 (IWM).

A Finnish mobile kitchen (IWM).

A column of Red Army POWs after Suomussalmi, January 1940 (IWM).

Two Finns walk past some of the remnants of the Red Army's 44th Division after retaking the field. Suomussalmi, January 1940 (IWM).

Karelian refugees prepare to leave their homes, March 1940 (IWM).

Preface

FOR ANY STUDENT OF international relations, let alone those purely military matters that arise from them, the history of Finland is of unique importance in the general European context, let alone the narrower Nordic one. This book examines the short, savage war that erupted between the Soviet Union and Finland in late 1939 – the Winter War.

Counter-factual history is an amusing parlour game, but seldom anything more. To speculate upon the great what-ifs of the past is generally a fruitless or frustrating exercise, but the first question that *naturally* arises when surveying the course and outcome of the Winter War is one of particularly high impact. Had this unique conflict led to a different outcome, would Operation Barbarossa have even been possible? For once, perhaps, that question is worth asking. Certainly, Soviet policy with regard to Finland was intended to forestall such an event as Barbarossa and as such it clearly failed – but why? How on earth did the largest force ever assembled, with total numerical and technical superiority in every arm, manage not to annihilate one of the smallest?

My own interest in this subject goes back to the 1970s, when, as an undergraduate reading International Politics, I found myself studying the Russian foreign policy of 'forward defence' and, not unnaturally, the role played by Finland in defining (and serially frustrating) that policy. The price it paid for doing so emerged rapidly, if not necessarily very clearly. This is partly due to the fragmented nature of published documents, given the unique nature of Russo-Finnish relations, which very often functioned at a highly personal level. Although there was little love lost between the two cultures as a whole, there is ample evidence that the ebb and flow of actual relationships played an extraordinary function in the broader bilateral one. The tangled but very intimate nature of these matters even gave rise, post-1945, to a new word – *Finlandization*, more or less defined as the attempt to exercise control over the internal affairs of a neighbouring nation-state without actually possessing its territory or even colonizing it.

The present work is an attempt to account for the necessity of such a policy, and to explain how it came into being – to examine the attempt made by the Soviet Union on the last day of November 1939 to effectively annexe the territory of Finland by invasion, why they failed, and to introduce the reader to some of the consequences.

This is a complex European story – the United States plays only a marginal (and less than triumphant) role in it. The painfully convoluted development of Anglo-French relations with both the Soviet Union and greater Scandinavia are basic to it, but at the core of the story is that uniquely tough body of people, the Finnish nation.

Robert Edwards
SOMERSET, 2006

Introduction
An Awkward Little Country

When you have a hammer, all problems look like nails.

Proverb

THE GREAT NORTHERN CRISIS of the winter of 1939–40, that period of uncertainty triggered by the Soviet invasion of Finland, was a unique and dislocating event during the first full year of the Second World War. It was by any measure a one-sided struggle, involving at its height well over one million Red Army soldiers against rather fewer Finns, and yet the Finnish fought the biggest army on earth to a virtual standstill, on occasion inflicting such shocking casualties that Stalin started to face the prospect of military as well as political defeat.

There was no event during the 'phoney war' period that served to question more the organization, structure, motivation and effectiveness of not only the Red Army, but also the Western Allies, who, although officially uninvolved in the actual fighting, none the less viewed the Finnish war as an opportunity to 'change the subject'. The attempts of a split Supreme War Council to manage its way through a situation that was on the one hand a tremendous *cause célèbre* (even a *casus belli*), but on the other clearly a hopeless undertaking, revealed more than anything else the total unsuitability of these men to make effective war in either Britain or France. This failure of policy led to the immediate collapse of the Daladier government in France, and later – after the Anglo-French-Polish Finland relief expedition was given more limited objectives in Norway – the fall of Neville Chamberlain. Chamberlain's eclipse did not, of course, take place until the war in Finland was over, and the plan, originally conceived as an expeditionary effort that would both aid the Finns and (more importantly) cut off German access to Scandinavian iron ore, was put into effect a month later with famous results – the first encounter between Allied troops and the Wehrmacht in Norway.

The remarkable 'shadowing' of the Berlin regime by the Soviet one is evident from the outset of the story, and the attempt by the Red Army in Finland to 'outdo' the German attack on Poland – even down to the creation of a border incident to justify invasion – is chilling in its cynicism, even given what we now know about Stalin's regime.

The most notable aspect of this story, however, is not Anglo-French incompetence, or the manifest failures of a blundering, lobotomized Red Army, or even the signal uselessness of the League of Nations (rather a given, by then); rather, it is the extraordinary resourcefulness and resolution of the Finns themselves. For 105 days, the tiny, under-equipped Finnish armed forces fought the Red Army (and themselves) to a standstill; by March 1940 the Finns had nothing left and were short of ammunition, food, sleep and, critically, people – Europe, and particularly Britain, marvelled at their absolute refusal to surrender. It was in all ways a prefiguration of the 'Spirit of the Blitz', a phenomenon that Britain has traditionally made its own, but in truth was born in Helsinki, Turku, Tampere, Kekisalmi, Viipuri and Sortavala, place names that, for a few months, became familiar to those who followed the highly imaginative, but largely inaccurate reports and dispatches that filled the front pages of the Western press.

There were other aspects to this extraordinary war that made it quite unique; the way in which the Red Army was assessed – incorrectly, as it turned out – by observers, particularly the Germans, who in a sense drew what they wanted from the embarrassing early failures of the Russian war machine. The German High Command came to its conclusions about the Red Army far too soon – bizarrely, it did not listen sufficiently to its Finnish counterpart, who had rapidly developed, at the combat level, a robust respect for the individual Russian soldier.

Inevitably, by invading in 1939, the Soviet Union turned Finland from a disinterested, isolated but essentially neutral neighbour into an enemy (with a massive border). German opportunism (and a military/economic 'protection' racket) rapidly converted Finland into a co-belligerent for Hitler's great doomed undertaking, the smashing of the Soviet State by Operation Barbarossa in the summer of 1941. Without the cooperation of the Finns, who shared the longest western border with the Soviet Union, Barbarossa was not technically possible as it initially stood.

And yet the core stated objectives of the original Russian attack – the provision for the defence of Leningrad against German attack being the main one – were not the basic motivations for Finland to join this fight; indeed, the refusal of the Finns to participate in the destruction of the city became a cause of serious friction between Helsinki and Berlin later in the larger war. Finland merely wanted its territory back; it had fought for it twice already, after all.

Perhaps the most remarkable aspect of the whole short conflict was the complete inability of any other great power to coordinate itself in a manner that could be of constructive use to the Finns, particularly the United States of America. President Roosevelt, hampered in his objectives by his Secretary of State as well as the powerful isolationist lobby, struggled (not very hard) throughout the duration of the war to provide assistance. In this, he utterly failed. However, Roosevelt's experience in the matter of the Finnish war would stand him in good stead when it came to providing assistance of a more useful kind later on, particularly for Great Britain and even, with great irony, for the Soviet Union. In the former case, he even employed the same imagery, of the neighbour's house aflame.

As a direct result of the Winter War in Finland, the Soviet Union became and remained isolated from every great power save Germany. By its conduct, the Soviet Union had revealed two very important characteristics about itself; the first being that the regime had no qualms concerning the acquisition of territory (in total contradiction to publicly stated policy) and the second that it was, despite the signature of the August 1939 non-aggression pact and the shared carve-up of Poland, still terrified of a German attack – correctly, as events turned out.

When that invasion came the result, famously, was the near destruction of the Red Army itself. We can only speculate as to what would have happened if the Soviet Union had had to face the Nazi invasion in the same military state it had been in in September 1939. Finland's Winter War did not, of course, change all that, but the shortcomings of the Red Army as it attempted to simply roll over its western neighbour revealed some terrifying truths, the most obvious being that it was not ready for war. This was ironic, given that the Red Army under Georgi Zhukov had delivered a very competent victory over the Imperial Japanese Army the previous September. But that had been an engagement fought over entirely different terrain and against a radically different enemy, in radically different weather.

Inevitably, the Winter War invites comparison with the Spanish Civil War, in so far as it nearly became a proxy conflict, but in truth the differences were vast. Anglo-French policy was also different – from strict(-ish) non-intervention (which included on the part of the French the questionable tactic of interning members of the Comintern's International Brigades as they straggled back over the Pyrenees) it now segued into a weird hybrid, which outwardly supported the Finns while at the same time used the huge public sympathy which that nation's plight generated at home to justify armed intervention on the Scandinavian peninsula for an entirely different reason.

BY THE TIME OF the *Anschluss* of 1938, the Soviet Union had become conservative, even imperial, in its outlook. It had achieved great power status without major conquest, but only because all its foreign efforts had failed; all it had had to do was survive its own gestation and the vengeance of those it had threatened, whose friends it had killed. To many in the West, whether fellow-travellers, class warriors or merely wishful liberal dupes, the USSR had performed a great miracle. Outwardly, of course, this was so – the Russian project had worked. It had become an economic giant; by Western standards an export-driven money machine. Internally, though, it was clear that this was a nation literally and metaphorically sacrificing its own children. Further, it was generally perceived that the Workers' and Peasants' Red Army was the most well-equipped and best-led force on the planet, a military machine easily the equal of the 'economic titan' that had forged it. Until 1937, this was probably true.

On the north-western border of the USSR lay Finland, an equally young nation-state and equally wrapped up in a project of its own – the creation of a socially democratic and mixed economy. Finland had declared, and then fought for, its independence from Russia at the earliest opportunity that the Russian Revolution had offered her, and a bloody civil war had been the result. The 'Whites', under the military leadership of Baron Carl Gustav Mannerheim, had won, and this remarkable soldier had suppressed the forces of Bolshevism with a Cromwellian ruthlessness, which left the country bruised, angry at itself, but basically whole. The civil war in Finland had, though, offered a dreadful hint of what was to come in greater Russia. By the time the great political crisis – the dictators versus the democracies – arrived, Finland, still gasping from its narrow escape, had taken its place in the ranks of the most advanced nations of Europe.

This had been a gruelling birth for a new nation and of course costly; economically the Finns had since focused on the repayment of the huge foreign loans that they had been forced to assume in order to rebuild their country; by the time of Hitler's *Anschluss*, (and even before) they had repaid nearly 90 per cent of the principal, even through the teeth of the global slump. Many other nations had not. Repudiation of obligation was simply not a notion that seemed to occur to the Finns. This was an extraordinary achievement (probably unparalleled in economic history, and a course that many nations had eschewed, preferring to default), but as nothing compared to the military accomplishments that the Finnish would shortly demonstrate.

Finland, as a 'value-added' commodity-driven export economy (and a small one) was well placed to profit from the general economic upturn that took place from the spring of 1932 (Dow Jones Industrial Average: 44) and so prospered by comparison with its more industrialized and commodity-short associates and neighbours, particularly Germany. But as Germany started to re-arm, followed by the USSR, Finland remained bent to its task of servicing a crippling level of foreign debt and polishing to perfection its own pet project (and a useful hard currency earner): preparing for the 1940 Olympic Games, to be held in Helsinki. A splendid stadium complex, the work of Finland's advanced, dreamy and minimalist architects, was nearly ready; nothing would be too good for the hordes of interested visitors who would flock there. Finnair (established in 1924) had already expanded to carry the expected traffic. None of the Fascistic grandeur of the 1936 Olympics would be present; Finland had almost solved its 'right-wing' problem by then. Finland was working, it paid its debts, it was clean, bright, new and – most important to the economic environment of the 1930s – solvent. The nation looked forward to giving the world a guided tour.

Within two years of that annexation of Austria, however, Finland's economy was in smoking ruins; over 25,000 of its people were dead and many more were injured or dispossessed. It lost 11 per cent of its territory and 30 per cent of its economic assets.

The Stranger from a Sunken World

Now, the General is the protector of the state. If this protection is all-embracing, the state will surely be strong; if defective, the state will certainly be weak.

Sun Tzu

HELSINKI, 4 JUNE 1937: As birthday parties went, this one was rather unusual and had clearly been choreographed down to the tiniest detail; it looked like an informal stroll of uniformed notabilities through the packed streets of the Finnish capital, but there was more to it than that. The only potential variable was the weather, which threatened rain, but undeterred by the prospect of damp, the streets and office windows were lined with a largely good-natured crowd of patient well-wishers; Finns are, perforce, used to unpredictable weather. In the event, they need not have worried.

At noon, the man whose anniversary this was stepped through his front door. At six feet two, booted and spurred, his height accentuated by a splendid snow-white fur hat and his upper-body breadth by a chestful of decorations from several grateful nations, he was an impressive figure. Cavalry sabre at his hip and marshal's baton in his white-gloved hand, he was greeted by blushing, reverential maidens in flowing pale blue gowns, who gracefully strewed great bunches of summer blooms in his path.[1] It was a scene of Ruritanian splendour and perhaps one rather untypical of Finland, but calculated to transmit a simple message to a confused and nervous public: all was well. For Field Marshal

Baron Carl Gustaf Emil Mannerheim, 70 today, this occasion marked a return to public life for which this last remaining 'White' general had worked hard. Some whispered, perhaps a little *too* hard.

An event not unlike this, complete with floral tributes, had happened once before, more than nineteen years previously, on 16 May 1918, the day on which modern Finland had been born; that Mannerheim had been the architect of that moment, by his brilliant, authoritative and unorthodox conduct of a savage civil war, was known to all. However, the legacy of that war, a sulphurous resentment on the part of some elements of the working classes, enthusiastically supported by Soviet agitprop, of what they regarded as bourgeois repression of a populist movement, had made for a delicate political tightrope upon which Mannerheim, in the judgement of a traumatized civil administration, had then been considered perhaps unsuitable to step after he had served briefly as regent. In this he had been treated shabbily, but necessarily so, and most of Finland knew it.[2]

Part of this hatred of him by the left was based on experience, for although 'White' Finland had fought with both determination and flair, the aftermath of the struggle had been utterly ghastly. No exact records remain of the tally of 'Reds' who perished in the internment camps, but it certainly ran into the high thousands; those whom the influenza pandemic did not kill starved to death.

Lenin's assessment of the country (in which he had been an *émigré* more than once) had given him high hopes in terms of combining it into the Soviet project. He had written in March 1917: 'Let us not forget that we have, adjoining Petrograd, one of the most advanced countries, a real republican country, Finland, which from 1905 to 1917, under the shelter of the revolutionary battles in Russia, has developed its democracy in conditions of relative peace and won the majority of its people for socialism.'[3] Mannerheim and his scratch army had comprehensively wrecked that.

Gustaf Mannerheim was and is a controversial but most

absorbing figure. To a large section of his 3.8 million countrymen he was the Father of the Nation, this man who had almost single-handedly forged a resolute yeoman army out of a cowed, hungry and terrorized population, equipped it with the bravely captured weapons of its foul and godless enemy and given Bolshevism a sound thrashing, driving it from the land in 1918. To many others of more 'progressive' sentiment, however, he was a monster: Mannerheim the White Butcher, a bemedalled dictator-in-waiting, swaggering and heartless, itching to crush the workers under the heel of his immaculately cobbled riding boot. Perhaps the paradox was best summed up by his decorations – both the Cross of St George, awarded by an appreciative Tsar Nicholas II for fighting the Kaiser, and the Iron Cross from an equally complementary Kaiser for fighting the Russians.[4] A unique achievement, perhaps, but only one of many.

To modern eyes, Mannerheim is a man of apparently bizarre contradictions, but it did not necessarily seem so then. A blood-thirsty big-game hunter who worked tirelessly in the cause of child welfare?[5] Quite normal. A political reactionary who also chaired the Finnish Red Cross? Perfectly natural. Even then, however, he was well-nigh unique in Finland; one who knew him well described him as 'a stranger from a sunken world'.[6] It seems appropriate, for that world had been Tsarist Russia, a place which Mannerheim had come to love more deeply than almost anything. 'Socialism,' he declared, 'was incapable of defending Democracy.' And yet democracy itself rather pained him; a tedious process, which seemed too often to thwart the efforts of well-intentioned (and well-bred) men. He had emerged in Finland (in full dress uniform) serene but unsmiling from the wreckage of the Revolution in the middle of December 1917, his worldly goods packed neatly into two valises and carried by a faithful Russian batman on the journey from the Finland Station in Petrograd. He had simply taken the train home. He'd also taken one glance at the Revolution and decided that it was not for him: 'It disgusted me to see generals carrying their own kit.'[7]

THIS BOOK IS NOT a biography of Carl Gustaf Mannerheim, for there are several already.[8] Yet he is an extraordinarily important figure and one often overlooked, partly because the complexities of his motivation are extremely hard to pin down and indubitably because his very existence (and success) sits rather unhappily with certain modern notions. One important aspect of his own world view was an anti-Bolshevism that had bordered on the hydrophobic at the outbreak of revolution, but which later segued into a resigned acceptance as it became clear that, rather like the duodenal ulcers that plagued him, it would simply not go away, and he did not have the resources to fight it (until 1941). He had schemed for the destruction of the Soviet regime, but at the time had been unable to persuade powerful but divided White Russian elements that Finland could deliver a knockout blow to the weak, enfeebled and beatable Bolsheviks, the price for which would be Finnish independence from a reinvented Tsarist state. He had been languidly rebuffed; as a result, by 1937 Mannerheim remained the only 'White' from the Court of Tsar Nicholas still active in serious politics anywhere. All the others were dead, senile, drunk or, as the black joke went, driving taxicabs in Paris.[9]

That this had been profoundly depressing to Mannerheim was clear; his residual irritation with, and disdain for *bien pensant* Social Democrats had been only one result; another, more important given his contempt for anything so vulgar as party politics, which would always isolate him, had been a fervent but frustrating campaign for Finland's hard-fought independence (largely his work) to be offered some measure of guaranteed security by the simple ability to defend herself. For whether or not Mannerheim was a schemer, an intriguer or even (as some muttered) a Crypto-Fascist,[10] he was above all a soldier, and a very good one. How good, the assembled thousands lining the streets on that June day would find out, and rather sooner than they would like.

For, in 1937, Finland seems to have had little concept of the world that was rapidly evolving around it. To be sure, Finns were aware that they sat on the Lip of the Bear, but the fact that the bear now wore a red suit was actually neither here nor there, for while Russia was still generally regarded by the bulk of the country as the *perivihollinen*, the traditional enemy, it was also true that a large minority of Finns embraced some version or another of the Marxist-Leninist agenda.[11] This created problems on more than one front, a vociferous far-right wing being only one. Tales of Moscow's Finnish fellow-travellers being beaten up and thrown ceremonially (and none too carefully) back over the Russian border, from whence they were deemed to have come, were common.

The legacy of Finland's civil war was a heavy burden and several times serious friction had broken out. Finland's civil solution had been straightforward: redistributive social democracy, punctuated by hard and resolute police action. As a result, as this agreeable birthday parade made its way around the streets of the capital, the nation could now look with some pride at its achievements since independence: a literacy rate (in one language or another[12]) of 100 per cent was the most encouraging sign for the future, but the economy as a whole was also in a very healthy state.

Relations between these two new neighbour nations, both of a similar age, were *de minimis*; while foreign trade in Finland was booming, little of it was with Russia. In fact Finns did more business with Greeks than they did with Russians, but none more so than with Britain; it was not a situation that anyone was particularly anxious to correct as Finland turned its collective back on Russia and bent to its task of creating a robust, durable and inclusive social democracy. Nothing, it was reasoned, could be allowed to stand in the way of that, for the price of failure would be total. No individual career was a card of high enough value to justify any amendment to the commonly agreed agenda, the international recognition of which was now on the horizon – in August 1940, Finland was due to host the Olympic Games. For a culture that so respected physical prowess as this one did, it was the perfect endorsement.

It was now becoming clear, however, that this extraordinary progress had been accomplished at huge risk. A comparison of expenditure on national defence and national education (about the same) revealed that while secondary school fees were actually lower in Helsinki than they were in Moscow, the nation was only militarily equipped to defend itself against an aggressor from perhaps forty years previously. As the world political crisis accelerated, in both Spain and Asia, with the same dizzying pace as a tipsy Karelian farmer hurrying home on an ice road in his (probably British) car, it was clear that something had to be done. Hence this parade – a very untypical piece of political theatre. With Mannerheim now back on public display (and perhaps, for his critics, safely close to retirement), the message was going out.

In Moscow that June, matters could not have offered more contrast. Another marshal, also late of the Tsar's army, was about to meet his own fate, his blood-spattered confession even then being thrashed out of him. He would confess to a raft of trumped-up charges, which included Bonapartism, treason and sexual depravity, none of which, of course, were true. With Bolshevik thoroughness, Mikhail Nikolayevich Tukhachevski – 'the violin maker'[13] – was being comprehensively dismantled as a hero, a public figure, a soldier and a man. His real crime dated back to the Polish campaign of 1920, when he had had the temerity to express his contempt for the military efforts of three martial mediocrities: Stalin, Voroshilov and Budenny. Unhappily for Tukhachevski, these men were now rather important and, as soon as it was safe to move against this gifted but arrogant soldier, they did, and swiftly. He would be shot in the early hours of 12 June 1937, as the great purge which had swept the USSR in the wake of the death of Kirov suddenly stepped up a gear. The 'Party of Lenin and Stalin' turned on the armed forces and the men who commanded them, fearing that they were powerful, accomplished, cynical and a threat; as the Party was clearly failing the State, the State, rather than the Party, had to suffer.

The blood-letting of the purge was almost unparalleled in history, perhaps the closest previous example having been the mass public 'sniffings-out' conducted over a century before in Zululand, and indeed there is much in common between Josif

Stalin and Shaka the Zulu king. For the purges were just that, the sniffing-out of traitors, plotters, wreckers and schemers by a *cadre* of magicians, in this case the NKVD[14], whose personnel could conjure up a confession to the most improbably outlandish of crimes by the simple expedients of barbaric torture and blood-curdling threats to friends, family and colleagues.

Tukhachevski had been perhaps the perfect revolutionary soldier, 'brilliant, quick of mind, with a streak of cruelty allied to an impetuousness which bordered on the rash'.[15] This remarkable man had by the time of his death forged the Red Army into the most feared military instrument on earth. Unlike certain of his contemporaries, he had studied the military art in whatever form he could obtain access to it. His passing would serve to put the Workers' and Peasants' Revolutionary Army into far less careful hands as it gave the signal for the wholesale arrest, torture, imprisonment and execution of a great swathe of the Soviet command. 'Never', wrote the historian Roy Medvedev, 'has the officer corps of any army suffered such losses in any war as the Soviet Army suffered in this time of peace.'[16] Catastrophic though these losses would be for the Red Army, they would have their effect elsewhere as the 'time of peace' started to look more and more finite, particularly for Finland, the country most easily within reach of a Soviet government that was starting to behave like a large and unpredictable drunk, slumped angrily against the same bar top that the Finns were forced, by reason of geography and history, to share. It was not a happy position in which to be, particularly with no army to speak of.

As these matters chugged into the public domain, no one was less surprised than Mannerheim, whose opinion of Bolshevism had been forged in 1917 and had not wavered since. His appointment as chairman of the Defence Council – a part-time role, subsidiary to the Defence Ministry, which carried the equivalent pay of an army major – had been made in 1931 but not specifically to combat external threats, as the economic fortunes of Finland, with its unique mix of political interests, subtexts and sentiments, suffered a reverse as savage as any in the wake of the world depression.[17] Issues of internal security came strongly to the fore as the vociferous Marxist interest stood up to be counted (and frequently suppressed). It was not perhaps a coincidence that 1931 was also the year in which the Communist Party was declared illegal. The rehabilitation of Mannerheim as a public figure, even a part-time one, sent another eloquent signal to those who had begun to feel that the country was going to the dogs.

In fact, the Finnish Ministry of Defence, showing an unerring misapprehension of military custom, did not even acknowledge that field marshal was a military rank. Technically, therefore, Mannerheim was not a member of the Finnish armed forces, but would become their commander-in-chief if, and only if, Finland found itself at war, and this arrangement was initially made only on an informal basis; successive governments seemed to detect in Mannerheim a streak of impetuosity. He *was* commandant of the Defence Corps, however, and this historically 'difficult' (i.e. conservative) organization, together with its female equivalent, the *Lottas*, can be said to represent Mannerheim's peacetime power base under arms. It is also true that these organizations, if asked to choose between their loyalty to the State and their loyalty to the Marshal might at least have paused for thought before choosing the State.

The Defence Corps had evolved into a civic *gendarmerie* after the war of independence. Politically it was predictably reactionary, with the odd extremist in its ranks. Outside the Defence Corps, in the world of party politics, the contrasts were more extreme, or perhaps merely more clearly drawn; the Patriotic People's Party (in Finnish, the IKL) had not, despite (or perhaps because of) its clear agenda, been declared illegal, and actually had a representation of fourteen seats in the 200-seat Diet.

Politically, then, Finland was a very rich stew indeed; a disenfranchised but vociferous Communist minority railed against the iniquity of having no parliamentary representation, while the far right, as expressed by the IKL, lounged smugly in the Diet. The middle ground, occupied by Conservatives, Liberals, the Agrarian Party and the Swedish People's Party, tended to cluster, in tension with the Social Democrats, who while they were intellectually and even emotionally Marxist, were also practical men, and no one more so than their leader, Väinö Tanner. Further, the perception (in such an introverted environment) that perhaps Mannerheim's demands for military expenditure reflected more his desire for internal rather than external security went deep. There is little evidence for this, but propaganda can bite very deep in times of uncertainty.

Finland's core difficulty, of course, was simply the length of its border with the Soviet Union. From the Gulf of Finland in the south, to the Arctic Ocean in the north, the border stretched over 800 miles. To defend it, Finland could only put an army in the field of ten under-equipped divisions.

CHAPTER ONE

Naboth's Vineyard

Should one ask: 'How do I cope with a well-ordered host about to attack me?' I reply: 'Seize something he cherishes and he will conform to your desires.'

Sun Tzu

THERE WERE TWO CLEAR imperatives governing the Soviet Union's attitude to its north-western border by April 1938; the first was concerned with the recovery of Tsarist territory lost during the chaos of the Revolution and civil war, most of which had been confirmed by the Treaty of Tartu in 1920.[1] The second stemmed from that: the realization that the Tsar's state had been a perfectly viable nation and that these carefully assembled western frontiers reflected an optimum balance between security and territory. By the time Austria ceased to exist, Stalin was less concerned about the Treaty of Tartu (although it had marked a significant humiliation for him as a commissar signatory) but was looking back with evident interest exactly two hundred years prior to that, to the Treaty of Nystadt, the last great territorial transaction to bear the signature of Tsar Peter, and whose core strategic importance had been to protect the approaches to his new capital, St Petersburg, by means of the acquisition of the states of the southern Baltic littoral (then Livonia and Estonia) and to the north-west by extending Russia's borders all the way across the vital land-bridge of the Karelian Isthmus, which separates the Gulf of Finland from Europe's largest lake, the Ladoga: 'The ladies of St. Petersburg could not sleep peacefully as long as the Finnish frontier ran so close to our capital', he had announced grandly, by way of justifying his conquest of Viipuri and Karelia.

Tsar Peter's border was an astute one; it allowed no latitude for Sweden or Finland to defend it (it was far too long) and with the vital Isthmus, controlled from the massive medieval fortress of Viipuri (Vyborg), in Russian hands, any invader headed for Peter's capital, (for which read a cowed but resentful Sweden[2]), would be forced to trek north, around the top of the Ladoga, whereupon they might well find themselves starving in an inhospitable and unexploitable wilderness. By 1938, however, Sweden was no longer the potential, or even the natural, enemy.

More than this, though, was the embarrassing counterpoint to the Soviet Union which the evident success of the Finnish project (as compared to the Soviet one) pointed out. The two undertakings (in these iterations, at least) were of an age, but the contrasts could not have been stronger. In Finland, the industrious population enjoyed 100 per cent literacy (in either Finnish, or Swedish). A policy of state-sponsored redistribution of land had led to the break-up of the great rural estates which had characterized the country before the civil war, augmented by the strategic release of much state-owned acreage.[3] Critically for the fortunes of the rural population, the country had no history of serfdom; thus the change of state which the Russian peasantry had undergone in 1861 (and which had left them little better off) was unknown. The population was rising as the birthrate edged up from a very low base and thus the school population was burgeoning, reflecting that vital demographic essential for progress. With great irony, secondary school fees were actually lower in Helsinki than they were in Moscow. These were subjects about which Moscow naturally maintained an embarrassed silence.

Further, Finnish industrial and agricultural production had leaped over the period by amounts which still beggar belief, particularly the latter, which was extracted from (outside the Pripet marshes) one of the most agriculturally unpromising chunks of real estate in Europe. Agricultural production had increased by an *average* of 400 per cent, paper production by the same and lumber

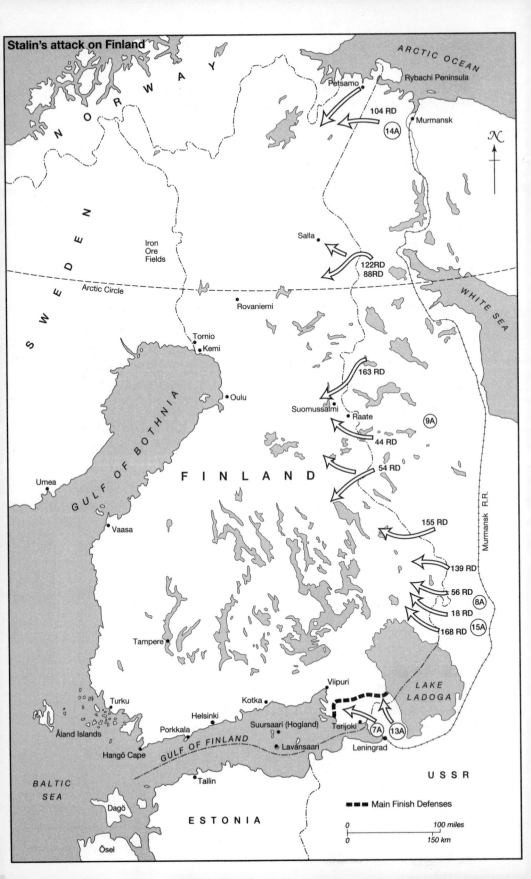

Stalin's attack on Finland

output by 550 per cent. The number of independent farmers had increased by 250 per cent to 300,000 as the great estates, which had characterized rural life in Finland at the time of the Great War, were broken up and handed to their tenants on agreeable terms. In short, Finland was accomplishing astonishing growth by the very opposite means to those employed by her giant neighbour to the east, where the attempts to collectivize farmland had led to class war of a different kind.

In step with this progress, the State infrastructure had blossomed in terms of post, telephone services and the rail net. Finland's economic progress since independence reflects an extraordinarily well-kept secret of history, and business with Britain accounted for 60 per cent of the credit side of the balance of trade. Trade with the USSR, by contrast, amounted to less than 1 per cent on the same basis of calculation. Indeed, trade with Greece was more robust. There was little the Finns wished to buy from Russia, and the reverse proposition reflected the simple truth that the Finnish markka was strong, at nearly 200 to the pound sterling and firming, whereas the Russian rouble was effectively wampum, and had been since the breathtaking incompetence of the Bolshevik regime had been unleashed upon a reasonably effective, if agrarian economy.[4] Population growth in the Soviet Union was on the verge of collapse; in the countryside as a result of famine, in the towns as a result of the institution of marriage wilting visibly under the vast and insistent social pressure of the Stalinist state. Professor Geoffrey Hosking reports that abortions had outstripped live births by nearly 200 per cent in Moscow in 1934.[5] Whatever interpretation one may put upon the sociological implications of such a statistic, economically, it was not an encouraging ratio.

So, on the eastern side of this vast 800-mile border, things were rather different, for the Soviet economy was managed by the *knout*. A burgeoning network of inefficient satrapies characterized by the slave camp, the firing squad and, dominating all else, the Great Purge, rather typified it. It has been estimated that by 1938, the population of the Gulag system was between 8 and 12 million, or at the very least, more than twice the population of the whole of Finland.[6] This unpromising foundation was further hamstrung by the destructive policy of setting quite ridiculous output targets – *Normy* – which, if met or exceeded (always hard to prove within the chaotic reporting system) would propel the manager responsible quickly up the party hierarchy and therefore away from trouble. In truth, Soviet industrial production was, save 'hero projects' and defence material, almost stagnant, and agricultural output (as a natural result of forced collectivization and tactically imposed terror-famine) languished below First World War levels. Output numbers, like so many official Soviet-issued statistics to be found elsewhere in this book, are highly suspect, but gained credence in the West as a result of the remorseless propaganda which attempted to characterize the USSR as an economic miracle; but the Soviet Union represented central planning at its worst. Never has a political–economic structure been hijacked and wrecked in such a comprehensive manner – until Robert Mugabe's Zimbabwe. As the Revolution devoured its children, so the hapless peasantry was sometimes forced to take the route of desperation and devour its own.

Naturally, the Soviet party *apparat* had a way of dealing with this unhelpful cross-border comparison with Finland – the prolonged, extravagant and repetitive sledging of successive Helsinki regimes. To the average Russian (particularly a Leningrader), Finland, according to the Party orthodoxy, represented nothing more or less than a 'vicious and reactionary Fascist clique'. Marshal Mannerheim was a particular hate figure, but he was not the only one: Väinö Tanner, leader of the Finnish Social Democrat Party, was the recipient of a volume of Soviet contumely in exact proportion to the success of his various enterprises, only one of which was politics. For Tanner, things would get much worse.

Väinö Tanner ruled the Social Democrats with the proverbial iron hand in a velvet glove. As the chairman of the ELANTO consumers' co-operative concern, as well as being the architect of the wider co-operative movement,[7] which was as close to all-powerful as any institution in Finland could be, Tanner could easily have forged a career in capitalistic business, but politics, particularly Social Democrat politics, fitted in rather neatly with his activities. In the West he was respected, particularly by the labour movement in Britain, where the great and the good of the British left (or at least a large part of the right wing of it) thought very well of him. Others, more in thrall to Moscow, would obediently follow *Pravda*'s line, and refer to him routinely as 'Ramsay MacTanner'. There is no evidence that he cared remotely, one way or another. Tough, tactless, stubborn and frequently bloody-minded, there is something of the Boer farmer about him. At this stage, Tanner himself regarded Mannerheim as perhaps a dangerous schemer and the Marshal was distrustful in return, blaming Social Democratic tight-fistedness for the parlous state of his beloved army. The two men would soon revise these mutual opinions, but not before some friction.

The real architect of the rigorously executed economic policy that had delivered true miracles, but which had left little room for the expensive matter of defence, was not Tanner, but one of Europe's most sophisticated and imaginative central bankers, Risto Ryti, who exercised the same rigid control over the Bank of Finland as Tanner did over the Social Democrats. The result had been a startling increase in personal credit and consumption, and even when the global economy had shuddered to a halt and slipped into reverse, Ryti had taken precautions, urging that the violent deflation (which since 1928 he – virtually alone – had been convinced would happen) warranted extreme care. Finland had listened and as a result, what might have been a disaster turned into a mere inconvenience; at the darkest point of the global depression (with the Dow Jones industrial average at 44) in the spring of 1932, Finland's unemployment was a mere 2.4 per cent.

Ryti's policies had been selectively Keynesian; by effective management of public debt, Finland had been able to provide the essential shock absorber for its economically harassed population and was able to act contra-cyclically, drafting otherwise unemployed workers into government-sponsored civic programmes which served well both to develop State infrastructure and maintain social conditions, so that the massive land distribution which had taken place, fuelled by levels of credit (nothing was for nothing) which appeared eye-poppingly unwise, allowed the State to be the employer of last resort, hand in hand with the Bank of Finland being the lender of last resort. One hand thus washed the other and once raw material prices started to rise, a vast potential problem, which elsewhere had given rise to unhappy political solutions, had been more or less avoided. Ryti's well-deserved reputation (perhaps, even, as one of the world's first *modern* central bankers[8]) had established him as a clever man who was prepared to take risks. Quite properly he regarded Treasury matters to be essentially disciplined but creative ones, and in this particular he had earned the unlimited respect of Mannerheim, whose own tenure as a bank chairman (a purely letterhead appointment – Mannerheim was certainly no financier) had not marked out for him a period of unalloyed pleasure.

Politically, Ryti was a Liberal, and far to the right of most Social Democrats. This particularly showed when he insisted that workers should cut their coats according to their cloth; as a result, wages during the depression plunged more in Finland than anywhere else in Europe, even if the absolute level of unemployment remained the lowest.[9] The three long years of belt-tightening that resulted caused some measure of unrest at both ends of the political spectrum, although massive economic hardship was damped by the proactive role played by the co-operative banking system, which, however much it may have creaked, never broke. This double act of Ryti and Tanner, the one a conservative Liberal, the other an intellectual Marxist (although Tanner insisted, with a rather splendid cussedness, that he was a *Menshevik*, on those rare occasions when he actually spoke to a Russian) had few parallels, perhaps not since 1903, when Rolls met Royce; the partnership assured that a reasonable level of prosperity in Finland was both broadly constant and, more importantly, repeatable. Tanner's political task, as one commentator put it, was to treat the Social Democrat Party like a radish; to peel off the red, revealing the white beneath.[10] Not an easy task given the grim legacy of Finland's civil war, but the Social Democrat Party had suffered badly from the Trojan horse wheeled up to its door by Lenin; Tanner was the man who would hamstring it.

So, to the fellow-travelling left, Tanner was anathema. Otto Kuusinen (of whom more later) declared him to be 'the devil in human form', a phrase which makes up in vitriol some of what it obviously lacks in originality, but the neat turn of phrase was never Kuusinen's strongest suit; he seemed ever to think in threadbare clichés. And yet, Tanner's far leftward political credentials had once been impeccable. When an American reporter asked him if the whispered rumour – that in his days as a putative revolutionary he had once helped a starving Stalin with money – was true, he replied crisply: 'It wasn't Stalin, it was Lenin. And it wasn't me, it was my wife.'[11] For the revolutionary left, however, his crime had been to reject the failed efforts of 1918; elected to the first unicameral Finnish Diet in 1907 as a 28-year-old firebrand, he had spent twenty years moving remorselessly to the centre-right.

As for Mannerheim himself, he clearly thought himself above party politics; he had given a cursory inspection to most of the groupings in Finnish politics, but had allied himself with none of them; indeed, when the right-wing Lapua movement attempted to embrace him, he stepped backward sharply. By breeding Mannerheim was an aristocrat, by cultural descent he was a Swedo-Finn and by political outlook he was unfashionably paternalist. That he was no particular friend of the working man for his own sake (unless uniformed) was fairly well known, and, while he may well have found certain elements of the *dirigisme* that had rapidly developed in Finland's political life useful, he was also on record as saying not only that 'socialism could not defend democracy', but also democracy itself was perhaps sometimes a questionable objective. All of which made him, too, a hate figure for the far left; his natural political constituency, wherever it lay, was certainly not with the Neanderthal right (he considered Nazis, above all other things, to be irredeemably vulgar) but neither was it with the resolutely urban *bien pensants* who, rather like the earthier Tanner, viewed him with some suspicion.

For it was axiomatic to a certain type of twentieth-century Social Democrat that a badly-equipped and therefore ineffective army was somehow less *immoral* than one that did its job well. It was further held that due to this deliberate oversight, an inevitably slavish dependence upon multilateral institutions would somehow take up the resultant political slack. The heavy cost of this point of view is seldom borne, either directly or immediately, by its proponents; one thinks like a sovereign nation-state, or one does not. When the wheels fall off the wagon of policy, the armed services often pay the price.

In Finland's case, the tensions between Mannerheim and his circle on the one hand and the dogged determination of a series of governments (to pay their debts and balance their books) on the other, were particularly marked. Unhappily, despite the fact that Finland had been turned inward upon itself since full independence (and to a purpose that still sets standards to which most cannot aspire today) the country had done so with a breathtaking disregard for the brutally Hobbesian world that was rapidly evolving on its eastern and southern borders, for by trade, debt repayment and all other commercial considerations, Finland had been looking to America and Western Europe, particularly Britain. Politically, the Finnish were constantly attempting to align themselves with Scandinavian neutrality, particularly with regard to Sweden; the central plank of the two countries' common ground being the question of the Åland Islands.

This sprawling archipelago had been demilitarized as part of the 1921 settlement, and with understandable reason.[12] If properly armed and garrisoned, the Ålands would control not only access to the Gulf of Bothnia, but also to the western approaches of the Gulf of Finland, even the upper reaches of the Baltic Sea itself, which is why the islands had always been a cornerstone of Tsarist geopolitical strategy. Like Finland, these islands represented lost territory to the USSR; Finland had rather grabbed possession as part of its leap for independence, and the League of Nations, as ever storing up trouble for later, had acquiesced meekly to Finland's demands. Ethnically and emotionally the Åland islanders were, however, Swedish and it was under pressure (and supervision) from Stockholm that Tsar Nicholas's magnificent 1914 fortifications were meticulously demolished. Moscow had denounced the 1921 convention as an 'Imperialist intrusion into the Baltic area'[13] and had been grumpy about it ever since, powerless to act after the civil war, and really lacking a reason, until Germany started stirring.

This matter had thus become important by 1938. It had been forgotten by no one, least of all the Swedes and the Russians, that the jumping-off point for the German Expeditionary Force to Finland of 1918 had indeed been the Ålands (as a territorial gesture as much as anything else). To Finland, however, this contentious piece of real estate also served another vital purpose as, in the light of the obvious deterioration of European tranquility, public consultations were undertaken between Sweden and Finland with a purpose of remilitarizing the Ålands, about which the Soviet Union could do little short of declaring war, as Germany, France and Britain had also signed the convention which made the islands Finnish property. The Finnish objective was to establish a military–political joint venture that might serve to bind Swedo-Finnish interests together; if Stockholm undertook to assist Finland in fortifying its own territory, then an important and useful precedent might be set. For despite the admiration that the Finnish project had generated everywhere outside Russia, Finland was functionally isolated: Cinderella's dance card would remain resolutely unfilled while she was handcuffed to her ill-tempered and distinctly ugly ex-sister. Politically, as a previous possession of Russia, it seemed likely to the whole of northern Europe that one day Russia would want Finland back, willing or not; and both the Ålands and Karelia were well known as unfinished business.

There was at least one Swedish politician who felt differently: Rickard Sandler, the foreign minister. Sandler spent much of his time attempting to produce a diplomatic solution whereby Scandinavian interests could be pooled, with a resulting neutral bloc, which would include Sweden, Denmark, Norway and Finland. The Åland question would be a neat way of producing a fait accompli of common ground, for his fellow cabinet ministers were less than unanimous in supporting this objective. As a result, he trod softly, but needless to say, he was a popular man in Finland, not the least reason being that he had bothered to learn the language.

Swedo-Finnish military cooperation represented a rich vein of shared history in the culture of both nations, the common link being Gustavus II, Adolphus, whose army during the Thirty Years' War, referred to in Finnish history as the 'Years of the Great Wrath', descended upon Pomerania and contained within it a significant leavening of 'squat and swarthy Lapps' as well as 'lean, colourless' Finns.[14] The martial aggression of these soldiers had been remarked upon by all who had seen it, for they had represented the backbone of Gustavus II's remarkable cavalry arm.[15]

By and large, Finland had been a contented place under Gustavus and his Vaasa successors; there were definite advantages in being a possession of Sweden as opposed to any other alternatives, which is perhaps why the pressure for independence, a Finnish nation-state, did not emerge until after the country had been handed over to Alexander I of Russia at the Treaty of Tilsit in 1807. Within two years Finland, nominally an autonomous Grand Duchy, was overrun by Russian troops, as the Tsar realized that if he wanted this territory he would have to fight for it.

THE TELEPHONE CALL received from the Soviet legation by the Finnish foreign minister Rudolf Holsti in April 1938 was, to say the least, unorthodox, but probably more welcome than a call from the minister himself, the obtuse and plodding Party hack Vladimir Deravianski, who was something of a cartoon Bolshevik. The caller was one Boris Yartsev, a lowly second secretary at the legation, but by comparison he was, or appeared to be, a breath of fresh air.[16] This affable young sprig apologized for the breach of protocol, but requested an urgent consultation, which he was granted with Holsti's usual grave courtesy, for 14 April. Holsti knew perfectly well that Yartsev was no junior diplomatist; both he and his wife, 'a fine-looking woman past her first youth', as Väinö Tanner rather ungallantly put it later, were an observable feature of the social scene of the Finnish capital. It was assumed, rightly, that they were both officials of some rather higher organ of the State than that represented by Deravianski, (probably the NKVD), if only because they seemed to enjoy a freedom of movement not actually enjoyed by the Soviet minister himself, who constantly dreading recall, tended to stay in or near the legation. Yartsev, when he appeared on 14 April, bore on the face of it startling news. He had just returned from Moscow, where he had received instructions to investigate the possibilities of 'improving' Soviet-Finnish relations which were, he conceded, *de minimis*.

Two days before, an event had taken place, which, in the context of the recent events in Austria, might have been considered tactless, if only in retrospect. It had been the twentieth anniversary of the liberation of Helsinki by Mannerheim's yeoman army, supported by the German Expeditionary Force under General Count Rüdiger von der Golz. Mannerheim and von der Golz, both men slightly creaking by now, had attended the celebrations, while a Finnish Army band (within earshot of the Soviet legation) had thumped out, with some enthusiasm, Wilhelmine marching songs in honour of the host of German veterans also present. The fact that no Finnish cabinet minister was present (in an official capacity, at least) may or may not have been appreciated.

In terms of the reasoning behind the Soviet initiative, Yartsev was unusually open, confirmation (not that much was needed) that he was sparring far above his diplomatic weight. As recent events in Austria proved, Germany was clearly on the move and probably poised to attack the Soviet Union. It was likely, stated Yartsev, that Germany would attempt to use Finland as a base of operations for an offensive towards Leningrad, and, should that prove to be the case, Moscow needed to know what Finnish attitudes would be. He did not add, nor did he need to, that the echoes of '*Alte Kameraden*' had barely died away in the streets outside. Should it transpire that German troops appeared on Finnish soil, Yartsev continued, then the Red Army would have no hesitation in advancing to meet them, but if Finland chose to resist the blandishments of Berlin, then the Soviet Union would offer '... all possible military and economic assistance and undertake to withdraw its troops as soon as the war was over'.[17] If this was not sinister enough, Yartsev added that without Soviet assistance, Finland would not be in a position to resist Germany; it was well known in Moscow that any attempt to deter Germany would lead to a Fascist coup in Finland, which would welcome Germany with open arms. Unsurprisingly, this was news to Holsti.

This mild Russian obsession as to Finnish intentions vis-à-vis Germany was not a recent one, and dated back to the civil war. What was not perhaps perceived, however, was that there was a distinct separation in public opinion. If Russia failed to grasp this, then Germany did not. The German minister in Helsinki, Wipert von Blücher, penned a long memorandum on the subject a few months after Yartsev's visit:

> In a war Finland can only be a loser. She is today a 'have' Nation, which is interested in the preservation of the status quo. Public opinion in the event of war will in large part instinctively turn against the power which is thought to be guilty of aggression. In deciding who is guilty, public opinion will be under the influence of Stockholm and London. As long as the belligerents respect her integrity, Finland will do her utmost to stay outside the conflict. The sympathies of the military and right-wing circles will be on the side of Germany. But for the left-wing circles who are in power, the cause of the war, the attitude of the Western democracies and other factors will be more important than Soviet participation in the war.[18]

As an exposition of informed opinion, Blücher's memorandum is quite masterful; it went a long way toward forming opinion in the German Foreign Ministry, under both Konstantin von Neurath and Joachim Ribbentrop. Von Neurath had been scathing in his initial assessment of Holsti, as 'mediocre, timid, and perhaps scheming'.

HIS BREAKFAST RUINED, Holsti attempted to allay his visitor's concerns. He explained that the government was well supported by a healthy majority in Parliament, that such relations with Germany as Yartsev feared were incompatible with Finland's policy of Scandinavian neutrality, and that the international situation, although serious, was surely not that grave.

Yartsev changed gear. The Soviet government needed, nay, demanded, 'guarantees' that Helsinki would not side with Berlin in a war on Russia, but crucially he refused to elaborate on what the nature of those guarantees might be. He had, for the moment, shot his diplomatic bolt and reached his level of competence. All other issues would be a matter of negotiation between the two governments. He was able to offer some concessions, though; the Soviet Union was in a position to buy 'limitless amounts' of Finnish raw materials and agricultural products.[19]

It is a measure of the success enjoyed by Mannerheim's persistent agitation that Holsti – perhaps tactlessly – enquired about the possibility of arms sales to Finland, at which point Yartsev replied that such matters were feasible, provided the 'guarantees' to which he had alluded were met, but about which he could speak no further. Finally, he added, neither Deravianski nor anyone else from the Soviet legation should know about this rather one-sided conversation. Politely, Holsti showed him out.

Yartsev went immediately to Moscow, reported, and proceeded then to Stockholm, where he had a detailed conversation with Foreign Minister Rickard Sandler. Unsurprisingly, the subject was the Åland question; despite Sweden's insistence upon the destruction of the Tsarist fortifications, the archipelago had lost little of its strategic importance, merely reverted to being a brown-field site for a military developer. For the Swedes, however, it was bad enough that the Ålands were Finnish territory, so the prospect of Soviet hegemony over them was a clear anathema; Napoleon had been rather stating the obvious when he had said that in the hands of a great power, the Ålands were a 'loaded pistol aimed at Stockholm'.

Despite Yartsev's faintly theatrical injunctions to secrecy, he had not kept silent on the matter elsewhere in Finland. He had, apparently upon his own initiative, talked at length to at least one staff officer, General Sihvo, as well as Prime Minister Cajander's assistant Arvo Inkalä, not to mention Moscow's fellow-traveller, the eccentric left-wing playwright Hella Wuolijoki (née Ella Murrik), who had 'form' in this matter.[20] In the latter case, Yartsev was rather singing to the choir, as Wuolijoki marked perhaps the most obvious link, not only with O. V. Kuusinen the thwarted Bolshevik exile, but with a wider Communist audience outside Finland.[21] Her sister Salme was married to Rajani Palme Dutt, the Swedish/Indian theoretician who ran (in uneasy alliance with the ebullient Harry Pollitt), the British Communist Party. Clearly, the ground was being prepared; an inveterate gossip anyway, Wuolijoki could be expected to pass on Yartsev's *obiter dicta* to her sister, to augment the Comintern's instructions, which, as this crisis developed, would become less and less consistent.

Arvo Inkalä chose to exercise his own leisurely discretion in bringing the matter of Yartsev's approaches to his boss's attention and two months later, at the end of June, Cajander saw the Russian, apparently with little outcome, save to arrange a meeting for 11 July, after which Väinö Tanner was informed of the affair.

Tanner, who met Yartsev on 30 July, was important not in the sense that he held relevant office (he was minister of finance at the time) but because of his leadership role within the Social Democrats. In truth Tanner, in keeping with his remit (and his instincts as a trader), was naturally keener to discuss business, which was difficult on two grounds: firstly, that trade talks could only spring from political ones and second, Yartsev knew little or nothing about the subject, save that it was at present almost non-existent.[22] It was clear that Yartsev's role was that of herald rather than principal and that he enjoyed an almost unique, but rapidly closing window of opportunity – although personally he was probably under less immediate pressure, as a serving NKVD officer, than certain other Soviet diplomatists, many of whom sat in paralysis, dreading recall to Moscow 'for consultations' and to share the fate of so many others at that time.[23]

WHAT IS PERHAPS startling, given the proximity of the two countries, is the extraordinary poverty of Soviet intelligence concerning the nature, priorities and ambitions of the Finns. It is not hard to imagine – given the tectonic shift in relations between the ruling elite in Moscow and the rest of the Party globally, the result of which was a blood-letting on an unprecedented scale – that there would be a natural instinct on the part of the interested reporters of these events to spin the realities somewhat. But the Soviet assessment of conditions in Finland fell so wide of the mark that they might well have been referring to another country entirely. The reason for this was simple – the Communist Party was an illegal organization in Finland – its nearest official representative, Arvo Tuominen, lived in exile in Stockholm.

Much of the Soviet attitude had its roots in a doctrinaire interpretation of the chain of events since Finnish independence, ratified at Tartu. In the wake of that, Stalin[24] had written:

> The revolt of the Finnish workers and agricultural labourers ... demonstrated the completed isolation of the government from their own masses. Utterly defeated, the government were obliged to appeal for aid against their own workers and peasants to the imperialists of western Europe, the age-long oppressors and exploiters of the small nations of the world.

The very fact that Stalin, as Commissar for Nationalities,[25] had his name on the treaty reflected the reality of that event. His piece, which appeared in *Pravda* at the end of 1920, reflected a dutiful disappointment at the Soviet Union's inability to foment a successful revolution in Finland. As the thwarted fellow-travellers trailed back to Russia, many were enlisted as front-line Comintern propagandists in what now was to become the major front of Soviet diplomacy in the West: the recreation of the territorial status quo of the Tsarist state in the light of the relatively serious failure in Finland and the catastrophe of Poland.

The most well-known Finn among these exiles was Otto Ville Kuusinen, who swiftly rose within the executive committee of the Comintern, developing a life-saving line in humourless toadying which would allow him, adroitly, to survive successive purges.[26] He was in constant and close contact with Wuolijoki and (via her sister Salme) Dutt.

Naturally, given the arms-length nature of both commercial and diplomatic contact, the Soviet justification for Soviet-Finnish relations needed to be spun somewhat. Rather than concede that independent Finland had little use for the Soviet project, and was prospering very well on its own, the orthodoxy developed that not all was well; another fugitive Finn, Yrjö Eljas Sirola, People's delegate for foreign affairs in the short-lived administration, had announced to the sixth Congress of the Comintern in 1928:

> We see a country where internally, under a façade of parliamentary democracy, a reactionary and indeed Fascist minority, with a long record of bitter hostility to the USSR, exercise the whole reality of power over a courageous and intelligent but oppressed minority [sic.[27]]; and in foreign relations, under a façade of independence, that same ruling minority accepts the position of a 'client state,' a colony, almost a military outpost, of Great Britain.

Once again, reactionary equals Fascist; the core assumption behind the Marxian analysis of its revolutionary rival is, of course, that Fascism must be the agency of the bourgeoisie, if only because Communism is the natural agency of the proletariat.

The response of the Comintern to this and other similarly frustrating matters was to take the gloves off with respect to Moscow's relations with left-leaning movements globally. *Class against Class*, a policy introduced just in time to split the left completely against the rise of Fascism, was not a strategy with which all agreed outside the USSR, but hardliners such as Kuusinen and Dutt pressed the point that to cooperate with Social Democrats was now, formally, a Stalinist heresy; Moscow had said so.

The Comintern's policy, triggered initially by the death of Lenin in 1924 and the resulting squabble for power within the Kremlin (the first casualty of which was Trotsky, expelled from the Politburo in 1926), proved with hindsight to be a disaster for the foreign policy of the Soviet Union. The three-cornered fight between Stalin, Kamenev and Zinoviev, which Stalin did not win until 1929 (and would not confirm until 1934, when he killed his old rivals), left the CPSU in a state of nervous collapse. Thus, in October 1929, when the capitalist West lurched into the greatest economic crisis of its history, the spectrum of the broadly left wing of world politics was, thanks to Moscow, splintered almost beyond repair. Into the vacuum stepped a much greater (and more organized) threat.

The rapid rise of the far right in opposition to accelerated agitprop took many forms. In much of Europe, the ranks of fellow-travelling Fascism (and, after 1933, Nazism) were filled by disillusioned alumni of the left, simply exchanging one workers' movement for another. The response of the left to this was frequently chaotic and reeling, and the 'Popular front' concept, hastily cobbled together alliances of all parts of the left-of-centre spectrum, from Spartacist to Liberal, could not be expected to prosper, given the icy indifference of orthodox Stalinist activists to the belated efforts of sundry liberals responding, too late, to the new threat from the bomber right. In some cases, the renewed but uncoordinated vigour with which the broad left attempted to articulate its position on the general economic crisis served only to increase the ardour of the non-revolutionary, (merely reactionary) right, particularly in France and, to a lesser extent, Britain.

In Finland, matters were particularly sensitive; despite the minor economic miracle that had taken place by the early 1930s (at least, relative to other states), memories were still long enough to recall the horrors of the civil war and there was political (and social) tension at many levels. For the civil war (usually – and not inaccurately – referred to as the War of Liberation) had savagely depopulated the country, not only by direct conflict casualties, but also by deaths from influenza and starvation, execution and the further insidious effects of large-scale emigration of (particularly) Karelian Finns, mainly to America.[28] Many of these 'American Finns' had in fact been lured back to the USSR just in time for the first of the Stalinist purges, signalled by the murder in Leningrad of Sergei Kirov in December 1934. Further, many (Arvo

Tuominen's account says 'all') of the Finns who had fled into the USSR after the war were rounded up and 'suppressed'.[29] Bar one, at least; Otto Kuusinen, the ultimate survivor, happily acquiesced in the wholesale slaughter and imprisonment of his countrymen with apparent enthusiasm.

Kuusinen was not the only prominent non-Russian active in the USSR during that period, but in common with many other hard-line Bolsheviks, he viewed the importance of the Soviet project (disastrous though it was proving) in essentially international terms. The Soviet Union was merely 'the base' (in Arabic, *al Qa'eda*) for world revolution, but he was Finn enough, and parochial enough, to imagine that his native country was an obvious target. Further, his lack of pity reflects a characteristic which we see again throughout history, that an undertaking (in this case the Finnish revolution of 1918) having failed, then the citizens of Finland did not deserve his sympathy. Perhaps the purges of the 1930s in the USSR were as a result of a similar sentiment on the part of Stalin – certainly the domestic condition of the USSR was not suggestive of a successful outcome to the project. To Kuusinen, the opportunity to foment revolution was partly a matter of policy and partly a matter of revenge. But, intelligence – information – is everything.

THE CORE OF THE right wing in Finland lay in the Civil Guard,[30] which had started life as the cadre of White Guard militia that had come into being in 1905 and which had formed the core of Mannerheim's civil war force, when leavened with returning volunteers from both the Tsar's and the Kaiser's army. Twenty years on, it had, as an organization, survived more or less intact in spirit, and in civilian life, represented essentially a middle-class interest of teachers, lawyers, yeoman farmers and industrial and commercial managers. By now, it had a female equivalent, the *Lotta Svärd* [31] organization which, in time of war, would take over a host of military functions: medical, clerical, transport driving, anti-aircraft spotting and, it transpires, combat and logistics being only a few of them.

The *Lottas* were, therefore, something rather more than a Women's Institute, although that is how they had initially been envisaged in 1919. Twenty years later, they were uniformed and badged and, importantly, over 80,000 strong. They would prove vital, releasing scarce soldiers for active duty elsewhere, but at the same time allowing an element of 'class war' into the analysis of the coming conflict, at least on the part of Finland's critics.

AT THIS POINT, after Yartsev appeared to have reached the limit of his remit, the Finnish Cabinet chose to offer a gesture, as much as an act of good faith as anything else. On 11 August, Tanner, standing in for Holsti, submitted to Yartsev a written draft for a treaty, which the Finns would find acceptable. Part of it read:

> The Government of Finland, which adheres to Scandinavian neutrality, will not permit any violation of the territorial integrity of Finland and will therefore not allow any foreign power to use Finland as a base of aggression against the Soviet Union. The Soviet Government, which undertakes to respect the inviolability of Finnish territory in regard to every part of the country, does not object to Finland's taking, even in peace time, such military measures as are required for ensuring to the fullest possible degree the inviolability of Finnish territory and the neutrality of the Åland Islands.

Yartsev was not impressed, but at least he had fulfilled his diplomatic function and opened a discussion. He then disappeared, returning (suspiciously quickly) a week later, with a written response. Tanner assumed at the time that the rather cobbled-together document he produced originated with *Narkomindel* (the Soviet Foreign Ministry) and Maksim Litvinov, but it is quite possible that it did not; certainly it bore no trace of 'indivisible peace', the policy by which the Soviet Foreign Commissar was best known. In its tone, it was pure Andrei Zhdanov: 'If the Finnish Government cannot enter into a secret military alliance, the Soviet Union would be satisfied with a written undertaking that Finland was prepared to resist German aggression and to accept for that purpose Soviet military assistance.'

Interestingly, this time there was no mention of stationing troops on Finnish soil for the purposes of 'forward defence'; rather, the security needs of Finland would now be met by a combination of arms supplies and the good offices of the Baltic fleet, which would, Yartsev added, need to take over and fortify the island of Suursaari (Hogland) at the Leningrad end of the Gulf of Finland. Further, the fortification of the Åland islands would be acceptable, but should now be a matter for the Soviet Union and Finland *together*, with no mention of Sweden. Soviet 'observers' would remain, to ensure that no German incursions took place.

This was particularly uneasy news; to seek protection in this way would prevent any meaningful exercise of a policy of Scandinavian neutrality on the part of Finland as well as destroy – utterly – any hope of a military alliance, however tangential, with Sweden, which was, of course, exactly the point. Russian policy, unchanged in 130 years, was to separate Finland from its northern neighbours and bind it, in whatever way possible, to the east. To make the Ålands a Soviet *casus belli*, particularly given the rapidly deteriorating international situation, was simply to play Russian roulette. Clearly though, the USSR wanted Finland back, if not as a vassal state, then certainly as a military dependency. Finland, to Moscow, was Naboth's Vineyard.

In this, the Soviet Union faced a ticklish doctrinal problem. It was not, in Leninist theory, *correct* for armies to be used for limited territorial gains, being against the spirit of world socialist revolution – a nicety of which the Poles had probably not been aware in 1920 – which had given rise to the tortuous, legalistic diplomacy of the type which Tanner was now experiencing, and which had already come to characterize the Soviet State. In the event, the Russian solution to this 'moral dilemma' was less than elegant.

The Finnish Cabinet rejected this latest proposal out of hand on 29 August and, weary of the whispered conversations with Yartsev, instructed Holsti to take the matter up with Litvinov directly in September, when he was due to attend at the League of Nations. This Holsti did, and was somewhat curious to learn that Litvinov appeared to have little or no knowledge of the Yartsev conversation, and certainly not of the recently rejected written proposals; this led the Finns to assume (or at least consider) that the Foreign Commissar, who was generally respected, was no longer the master of his brief, nor even in charge of events.

The Munich crisis at the end of September 1938, the apparent solving of which by Chamberlain served to send a wave of optimism through Western Europe, had rather the opposite effect in the north, as the Soviet Baltic fleet promptly mobilized, surface craft and submarines pouring out of Kronstadt and crowding the Gulf of Finland, with several violations of the territorial waters of both Finland and Estonia. Clearly, nerves were tightly strung in Moscow.

As they were in Helsinki and Stockholm. The news that there would be no immediate war caused a wave of relief to sweep through both capitals and mobilized reservists stood down; it was generally held that a war between Germany and the Western powers would be a catastrophe for Finland, and therefore Scandinavia. Czechoslovakian independence was a small price to pay. Mannerheim used the September crisis to carry out a swift audit of the armed forces, which he would command in the event of war.[32] The tone of his report was bleak:

> The recent crisis has confronted us with a hopeless picture as regards the armament and equipment of the forces which we would have to put into the field in case of war. Finland's field army would have to be thrown against the enemy completely without protection against armour and aircraft, supported by artillery weak in both quality and quantity, and to a degree lacking in individual equipment. When one realises the equipment and arms of the presumptive enemy, the situation of the Army appears even more hopeless. The same can be said of the Navy and the Air Force. In a word, the armed forces must at present be described as totally unfitted for war.

And, as for the Isthmus:

> ... the slowness with which the fortifying of the frontier districts is proceeding deserves to be especially emphasised and is due mainly to

> the almost total lack of technical personnel. To put it shortly our country
> is at the present time not in a position to be defended. The events of
> the last few weeks show that our respite may be very short.[33]

Shortly afterward, Mannerheim embarked on a lightning visit to both Paris and London. What he encountered in Paris dismayed him somewhat, in the person of General Gamelin, who was, reported Mannerheim, 'shocked' at the state of the French Army.[34] In London, Lord Halifax gave him a grand lunch and Mannerheim took the opportunity of asking the Foreign Secretary whether he could impart the news in Finland that: 'England was arming as if she were already in a state of war.'[35] After 'some moments of reflection', Halifax assented.

Equipped with this information, Mannerheim busied himself with renewed appeals to President Kallio concerning military estimates, the current 1939 amount having already been spent, and with little, as his report reveals, to show for it. He urged Kallio to authorize an increased budget of 500 million markka for the next year. He got 350 million, to commence in the spring – six vital months away. The news that a second 200-million-markka public bond issue was also under subscription may have pleased him, until he discovered what it was for – the 1940 Olympic Games.

YARTSEV, MEANWHILE, had not given up and nor had Litvinov, despite the fact that his policy had been consigned to history at Munich. Holsti, however, resigned as foreign minister, although not for reasons particularly associated with the USSR.[36] The fact that Holsti was rather anti-German (and, reciprocally, they he) served to start rumours that somehow Berlin had engineered his downfall.[37] His place was taken by Eljas Erkko.

In a curious attempt to appear to be even-handed, the Interior Ministry promptly issued an order banning the Patriotic People's Party (IKL) as the Communists had been banned, declaring it illegal. The minister in charge, Urho Kekkonen (later, after 1956, president) was to admit later that this was a simple (if crude) gesture, to suggest to Moscow that Finland would have no truck with German fifth columnists. The ban was later – rather awkwardly – reversed by the Finnish courts as being unconstitutional, but it served to rather confuse the issue of Holsti's resignation, as well as putting the relative fortunes of extreme right and extreme left into some perspective.

The diplomatic pressure now shifted ground. Given that the Finns had already rejected the Soviet proposals concerning the Åland matter, in January 1939 Cajander, Erkko and Tanner travelled to Stockholm to sign the revised 1921 convention with the Swedes. This was a significant moment in the execution of a policy of Fenno-Swedish collective security and the Russians tried very hard to sabotage it. Because the convention was a League of Nations matter, it required the approval of all those who had signed the original 1921 agreement, which did not, of course, include Moscow. None the less, as soon as the news broke that British and French approval was now being sought, the Soviet ambassadors in both London and Paris urged delay upon the British and French governments, citing a secret agreement between Finland and Germany that in time of war the Åland archipelago was to be placed at the disposal of the *Kriegsmarine*. Ominously, the same story appeared in the last week of January in *Krasnaya Zvezda* (*Red Star*), the official Red Army newspaper. The crude disinformation worked, eliciting the response to the Fenno-Swedish *démarche* in both capitals that presumably the Russians would find the new arrangements for the militarization of the Ålands agreeable? Otherwise ...

Under certain well-defined circumstances, they might. The lure of a trade agreement was once again used and, perhaps naively, a Finnish delegation obligingly appeared in Moscow – and waited. As they drummed their fingers in expectation, another face appeared in Erkko's office – this was one Boris Stein, who had been a predecessor of Deravianski's as ambassador to Helsinki. He had contrived to be 'passing through' as part of a rest cure – the media reported that he had been ill.

With a variation on the well-worn theme, Stein suggested that the island of Suursaari (Hogland) be leased for thirty years by the Soviet Union, together with four others in the eastern Gulf of Finland, all of which had been demilitarized by the Treaty of Tartu. In return, territory in Soviet eastern Karelia was to be offered in compensation. The familiar issue, the security of Leningrad and Kronstadt, in the event of German aggression, was cited. As Stein proposed in Helsinki, so too did Litvinov to Yrjö-Koskinen in Moscow.

This time, however, there was a difference. Erkko actually told Mannerheim what was happening – the Marshal had been rather kept out of the information loop during the Yartsev approaches, and what he now heard, that the Cabinet was not disposed to discuss Stein and Litvinov's proposition, quite appalled him. He urged concessions; Stein must not return to Moscow empty-handed. The islands in question were of little value to Finland and could not be used for offensive action against her, or even if they could they were of no more use than any other point along the 800-mile border. To lease the islands to the Soviets, he maintained, would pacify them and go a long way to address the serious issue of the security of Leningrad – a constant niggle which had surely driven Russian Baltic policy for over two centuries.

As soon as the terrifying implications of Moscow's demands were revealed by an embarrassed Cabinet to an incredulous commander-in-chief in waiting, Mannerheim's counsel was straightforward; given that the task of actually fighting the Russians was at present completely beyond the abilities of the Finnish Army (as he had already reported in the wake of the crisis after Munich), then negotiation was the only realistic option. To his consternation, the Cabinet viewed the matter rather differently – Cajander's view, that any government which offered territorial concessions to the Soviet Union would undoubtedly be ejected from power, did not impress the Marshal, whose opinion of political parties, as a clearly committed public servant (whatever his previous private agenda), was gloomy at best.

Once again, he found himself a voice in the wilderness; the Cabinet seemed to view the situation with a Zen-like calm, which was not justified by the brutal realities of what it was facing. The assumption, which the members of the Cabinet collectively made, that Russian demands were an opening gambit in a prolonged haggle, was essentially false, but it would take them vital months to arrive at that conclusion. As for Mannerheim's dissent, his well-known dislike of Communism, coupled with his uncomfortable Russian past made him an object of a certain amount of naïve suspicion. But the core misunderstanding on the part of Cajander's Cabinet was that it could negotiate with Moscow as an equal.

It was no particular secret, at least at the political level, that Marshal Mannerheim and Prime Minister Cajander did not necessarily find each other congenial, which may well be why they met so infrequently. Cajander was possessed of those immaculately liberal urban instincts, which can often display themselves as a mistrust of the military and all its 'toys'. Cajander had refused, serially, to admit that Finland was in any particular danger. The cloak of neutrality was enough, he maintained. Mannerheim thought him a purblind ass, an opinion probably reinforced by a series of ill-advised speeches which the Prime Minister was unwise enough to make, the first of them after the Molotov-Ribbentrop pact was signed – he jokingly congratulated the Finnish Army on not having received any new weapons: 'They would be rusty and obsolete by now!' Nobody laughed.

Cajander's handling of the diplomatic crisis with Moscow had been characterized by a singular lack of imagination. That fatal lack of vision, an inability to calculate what might go wrong if one is not careful, was coupled with a complete misappreciation of either Soviet needs or indeed Soviet intentions.

Adolf Hitler had not made the same mistake. Just as his policy had been the creation of a greater Germany, so he intuitively understood that the Kremlin's policy was the geographical re-creation of the Tsarist state; not merely the state of Tsar Nicholas, but the state of Tsar Peter, with borders in the west roughly defined in historical terms by the year 1721. There was no room in this plan for an independent Finland, autonomous Grand Duchy or not. Mannerheim and his circle realized that, for they had a greater strategic understanding of what Russia's security needs were than did the Finnish government.

The Tsarist state had been carefully assembled, particularly in the context of the Baltic. It had long been appreciated that the City of St Peter could only be protected by control of both sides of the Gulf of Finland as it narrowed to become what were now the roads of the City of St Lenin. That imperative had grown and matured as technology improved to the point where a capital ship could shell Leningrad at will or, more critically, modern artillery parked on the Karelian Isthmus could also do the same. The fact that Finland had no artillery to speak of was irrelevant, as it was a lack which could be surely filled with ease.

In the context of the Baltic states, then, this was the essence of the territorial aspect of the Molotov pact. In a secret annexe to the pact, the southern Baltic states of Estonia and Latvia (and, later Lithuania) were consigned to the Soviet sphere of influence and so, crucially, was Finland. In this way Germany could accommodate the Kremlin's imperial needs, and even pretend that the reason was to protect Leningrad from the Royal Navy from the sea, rather than the Wehrmacht on land. In Finland, the importance of this unlikely alliance was regarded along predictably party lines. Liberal interpretations of it concluded that Finland's undeniable prosperity – the success of the whole project – had made the country indispensable as a model social democracy; the world needed it as a neutral beacon of hope in a chaotic world. Others, Mannerheim included, felt that fine and splendid though this dizzying success was, it could all prove to be purely temporary if the Russians were not dealt with very carefully indeed; and, clearly, they had not been.

Mannerheim visited, in turn, President Kallio and Prime Minister Cajander, as well as browbeating Erkko on the matter. Their response was simple and consistent – the government would simply fall if any hint of this negotiation to dispose of Finnish territory was made public. Mannerheim, whose view of party politicians was well known, responded with an offer, which, to the slightly rattled government, might well have appeared suspiciously like a power-play: 'I was prepared', he recalled, 'to place myself at the disposal of the government, convinced as I was that my honest opinion would be understood. But I went still further and expressed the opinion that it would be to Finland's advantage to offer to move the frontier nearest to Leningrad westward by five or six miles against a reasonable compensation.'[38] On the one hand, this can be seen as a bluff, soldierly offer to carry the can of public opinion, but on the other, it was also perhaps an attempt to raise the already high stakes involved in upsetting the Russians. He stopped short of threatening to take the matter to the public, but it cannot have been very far from his mind; his patience with these woolly-minded liberals was wearing thinner by the day, particularly because his defence budget demands, although agreed at 350 million markka, were still unfulfilled.

The Cabinet was not confident enough of its position to take the issue to the Diet (and would not) so the country never knew what had been discussed, and Mannerheim, although clearly fuming, was forced as a result to again consider his position. Stein departed Helsinki on 6 April, and the Finnish trade delegation returned, equally empty-handed, shortly afterwards.

Between the departure of Stein from Helsinki and the commencement of direct conversations with Moscow, events elsewhere gathered pace, and while the Finns had been relatively relaxed concerning their ability to manage the clear agenda to their own satisfaction, the fast-changing relationships between the European powers rather served to put them on their guard.

Key to this was the constant Soviet desire to repair their western borders in the light of the Nazi threat, which, in the year elapsed since Boris Yartsev had first hove into sight, had been less than encouraging for the Russians, as it seemed to them that the whole of Europe had moved firmly as far to the right as Germany. In fact, it had not, but the collapse of the Popular Front in France, coupled with the final realization in Britain that some sort of massive rearmament was clearly necessary, served the Soviet Union notice that tensions were rising rapidly. As to who would fight whom, that seemed to Moscow to be an opaque matter; given the aggressive actions of the Comintern, and the logical response to that, it seemed as likely as not that the Soviet Union would be under threat from the entire Western European community, despite German unilateral action in Czechoslovakia, which had met with universal disapproval but no action. As we shall see, the Soviet perception of external threat still existed in predominantly civil war terms.

Maksim Litvinov had, since the very early spring, been attempting to duplicate his approaches via Stein in Finland with a useful dialogue with the Poles, who were just as recalcitrant, and with similar good reason. The Soviet Union had already attempted to liquidate Poland once as a viable state in 1919 and nothing in their present diplomacy seemed to suggest that, twenty years later, matters now lay any differently. Litvinov's stated policy, of indivisible collective security, met with scant credibility, as the statesmen in the West still seemed to mistrust the Soviet Union more than anyone.

For a while, the diplomatic pressure for concessions would abate, as the Soviet Union addressed itself to the issue of Anglo-French intentions, which, as was the custom, started with political discussions preceded by trade talks. At the heart of the Anglo-French-Russian military conversations in August was the agenda for the security of Europe against the clear designs of the Nazis. This was, of course, a simpler matter for the Russians than it was for either of the Western allies, as German propaganda relating to the 'Bolshevik threat' had not been either reticent or subtle, whereas Germany's foreign relations initiatives with France and Britain, particularly the latter, had been for some time sinuous and flexible, to say the least. Part of this was down to the observable level of appeasement in certain British government and establishment circles, another due to backslapping diplomacy (with very mixed results) from both Ribbentrop and Göring, but a far greater contribution was Britain's simple inability to yet fight a European war with any confidence as to the outcome.

The Soviet desiderata, however, included issues that went

against the very warp and weft of British policy. Implicit in the price to be paid for an eastern anti-Nazi bulwark would be free reign over the territories previously controlled by the man who had happened to be the last Grand Duke of Finland, Nicholas II. Further, the freedom to do so hinged around the concept of perceived *indirect aggression*. This term, it became clear, was a uniquely Soviet abstraction, and covered all eventualities, from the election of a potentially hostile adjacent government on the one hand, or an attempted *coup d'état*, (apart from one started by the Soviet Union) or even an ill-advised newspaper headline. It further became clear that the Moscow view of international relations was governed chiefly by a certain, justifiable paranoia. Moscow was touchy, and had much to be touchy about.

The British delegation did not hurry itself to get to Moscow – instead of flying, they steamed over at their leisure, which was the cause of some apparent impatience at their destination. So urgent was the matter, the Russian argument went, that there was no time to lose. In fact, talks had been going on at ambassador level for some time concerning a Russo-German trade agreement, and it was also clear that British policy would not countenance the annexation of other peoples' sovereign territory on the questionable (and unilaterally defined) pretext of 'indirect aggression'.

The issue of Anglo-French-Soviet cooperation hinged, famously, about Poland and, to a slightly lesser extent, Finland. These great gaps in the western defences of the USSR, already alluded to, required rights of transit for the Red Army to wherever its presence would be needed under the terms of any agreement that was hammered out. The Poles refused point-blank to consider it, and the Finns had already made their position clear to Boris Stein months before the opening of the three-power military talks in Moscow. No one had actually asked the smaller Baltic states their opinion. That this sequence of events is important is surely clear. The Finnish refusal to cooperate with Soviet defence needs actually came well before the Polish one, which only emerged as a contingent matter once the British and French delegates had sat down at Voroshilov's table on 11 August. But if neither Finland nor

Poland would have anything to do with the Red Army on their soil, a clear problem arose, at which point the military cards were laid on the table, almost literally.[39] It was clear that if these vulnerable countries between Germany and the USSR were to be protected by anyone in the event of German intentions becoming obviously hostile, then the only army which could even attempt to forestall them was the Red Army, a point of which the Poles were only too aware.

Voroshilov stated flatly, on 14 August, that the Red Army would be in a position to put 100 divisions in the field to counteract direct German aggression in Poland and the Balkans. Doumenc, the head of the French delegation, matched this with an equal balance, acknowledging freely at the same that the French forces were a long way away.[40] The British delegates, headed by Admiral Drax, were more circumspect, and were forced to admit that at present, British Army divisions were very few and far between.[41] The very fact that Drax was an admiral was perhaps intended to convey the implicit role of the Senior Service in this matter, as the British fleet was deemed unchallengeable, but suddenly, this had become a purely military matter, a bidding war for the hand of the Soviet Union, and the currency of choice at this auction was infantry.

The Russian response to the news that these putative allies had few resources to offer, and that they were unable to persuade either Poland or Finland to allow the Red Army access to their territory by treaty (this legalism was important to the Russians in the context of overall policy, given how they knew they would almost certainly abuse it) was simple. Voroshilov went off wildfowling, and the military conversations were over, almost before they had started. The Russians now knew that however large and well armed the French Army was (with some uncertain indicators of its readiness to act in the face of German aggression in Poland) the British Army was nowhere near its equal, not even militarily significant. This intelligence would find its way to Berlin in very short order. In return, Germany would provide equally useful information.

It was (in an unfashionable defence of British policy) a relatively honourable line that was adopted by London. There was surely little point in promising forces that were simply unavailable, and the French policy, which was to undertake to pressure Poland to accept the Russian territorial access demands without having the means to guarantee their safety, was perhaps less than straightforward in the light of the clear lack of interest that Poland had showed in being guaranteed by the Red Army. But further, the British government was, and remained, unhappy at the suspiciously loose definition of 'indirect aggression' as offered by Moscow, a matter that the French clearly considered a mere detail. Indeed, Doumenc was even authorized by George Bonnet, the French foreign minister, to accept, on the Poles' behalf, the Red Army's right of incursion should hostilities erupt. No one told the Poles, of course.

Famously, the talks were abandoned when Ribbentrop flew to Moscow and gave the Russians all they wanted, after which the British military mission made its way back home, curiously via Helsinki, where they were entertained to lunch by Erkko. The talk, perhaps predictably, turned to the possibility of a British naval presence in the Baltic: 'Possibly,' said Drax, 'and I'd know exactly what to do with it. I'd turn all the guns on Kronstadt.'[42] Such attitudes were, it must be said, far from rare in British establishment circles, but, interesting though this was to the Finns, the conversation went no further into detail.

CHAPTER TWO

Bear-baiting: The Emerging Crisis

First kill me before you take possession of my Fatherland.

Chief Sitting Bull, 1877

GIVEN HINDSIGHT, it seems quite bizarre that Winston Churchill, despite his responsibilities as First Lord of the Admiralty – and therefore the man who spoke for the largest and best navy in Europe – was not actually a member of the Supreme War Council. Neville Chamberlain had had little choice in bringing Churchill into the War Cabinet (indeed, back into his old job) the instant his own policy had come apart in his hands, but Churchill's very presence in government served as a constant reminder to all that Neville Chamberlain's best work as a politician was now clearly behind him.

As an engine for ideas, Churchill was very much in the Bugatti rather than the Rolls-Royce class. An unending stream of initiatives, suggestions, future policies and plans poured out of him, generating both heat and light in equal measure. He had, after all, run the navy before; he also had significant field experience as well as an intimate knowledge of the logistics of war. On a bewildering variety of topics, from the dreadnought to the cavalry charge, he could not be gainsaid, least of all by such unmartial figures as Neville Chamberlain, or the Foreign Secretary, Lord Halifax.

Despite (or because of) his lack of office, Churchill had served as a natural focus for dissident opinion as the policy of appeasement, which he had so bitterly opposed, quickly came unstitched and the first few weeks of war, with its attendant research, revealed the full horror of the state of the British Army, its manning, morale and equipment. Of the splendid sixty divisions – fit, motivated and superbly armed – with which Haig had finished the Great War on the Western Front, there was hardly a sign. The best army in the world had simply disappeared; it was now no better off (and in many cases much *worse* off) even than its Finnish counterpart. On the outbreak of war it disposed of – as current (i.e. instantly deployable) assets – only two fully fit divisions for the European theatre.

Much of this had to do with economy, but more than that it was the result of some clear cherry-picking on the part of government. For those who took the study of war seriously in the 1930s, it was clear that simple mass was no longer the answer – rather, it was technology, both in the air and on the ground. From Mikhail Tukhachevski to Basil Liddell Hart, most agreed that the future of offensive war revolved around the close coordination of combined arms, with fast, armoured vehicles, supported by the (subordinate) air arm, punching through to gain ground, with infantry offering support and consolidation.

From Britain's point of view, this may have been cheery news (at least financially) as it meant that the maintenance of a large Continental army, and its attendant cost, was now a dispensable luxury. Unhappily, the second element of this policy, that of sophisticated technology – good tanks and better anti-tank ordnance – had been left in abeyance for financial and policy reasons. For the nation that had invented the tank, this was embarrassing, to say the least, particularly when viewed against the integrated mobility of the Wehrmacht and the Luftwaffe, together now knifing through Poland.

So, on 7 September 1939, in an atmosphere of sepulchral gloom, General Edmund Ironside, the Chief of the Imperial General Staff, unveiled his preliminary plans for the army's war establishment needs to the Land Forces Committee. It was, not uncoincidentally, for fifty-five divisions from Britain, the Dominions and the

Empire, with full equipment for sixty. It was all to do. Like the auditor of a troubled corporation in receivership, Ironside went through the inventory point by point, remorselessly and in full: 'Winston and Co. were horrified when I produced the figures...'[1]

For any chief of staff starved of resources and – more critically – political support to his own satisfaction, a certain theatrical lip-smacking when pointing out the real effect of policy deficiencies is understandable – Mannerheim was doing the same thing in Helsinki. Worse was to come for the Prime Minister, though. At a War Cabinet meeting two days later it was decided to approve Ironside's estimates and prepare for a war of three years' duration. And, dreadfully (but inevitably), to inform the fourth estate. Ironside reported:

> When it was decided to dish this out to the papers the P.M. put his forehead down on the table and kept it there for nearly ten minutes. When he eventually looked up he looked more than ghastly ... When it was mentioned that the Chiefs of Staff were going to consider a recommendation of 'gloves off' [i.e. the bombing of Germany] in an Air War, he shook his head in a dull way as if it were too much to consider.[2]

For Chamberlain, who had become so personally identified with British policy, this must indeed have been a low moment and, for those witnessing the embarrassing spectacle of this uniquely personal crisis, one that must have generated at least mixed feelings. Worst of all was the clear realization (at least among those who did not know it already) that the guarantee which had been offered to Poland was, in the light of Ironside's disclosures, at best a rubber cheque and very probably a lot worse; an utterly false prospectus, the challenging of which by a puissant Germany had now led Britain to war. This was not a promising place from which to start.

Why did Chamberlain not resign? Clearly, to keep Churchill out of Downing Street. It must be borne in mind that the rivalry between these two men was almost Sicilian in its quality of mutual distrust, their differences over appeasement merely being one element of what amounted to a blood feud. At stake was not only the very soul of the Conservative Party, but also the resolution of issues which went back to their respective fathers. To Churchill's friends, he was but an imaginative scamp; to his opponents, he was little less than a gangster, and even worse, a gangster in a hurry. His choice of associates, even many who were agnostic about him agreed, seemed at best questionable.

What made Chamberlain's humiliation far worse was Churchill's steadfast refusal to glory in it publicly; a subtle and refined form of torture, we may regard it now, and infinitely more hurtful, changing the hapless Prime Minister's public demeanour, from the grave, industrious meritocrat,[3] noble and philosophical in the face of failure, to a mask of ungovernable, simian rage. From the hubris of Croydon airport to the nemesis of the Cabinet room had taken Chamberlain a mere fifty weeks, but it was upon the resolution of this man that so much now depended.

IN THAT SAME PERIOD, events had moved on in Helsinki, too, but if the Molotov-Ribbentrop pact had been a diplomatic embarrassment for His Majesty's Government, it marked potential disaster for Finland's. It took no great leap of logic to calculate that the stumbling blocks to the tripartite talks in Moscow – the delineation of the Soviet Union's sphere of influence, coupled with the problematic definition of that sinister phrase 'indirect aggression' – had been swept aside at the stroke of a pen. Given that the public version of the pact made no reference to either, it was widely assumed by those who had a stake in this that these must be matters covered in a secret protocol – and so it proved; ten days after the awful evidence of Britain's unpreparedness for war became public knowledge, the total dismemberment of Poland was undertaken by the Red Army and by 25 September it was all over. The Russians marched in with 470,000 troops, meeting only token resistance. The Polish Army had fought the Germans heroically, even inflicting a serious (and surprising) defeat on the Wehrmacht at Lvov, where General Sosnkowski's forces destroyed or captured eighty tanks (they had outrun their fuel bowsers) but it was not enough. With the entry of the Soviet Union, seizing territory in the way that a second lurcher seizes upon a weakened and bleeding hare, the Polish resistance effectively ceased, and what remained of the Polish General Staff slipped reluctantly over the Romanian border.[4] Behind them, the Red Army took over 400,000 Polish Army prisoners and established the new Russo-German border along the Bug, San and Vistula rivers.

The mass deportations east started immediately; the pact had survived its first test.[5] What was perhaps of more importance to neutral countries was that Anglo-French resolution had been tested and failed. There had been propaganda, to be sure, but the poverty of the British military balance sheet had been matched with a notable lack of resolution from Paris; the oft-promised move on the Seigfried Line, originally indicated by General Gamelin never – indeed, would never – take place. It had been scheduled for completion by 17 September, but events rather served to overtake it.[6]

For Moscow's cheerleaders in Western Europe, the Soviet action could not have come at a worse time. Already reeling from the profound shock of the Molotov-Ribbentrop pact (in response to which the broad swathe of progressive, pro-Soviet opinion had already scrambled to shorten the line in political debate) the Soviet invasion of eastern Poland was in all ways worse than what had already happened in western Poland. In this instance, the Soviet Union's action was only partly understood in terms of the doctrine of 'forward defence', a concept rather hard to sell in the light of the non-aggression pact of only three weeks before. To island Britain, and fortified France, the Russian annexation seemed at best opportunistic, and at worst begged the accusation of being an accessory after the fact; the obvious cynicism attendant upon such an action was rather a given. Others, perhaps relieved that there was no longer a Polish state to guarantee, even drew comfort from the joint communiqué issued (after four days of haggling) by Moscow and Berlin, that the Polish state had collapsed, effectively declaring *force majeure* on such diplomatic niceties as the 1934 Soviet-Polish non-aggression pact; no Poland, no pact, no problem. Germany had smashed Poland, and therefore the bilateral agreement between that benighted country and its eastern aggressor was now perforce in abeyance. Further, lest there be some misunderstanding, Moscow announced: 'The aim of these forces is to restore peace and order in Poland, which had been destroyed by the collapse of the Polish State, and to help the Polish population to reconstruct the conditions of its political existence.'[7]

Of course, nothing of the sort happened; far from it. For Moscow, the destruction of Poland, even the rump of it, was unfinished political business and had been since 1920 when the Red Army, accompanied by its many thousands of civil agitators,[8] had been repulsed in the westernmost extension of that same general war, which had already saved Finland from the fate that now befell Poland. 'If the Germans come', Marshal Smigly-Rydz[9] had stated only a month before, in August 1939, 'we lose our freedom. If the Russians come, we lose our souls.'[10] As things now transpired, they had lost both.

THE FAR LEFT IN Western Europe had spent much of the 1930s carefully building a link between anti-Fascism, Socialism and even (by a truly vertigo-inducing leap of logic) Christianity.[11] So successful had it been in doing this, and so ably assisted by Moscow, that one of the core precepts of Marxism-Leninism, that peace and war are merely two sides of the same coin, a period of peace merely being a hiatus in the revolutionary process, was rather forgotten, so that the association between anti-Fascism and the left (rather than anti-Fascism and the bourgeoisie), became in many ways implicit and thus interchangeable for the logically sloppy.

For the conservative right matters were more straightforward, and there was no better example of the embedded tension between the two extremes of the spectrum than that of Spain. In August 1938, a Conservative MP, Commander Bower, wrote:

> The average Conservative does not regard a Communist merely as a member of an ordinary political party: he regards him as a mortal danger to Christian civilisation ...[a] foul, cancerous disease of the human soul

... and the Spanish Government, if not Communist at the moment, is at least a 'contact' and going through a period of incubation. As we see it, Communism is something far more than a political or philosophical creed; it is the deadliest enemy of our very civilisation. Before its threat, the hypothetical dangers of a Franco victory sink into comparative insignificance...

The average Conservative dislikes dictators ... but we have one thing in common with them, a loathing of that bestial creed, Communism. The dictators may threaten us politically and economically, but (excluding, of course, Soviet Russia) they have no exportable philosophy with which to corrupt the very souls of our people. Reduced to simple terms, the Spanish war is a conflict between Christian civilisation and the Beast. That is why so many of us hope that Franco will win.[12]

No confusion there, then. Bower's view – a reasonably typical standpoint – seems uncompromising now, but given the outcomes in Eastern Europe in the wake of the Second World War, at least in terms of a strictly *libertarian* analysis, it is a difficult one with which to differ now.

The same woolliness of the left, in the light of its collective willingness to be duped by Soviet motives for intervening in Spain, also served to produce the profound sense of shock at the announcement of the Molotov-Ribbentrop pact. But, as J. F. C. Fuller has pointed out:

A fundamental principle in Marxian dialectics is verbal inversion. When the accepted meaning of a word or idea is turned upside down, not only are Communist intentions obscured, but the mind of the non-Communist is misled, and mental confusion leads to a semantic nightmare in which things appear to be firmly planted on their feet, but actually are standing on their heads.

And:

This process of mental contortion is to be seen at most conferences between Communist and non-Communist powers. Disarmament to one means one thing, to the other another thing; so also does peace. While to the non-Communist peace is a state of international harmony, to the

Communist it is a state of international discord … Communists hold that peace and war are reciprocal terms for a conflict which can only end when Marxian Beatitude is established; since their final aim is pacific, they are peace lovers.[13]

Apart from presenting a very tidy analysis of the roots of twentieth-century political correctness, General Fuller is describing perfectly the dilemma of the left Liberal in 1930s Western Europe; that, given Moscow's intentions were, in the longest possible term, clearly and honourably Utopian, obviously its conduct in the short term, therefore, was misunderstood only by reactionaries. Further, by a few eliminating pen strokes, cancelling out the moderate, the apathetic and, critically, the neutral, the algebra was reduced to the far simpler self-proving twin formulae, that anti-Communism equals Fascism, and, by deduction, that anti-Fascism can legitimately *only* mean sympathy with the Communist cause. A derivative supposition, that questioning but reactionary instinct *equals* Fascism, is still with us. But by that questionable reckoning, both Poland and Finland were Fascist; QED.

Thus was the ground prepared. Whole sectors of moderate thought, particularly the soft-left and pacific, were thus hijacked. From the Left Book Club to the Peace Pledge Union, the organization, operation and, vitally, the *soul* of these bodies commonly fell into the hands of the carefully placed cadres of steely activists.[14]

If the Molotov-Ribbentrop pact had stretched credulity (and it did), then the military-political alliance which seemed to be in place after the partition of Poland snapped it entirely. There was a rush to rationalize: on 22 September 1939, Stafford Cripps defended the Soviet action in Poland in the pages of *Tribune*, only a fortnight after he and Aneurin Bevan had encouraged Socialists to 'assist the forces of anti-Fascism' in the same journal, in a piece which of course had reflected only German actions; the Soviet invasion took place in the early hours of 17 September, before the copy deadline. Cripps's timing in this was at best unfortunate; it would cost him his Labour Party membership.

Certainly very few, if any, commentators viewed the extraordinary activity on the Soviet Union's western borders, of which the pact was merely the overture, as being essentially retrospective, a simple process of re-establishing a territorial *status quo ante*, but in effect, that is what it was. The careless but unavoidable loss of the western possessions of the Tsarist state in the civil war and its aftermath was a constant irritant in terms of the security of the Soviet one – the Central Committee simply felt naked without them – and it was, in effect, this desire to turn back the clock that had governed the signature of the Berlin-Moscow rapprochement of August 1939 after years, as Stalin himself eloquently put it, of 'pouring buckets of shit over each other'.

The fate of Poland was, of course, proof positive that the Soviet Union had been, according to the pact, allowed its own Monroe doctrine – free rein in its own back yard; to build up buffer territory under the polite fiction that it was the Western Allies, particularly Britain, who were the persistent and obvious enemy, and therefore one to be most feared by Moscow. The probability of secret annexes to the agreement loomed large, particularly in Anglo-French government circles, as much of the spring and summer of 1939 had been spent in attempting to come to some sort of agreement that might offer a coherent anti-Nazi policy, in effect recreating the pattern of alliances which had been in place until Brest-Litovsk in 1918.

IN KEEPING WITH THE orderly progression of events, which rather characterized the administration of Soviet foreign policy, and in delayed lock-step with Germany, the Soviet invasion of what was left of Poland took place only after the completion of unfinished Red Army business in Manchuria; the launch of the month-long campaign against Japanese forces on the Khalkin-Gol River, at Nomonhan, took place on the eve of the signing of the Russo-German pact. Only after victory there on 15 September did the Red Army occupy the space kindly reserved for it in Poland.

Within what was left of eastern Poland, which had become overnight western Ukraine, the new Soviet administration carried on where it had left off in 1920; as well as the remains of the Polish

Army, the country was purged of 'reactionary elements' as a savage class war was declared. Teachers, librarians, farmers, lawyers, and particularly landowners, were rounded up and the orgy of killing began. The Russians behaved with an irrational brutality that still beggars belief, grisly evidence of which was to be uncovered in 1941 by an astonished Wehrmacht and a much more thoughtful SS.

Beatrice Webb, clearly traumatized, observed twenty years of hard lobbying, together with potential future royalties, literally, going up in smoke.[15] Her diary entry for 18 September read:

> Owing to the lust for the old territories of Czarist Russia to be won by force, the statesmen of the U.S.S.R. have lost not merely moral prestige, but also the freedom to develop the new civilization, while the old western civilization was being weakened and perhaps destroyed by war. To me it seems the blackest tragedy in human history. Sidney [husband] observes that within a century, it may be a forgotten episode. He refuses to be downcast.[16]

The British War Cabinet issued a communiqué that evening: 'The British Government has learned with horror and indignation of Russia's invasion of Poland. Their obligations would not be altered by it and they remain confident that Poland would be restored at the end of the war.'[17] But no mention of even the possibility of a declaration of war on the Soviet Union.

The new territories of both the Reich and the Soviet Union were enshrined in a Friendship and Boundary Treaty, which was added to the text of the August pact, and in preparation for Ribbentrop's scheduled visit to Moscow on 27 September, Stalin informed von der Schulenberg that he intended: '…immediately to take up the solution of the problem of the Baltic States in accordance with the Secret Protocol and expected the unstinting support of the German Government. Stalin expressly indicated Estonia, Latvia and Lithuania but did not mention Finland.'[18]

In fact, Stalin had already started; even as the Red Army reached its new stations, the diplomatic pressure on the Baltic states to the north had commenced, starting with Estonia. As ever, there was a particular gripe; the damaged Polish submarine, Orzel,[19] had take refuge in Tallinn, on the southern coast of the Gulf of Finland and, it was maintained, the Estonians had been neglectful of their obligations to maintain security in the Baltic area by allowing it to escape. To say that this was a surprise to the Estonian Foreign Minister Karl Selter would be an understatement; he had been under the impression that he was in Moscow on 25 September to talk about trade agreements. Not so: 'Periscopes,' added Molotov, 'had been seen in the Baltic.' He then produced a ready drafted Soviet-Estonian 'mutual assistance' pact, upon which the ink was obviously already dry, and the only important clause of which, under all the boiler-plate, was the right of the Soviet Union to station up to 25,000 troops, already clustered at the Estonian border, at selected points about the country.

Selter attempted to rally, but was brusquely cut off; Molotov advised him not to force the Soviet government to use 'other, more radical measures to strengthen its security'. And, in case Selter was still unaware of the nature of what was really happening, he added menacingly: 'Don't imagine that Germany will help you; I am sure the German Government will approve of the proposed treaty.'[20] Further, Molotov went on, in as neat an exposition of Soviet policy as anyone had heard thus far: 'The Soviet union has become a powerful state with a highly developed industry, and in possession of a great military force. The status quo which was established twenty years ago when the Soviet Union was weakened by civil war can no longer be considered as adequate to the present situation...'[21]

Selter flew home immediately and consulted the German minister in Tallinn, Frohwein, who listened courteously and informed the Foreign Ministry in Berlin. Before a formal response could be given, poor Selter relayed the depressing news, on the 26th, that Moscow was demanding an answer: 'We are inclined to accept.' And so they did, signing this unavoidable and one-sided document on 28 September.

In the light of the foregoing, neither Latvia nor Lithuania were in any position to decline similar offers from Molotov; the Latvian Foreign Minister Vilhelms Munters arrived in Moscow on 2 October, signing his treaty three days later and his Lithuanian counterpart Juozas Urbšys's visit overlapped (they may even have crossed paths in Molotov's outer office), arriving on the 3rd and, doing his best, managing to hold out with some semblance of dignity, until 11 October.

But still, it seemed, all was not clear. Slightly bemused German Foreign Service officers reported that the small Baltic republics seemed to be *grateful* to Germany that the situations now imposed upon them had not been far worse, given what had happened to Poland. For this, they assumed that Ribbentrop had somehow intervened on their behalf. He had not. In the first week of October, the order went out that all *Volkdeutsche* (Gentile Balts of German heritage, birth, or even 'appearance') should be henceforth placed under the protection of the Reich and 'repatriated' if they so wished. Most did. What they discovered, though, was that they were to be resettled in what had been Poland, the German portion of which was already in the grip of an ethnic cleansing operation that, for the moment at least, seemed relatively modest when compared to what Russia was already doing to the east of the new border.

For Stalin and Molotov, this reacquisition of the entire territory to the south of the Baltic lost during the Revolution represented an astonishing *coup de main,* and, the minor losses in Poland aside, a bloodless one, at least for the Red Army. In three weeks, every square yard that had made up the western frontier of the Tsarist state southwards from Tallinn, to southern Poland, had been cowed into submission, secured and garrisoned. Aside from some desirable real estate (Bukovina) on the Romanian border, most of which was not addressed by the August pact,[22] the task of rebuilding the western defences was almost complete, only six weeks into the general European war. However, there was still Finland.

The meek and sequential compliance of the Baltic states could not have been expected to do anything but unsettle the Finns; since the Soviet invasion of eastern Poland, there had been little or no mention of Finland in any public pronouncement by either Hitler or Stalin. In Helsinki, not to mention the wider country as a whole, this silence, through which now echoed the previous words of Yartsev, Litvinov, Stein and Molotov, was uncomfortable. The apparent *impasse* was broken on 5 October. A note from Molotov was dispatched to the Finnish minister in Moscow, Baron Aarno Yrjö-Koskinen; it invited Foreign Minister Erkko to visit Moscow to discuss certain 'concrete political questions'. An RSVP was demanded within 48 hours.

With the events to the south demonstrating clearly that the Soviet-German *rapprochement* actually worked, there would be little point in Finland making bland assurances of neutrality; this was no time for bromides of the sort that had already irritated Moscow, and enough hints had been dropped over the previous eighteen months as to Soviet intentions that no one was in any serious doubt as to what these 'concrete political questions' would be. Whatever they were, they were unlikely to be to Finland's advantage. But first things first; orders went out to mobilize the border-guard element of the army and Erkko, as ever optimistic, dropped in to see the German minister, von Blücher.

Dr Wipert von Blücher, had, until that autumn of 1939, been serenely happy in his job. Although he was not a Nazi[23] (he was a little too grand for that), he was a first-rate diplomatist. He had been in post since 1935 and had developed an affection for Finland that went far beyond the ordinary. He understood how Finns felt, the structure and process of their constitution, and, as he was essentially a Wilhelmine Prussian gent who knew at first hand the perils of autocracy, he had also grasped (or attempted to) the essentially Athenian processes that Finland revered so much, a sentiment which he was starting, perhaps dangerously, to share.

His reporting telegram to the Foreign Ministry in Berlin went out on the evening of 6 October.[24] It bordered on the timid, as if his watered-down description of the peremptory nature of Molotov's summons – he described it as an *invitation* for an *exchange of views*[25] – could engage Berlin in some creative thinking:

The Foreign Minister [Erkko] remarked that if the Russian plans were directed towards Viipuri or Åland, as rumour had it, the Finnish government would have to reject them and prepare for the worst. The frontier guard has already been mobilized since last night.

He discreetly intimated that he would like to know whether Finland would find any support from Germany in the event of excessive Russian demands. In this connection he repeated a previous statement of mine that there were now only two great powers in the Baltic: Germany and Russia.

Later that evening, Hitler made a speech to a special session of the Reichstag, in effect a review of the events of the first month of war, with special reference to the Baltic. Ominously, he did not mention Finland, an omission which caused much consternation, although some assumed that he did not need to – relations were surely healthy and normal? Others, notably (but not solely) Mannerheim, took a more realistic view. Even before the entry of the Soviet Union into Poland, he had hoped that the Anglo-French forces were as well equipped as their enemy: '...otherwise we are all going towards slavery'. And afterwards, as he surveyed the smoking results of the joint efforts of the two tyrants: 'And whose turn is next, when the appetite of these two gentlemen has managed to grow?'[26] But these were private thoughts; professionally, Mannerheim had not enjoyed his summer. He had, since the Czechoslovakian crisis, taken a deeply gloomy view: 'It seems,' he had written in March, 'quite simply to be the aim to change the people of Europe into white Negroes in the service of the Third Reich.'[27]

IT HAD BEEN DECIDED, almost as soon as Yrjö-Koskinen's message was decoded, that Erkko was probably not the man to send to Moscow (Blücher's message rather tends to confirm this); rather, the man selected was Juho Paasikivi, now working his way towards a well-earned retirement as the Finnish minister in Stockholm, from whence he was immediately summoned.[28] He was nearly 70, and, although a well-respected Grand Old Man of the Conservative Party, had not taken an active interest in Finnish politics, foreign or domestic, since 1920, when he had led the

Finnish delegation, eyeball to eyeball with Stalin and Trotsky, at the Treaty of Tartu. Some later commentators have viewed Paasikivi as a tactless choice, but in truth, despite the ideological chasm between Paasikivi and Stalin, the Finn was a practical man, if inclined to despair from time to time, rather like Mannerheim. He was also, ironically, the man who had, with immaculately awful timing, attempted to reintroduce a monarchical constitution for Finland in October 1918, by inviting the Kaiser's brother-in-law to become King Väinö I, the strategy so effectively sabotaged, first by Mannerheim and more firmly by later events.

That this matter was urgent was left in no doubt on the evening of 7 October. Yrjö-Koskinen was again called round to Molotov's office to be reminded icily (in a straight reissue of his sinister remarks to Selter) of the 'other means' at Moscow's disposal in the event that Helsinki declined negotiation. That same evening Vladimir Deravianski turned up at Erkko's office in Helsinki – unannounced, and quite possibly more than a little drunk – doing what he did best: blustering that Moscow was 'boiling over' at Helsinki's discourtesy.[29] Clearly, Erkko's non-appearance signified that this process would not be any ritual show of obeisance. 'The place of a Foreign Minister is with his government,' responded Erkko, with a coolness he probably did not feel.

Wearily, Paasikivi prepared for his journey to Moscow. With him, he took Johan Nykopp, a senior Foreign Ministry official, and, upon Mannerheim's insistence, Colonel Aladár Paasonen, a noted authority on Red Army matters and, as important, one of Mannerheim's close circle. Since all three men spoke fluent Russian (although Paasikivi's was rusty), no interpreter was included. Paasikivi's brief from the Cabinet, drafted by Erkko, was very precise, more a straightjacket than an agenda. He was not authorized to discuss anything other than three small islands in the Gulf of Finland. The Ålands were off the menu, and so was Hanko Cape. As for the gulf islands (which did not, awkwardly, include Hogland), he was permitted to either lease them or swap them for border territory in Karelia; the Finnish Cabinet assumed that this modest real-estate transaction would be well within his capabilities – he had, since retiring from active politics and prior to his Stockholm appointment, been running a bank.

Von Blücher, meanwhile, had received an answer to his telegram on 7 October, and it was not the one for which he had hoped; indeed, it was the one he probably dreaded most. From Ribbentrop himself, it laid out in bleak terms the essence of German policy. It was copied to the legations in Estonia and Latvia (Lithuania was still stubbornly holding out in Moscow, plaintively haggling over minor territorial matters):

> During the Moscow negotiations with the Soviet government, the question of delimiting the spheres of interest of both countries in Eastern Europe was discussed in strict confidence, not only with reference to the former Polish state, but also with reference to the countries of Lithuania, Latvia, Estonia and Finland.
>
> …The [demarcation] line is identical with the German / Lithuanian frontier. Thus it follows that Lithuania, Latvia, Estonia and Finland do not belong to the German sphere of interest … You are requested to refrain, as heretofore, from any explanation on this subject.[30]

From elsewhere, however, there was some encouragement, albeit cosmetic. In advance of Paasikivi's arrival in Moscow, the ministers plenipotentiary of Denmark, Norway and Sweden presented identical notes expressing the hope that: 'nothing be done to prevent Finland from pursuing its full independence, her neutrality and her cooperation with the rest of Scandinavia.'[31]

Molotov refused to receive either the notes or the envoys who bore them.

BY THAT PECULIAR PROCESS of Brownian motion, which always seems to deliver the distribution of unwelcome news, the purpose of Paasikivi's mission appeared to be a matter of public knowledge by the time he arrived at Helsinki station at 9p.m. on the evening of 9 October. There had been no public announcement save a brief, non-committal statement that a delegation was going to Moscow.

To the trio's surprise, there was a huge crowd of several thousand present at the railway station. It watched silently as the delegation entrained itself, and then, spontaneously, gave voice. There were two choral themes in particular: the National Anthem and Luther's hymn ('*Ein Feste Burg*'), the latter properly delivered in Finnish rather than its native German. It was nothing more or less than a giant, spontaneous collective gesture, both calm and intended to be calming. Surely no modern diplomatist setting out to do his country's business has ever departed with such a simple statement of good faith. But neither has one been sent off with such an eloquent reminder of his responsibilities, should he fail. As the train pulled away, orders were cut for the full mobilization of the Finnish Army, under the guise of 'refresher exercises' for reservists. Contingency plans were also drawn up for the evacuation of women and, more particularly, children from the major population centres. Few believed there would be a war, but the Poles had believed that, too.

INITIALLY, THE MOSCOW talks went well, but were marked by a curious, unrehearsed character with no formal agenda. In a sense, one was not needed; it had been set over two hundred years before. The first encounter of this phase took place in the Kremlin on the afternoon of 12 October. Present for the Russians were Stalin, Molotov, Assistant Commissar Potemkin and Deravianski. With that menacing bluntness which had cowed Selter, Munters and Ursbšys, Molotov attempted to open the conversation. Would Finland accede to the same form of 'non-aggression' pact so recently signed by Erkko's Baltic counterparts? That was easy – *No*. This negative, expressed by Paasikivi so that there would be absolutely no misunderstanding, was careful to employ the word 'unthinkable'. Perhaps, unsurprisingly, the matter was not raised again.

Stalin now took the floor, with a six-point exposition of the terms needed to ensure the safety of Leningrad.

1 Finland would lease to the USSR the entire Hanko peninsula for a period of thirty years for the purpose of building a Soviet naval base, which would include coastal artillery. This would effectively seal off the Gulf of Finland and therefore the Leningrad approaches.

2 The Baltic fleet would have the right to use nearby Lappvik bay as an anchorage.

3 Finland would cede the Gulf islands already mentioned, as well as Björkö.

4 The Soviet–Finnish border on the Karelian Isthmus would be moved back, away from Leningrad.

5 The Finnish fortifications on the Isthmus would be dismantled (as clearly unnecessary).

6 The cession of the western part of the Fisherman's peninsula.

In other words, this proposal implied the confiscation of every single element of Finnish security to her east as well as the removal of the strategic integrity of the port of Petsamo in the far north. In return, Stalin offered a valueless, 3,450 square-mile slab of Soviet Karelia as territorial compensation,[32] an unsubtle sop to the rabid Karelian irredentists of whom he had heard so much from Deravianski, but who represented at best the thinly populated and eccentric end of the political spectrum.

There was one small, unforced concession; that of the Åland question, which was left open, provided that no other country participated in the islands' fortification. That could be Finland's privilege. The inevitable question – *with what?* – was left unasked. Finland could keep the Ålands, but the price would be the security of Petsamo. This was subtler than it seemed – to stake a claim on the Åland archipelago would be to invite some measure of Swedo-Finnish solidarity against Soviet pressure. (See page 80 *et seq*)

With that, the first stage of the talks broke up. There was nothing else that a sensible diplomatist – and Paasikivi was, despite his famously irascible temper, such a man[33] – could do. The Finnish delegation took their leave in order to reflect on what had been said, to read the written version of the proposals and take soundings in Helsinki. A further meeting was arranged for 14 October.

Meanwhile, Colonel Paasonen busied himself with a military critique of the Soviet proposals vis-à-vis Leningrad. In this, he would certainly have been briefed by Mannerheim and other colleagues – indeed, it is not impossible that the brief he produced, anticipating the initiative, had already been composed in Helsinki. The essence of his argument revolved around the central thesis that whoever held the southern shore of the Gulf effectively controlled all access to the Gulf itself. Now that the USSR had the right to Baltiski (Baltischport) in Estonia, as well as other newly-acquired southern coastal assets including Ösel and Dagö, then surely the Hanko peninsula and the Gulf islands, particularly Björkö, were surplus to requirements? Further, given the narrowness of the Gulf of Finland, the sort of assault the USSR feared was surely impractical, given the developments in ordnance which had taken place of late.

To say that the Finns were suspicious would be to understate the matter somewhat. The absence of the Ålands on the agenda was actually far from encouraging. The islands were Finnish territory by League of Nations convention – by the removal of Finnish mainland defences that Stalin's proposals implied the whole country, Ålands included, would now be a simple target. None of the delegates was yet aware that Finland had been abandoned to its fate by the August pact (von Blücher was maintaining a loyal silence, as instructed) but here now was a large hint that this might be the case. The Åland question had been the great Baltic *cause célèbre* since 1921 – a real Great Power issue – but here, it was not mentioned at all. The key issue for the Finns, in the light of Russo-German rapprochement, was obvious. From whom, exactly, did the Russians fear attack?

Courageously, Paasikivi read Paasonen's paper aloud, in Russian, to the meeting on 14 October. It fell on stony ground, but triggered an autodidact's disquisition by Stalin – a potted history of the region, in effect, displaying not only his remarkable grasp of detail, but more revealingly, his essentially civil war era strategic mindset. Then, the meat:

You asked which power could attack us. Britain or Germany. With Germany we now have good relations. But everything in this world can change. Both Britain and Germany are able to send strong naval forces into the Gulf of Finland. I doubt that you could then stay out of the conflict. Britain is already putting pressure on Sweden for bases [sic]. Germany is doing the same [sic]. Once the war between those two is over, the fleet of the victor will sail into the Gulf of Finland. Yudenitch attacked along the Gulf, and later the British did the same.

Right or wrong, all this had little to do with the border on the Isthmus, a subject to which Stalin now turned:

Since we cannot move Leningrad... then we must move the border. You ask why we want Björkö. I will tell you why. When I asked Ribbentrop why Germany had attacked Poland, he replied: 'We had to move the Polish frontier farther from Berlin.' Before the war, the distance from Posen [Poznan] was about 200 kilometres. Now the border has been moved 300 kilometres farther east. We ask that the distance from Leningrad to the border should be 70 kilometres. As to Björkö, you must bear in mind that if 16" guns were placed there, the movements of our fleet could be entirely paralysed in the far [eastern] end of the Gulf. We are asking for 2,700 square kilometres and offer in return 5,500. Would any other Big Power do that? No, only we are that stupid.[34]

Grotesque falsehoods anent Poland aside, Stalin revealed clearly that his suspicions concerning current events had their roots in the time of greatest danger from twenty years before, which made perfect sense of the otherwise apparently random selection of the Petsamo region as an objective – to provide security for Murmansk and, further west, Archangel, the latter being the area where the current British CIGS, Ironside, had last served actively abroad.[35]

In supporting this position, Molotov claimed that Paasikivi, in listening too closely to his military advisers, ran the risk that the stakes may even be raised, with dark hints about the frontier of Peter the Great. Whereas the Finns were minded to discuss the situation in terms of the Treaty of Tartu – which both Stalin and Paasikivi had signed – the Russians were now disposed to consider matters in a much grander, historical sweep, revealing the ancient geopolitical dispositions of a violent, creative, but ultimately unhinged, autocrat.

Suddenly, the situation for Finland looked bleak. Paasikivi, following both the letter and the spirit of his brief, pleaded time to return to Helsinki and consult. Stalin affably assented, but with the proviso that time was now of the essence. He observed that Finland had mobilized, and that Red Army units were now on the Isthmus, as Paasikivi would have been aware: 'This cannot go on for long without danger of accidents.' Otherwise, Stalin and even the plodding Molotov were now charm itself. As Paasikivi reminded them that a parliamentary assent would be required to discuss the issue, let alone approve it, and that if this were to be taken further, a five-sixths majority would be required, Stalin was jocular: 'Don't worry – you'll get 99 per cent!' Molotov added: 'And our votes on top. We'll sign an agreement on October 20th, and on the following evening, I'll throw a party for you!' 'Iron-arse' thus displayed a useful ignorance of the workings of a democracy, both in terms of time taken to ratify decisions, as well as the likely outcome.[36]

Paasikivi, Paasonen and Nykopp courteously took their leave and boarded the train from the October Station to Leningrad. From there, the journey from the crowded Finland Station, passing as it did through a milling confusion of Red Army soldiery, all apparently heading for the Isthmus, was sobering. The delegates arrived back in Helsinki on 16 October, where Paasikivi briefly addressed the waiting journalists. 'Mr. Stalin,' he stated dryly, 'was a pleasant fellow with a sense of humour.'

THE IMPLICIT CHALLENGE to Scandinavian unity from the absence of the Åland question on the Moscow agenda caused a predictable frisson of concern through the entire Nordic region, particularly in the light of Molotov's previous rudeness to the Scandinavian ministers before the Finns' visit to see him. Accordingly, a rare event was hurriedly laid on in Stockholm – the conference of the three kings – of Sweden, Denmark and Norway – attended by the singularly un-regal, aged and bowed (but movingly dignified in his hour of need) President Kyosti Kallio. Erkko accompanied him.

Predictably, the public appearance of Scandinavian solidarity in the midst of potential chaos was soothing, at least at the popular level. In government circles, however, it was all rather different. Rickard Sandler, the strongest advocate of a Swedo-Finnish solution to the Åland question, found himself marginalized, as his pet scheme had now been rather struck off the agenda. His enemies in the Swedish Cabinet were quick to exploit this, thus neatly playing themselves into Russia's hands. If the Ålands were not at present a Russian concern, their argument went, surely the Swedish military could not now be expected to transfer its attention to the Karelian Isthmus? If the sole basis for a military alliance – the joint fortification and defence of a *Swedish*-speaking archipelago – was no longer urgent, then there was little else to say.

As Erkko sat in conclave with three of his Swedish opposite numbers (Sandler attempting to be encouraging, the others merely gloomy), he felt his habitual bounce becoming rather subdued. Oddly, although he described Stalin's demands with some precision, Erkko did not mention war as a possible outcome. He, therefore, did not ask the vital question, probably because he feared the answer he might receive, of what assistance Finland might expect from its western neighbour. The feeling that dear friends had suddenly become mere acquaintances was a small but nagging doubt in his usually optimistic mind. The contrast between public gesture and private reality could not have been more marked.

The Swedish General Staff, the senior members of which were of a similar caste and outlook to Mannerheim, was assessing the matter rather more positively.[37] The Staff was at work to produce a convincing argument that Swedish support for Finland's clear plight should go further than merely the Åland initiative. It would conclude that Soviet intentions would not stop at Finland, and that Russia as a direct, odiferous neighbour would be a less than fine idea. A declaration of military support for Finland *at this moment* could save costlier measures later. It was nearly right, as events transpired, but it was not a view that would find much support, particularly not from the man who held the purse strings, Ernest Wigforss, the finance minister, and Rickard Sandler's openly committed foe in Cabinet. Wigforss later recalled: 'The most remarkable feature of the military reports was how quickly the scene shifted from the Åland islands to the Karelian Isthmus and to the question of how many Swedish Divisions might be needed there.'[38] Clearly, the traditional pacific Social Democrat distrust of the perceived military mindset – always wanting more tiresomely expensive toys, always spoiling for a fight – was alive and well in Stockholm that autumn.

In Helsinki, however, there was at street level at least a measure of collective euphoria. The prospect of proper, indivisible Scandinavian mutual security seemed now, to the uninformed, to loom large, and the Finnish government did little to disabuse the revellers of this notion. For there had also been a marked, almost overnight improvement in the state of social tension. The fact that Swedish-speaking 'Finlanders' were openly celebrating alongside 'real Finns' was enough to bring a brief, wintry rictus to even Mannerheim's stern aspect. But he was very worried; his private conversations would have revealed that however constructive his opposite numbers in Stockholm's General Staff were trying to be, the political acceptability of such an approach was always going to be questionable. Whatever Erkko's Tiggerish optimism suggested, it was common knowledge that at this moment if the single fundamental of Finland's foreign policy was Russia, then Sweden's was Germany.

And Erkko *was* optimistic, on the surface at least. After the anodyne post-conference communiqué, issued with great attention to detail by the Swedish government, was released – stating nothing but a continuation of *individual* Scandinavian neutrality – the question then returned: what to say to Moscow? More importantly, who to say it? The date of Molotov's putative cocktail party had been 21 October. It was on that day that the second Finnish delegation finally set off, by train once more, for the Finland Station in Leningrad.

Paasikivi had insisted that he be accompanied this time by a Cabinet minister and Väinö Tanner was the man chosen. As leader of the Social Democrats, it was held (quite wrongly, in fact) that a strong line carrying his authority would perhaps serve to convince the Russians that he bore with him the total support of the working class of Finland, who, as the bulk of the army, would naturally endure the worst of any potential conflict. The Finnish Cabinet had still to grasp the essential truth, that Social Democrats were anathema to hard Bolsheviks, and worse, that these particular Bolsheviks were now, all else having failed with Finland, of a firmly imperial cast of mind.

Like the first delegation, this expanded one was seen off with songs and late flowers. The train was slow, unavoidably delayed by troop movements, this time on the Finnish side of the border, as the mobilization orders were put into final effect and the tiny, ill-equipped Finnish Army moved towards its preliminary dispositions in front of Viipuri.

TANNER HAD NOT laid eyes on Leningrad in more than twenty years.[39] It had been St Petersburg then. It seemed little changed to him now, except for the unusual number of people who were gathered there to observe the arrival of this well-publicized second delegation whose agenda was so secret. They were merely watching; there was no singing here. Across the Neva River could just be glimpsed the Smolny institute, an edifice that had acquired all the significance of the Temple of Solomon in Bolshevik theology, where Andrei Zhdanov – curiously remote from these negotiations – now held court. It had once been an elite girls' school and, perhaps for that very reason, it had been selected as Party headquarters. In previous times, Mannerheim had sent both his daughters there.

The delegates entrained for Moscow in a very grand first-class carriage aboard the *Red Star Express* and arrived on the morning of 23 October. They were met by Deravianski, who was slightly uneasy at the presence of the three other Scandinavian ministers plenipotentiary, there to offer at least moral support. Packard limousines whisked the Finnish party to their own legation at breakneck speed, klaxons blaring. There was light traffic, but it was held up by imperious militiamen as the small convoy hurtled through the streets. Clearly, this was intended to be a visit of some moment.

At the Kremlin, where the delegation was greeted with an impressive courtesy almost Tsarist in its *punctilio*, the men were ushered into the presence of Stalin and Molotov. Paasikivi opened the discussion by reading a prepared statement, which indicated that Finland would be prepared to cede six islands in the Gulf of Finland. These would be sufficient to provide both observation points westwards as well as extra security for the massive island fortress of Kronstadt, headquarters of the Baltic fleet. Further, the memorandum stated, there could be border rectification in Russia's favour on the Isthmus of approximately 13 kilometres in the south-west, which, if it did not remove all of Moscow's concerns, at least went some way towards that objective. It also straightened out an obvious kink in the frontier which, in time of tension, might offer a strategically uncomfortable salient. Unhappily, the Hanko Cape was not up for discussion. In essence, this proposal was what Mannerheim had suggested offering Boris Stein six months earlier. The paper concluded with a few paragraphs of goodwill bromide concerning the 1932 non-aggression pact. There was a brief silence, during which Paasikivi asked if it would be permissable to speak in either English or German, as his Russian was clearly not as fluent as he had recalled it to be.[40] '*Nyet*,' said Molotov.

Stalin now took over. The Finnish proposals were insufficient, he stated. Russian demands were 'minimal' and also the 'very minimum' and therefore haggling over them was pointless. At this point, he launched into another situational assessment, which Paasikivi and the others had heard before, but Tanner, of course, had not. Again, Stalin stressed the danger from Anglo-French intentions, mentioning Germany only in passing.

Round and round the circular conversation went, always coming back to the same issues: Hanko, with a garrison of 5,000 men, and the border. Stalin then produced a map upon which he sketched, very roughly, his minimum requirements for the border

on the Isthmus. At one point, the Finns offered a small concession in the far north concerning the Rybachi peninsula, but this did
not deter the Russians. After two hours of this tedious haggling,
Tanner's patience, never particularly elastic, was wearing very
thin, and he made clear his view that the meeting was over.
Molotov feigned astonishment: 'Is it your intention to provoke a
conflict?' Paasikivi, visibly cross, snapped back on his colleague's
behalf: 'We want no such thing, but you seem to.' Stalin said
nothing, merely smiled behind his moustache. At 8 p.m., the
Finnish delegation departed, armed with Stalin's map. That, it
seemed, was that.

Back at the legation, the delegates pored over the proposals and
the map during a scratch supper. At 9 p.m. the telephone rang,
offering another meeting at 10.30 that evening at the Kremlin.
This was shortly afterwards put back to 11p.m. Another Packard
was waiting for them outside, and the delegation was driven back
to the Kremlin at the now clearly habitual Grand Prix speed.

Apart from Stalin and Molotov, a tiny concession also awaited
them. The proposal for the size of the Hanko Cape garrison had
been cut to 4,000 men. On the other hand, the border rectification was still insufficient. Tanner and Paasikivi could only attempt
to buy time citing, quite reasonably, that the Cabinet and the Diet
would need time to digest this matter. This time round, there
were no light-hearted remarks about majorities, nor was there
any mention of a party, although the farewells were as amicable as
the *impasse* permitted.

There was now some time for sightseeing and Tanner took the
opportunity, under the aegis of *Intourist*, to inspect, among other
things, Lenin's tomb. He had his own escort of NKVD men, who
were mightily impressed when he revealed that he had actually
met the great man, indeed shaken his hand, but he chose –
typically – to spoil the moment, by remarking, as he inspected
the shiny mummified remains, that in life 'his head had been
much bigger.'[41] The scandalized guards shooed him out into Red
Square. Having demonstrated that diplomacy was not his strong
suit, he proceeded back to the legation.

There were no more last-minute proposals for late meetings, and the thoughtful delegates departed from Moscow on 24 October. They left Leningrad's Finland Station the next day – this time, ominously, the platform was roped off and under an armed NKVD guard.

TANNER'S FIRST INSTINCT was to agree with Paasikivi, that a letter to the Swedes might serve to clarify their position on this issue, for with Swedish cooperation, they reasoned, a hard line concerning Moscow's demands could be taken with some confidence. Without it, both men were practical enough to realize that a diplomatic solution to this *impasse* would be difficult at best. The letter read:

> Brother,
>
> A grave matter occasions this letter to you – the gravest I have ever had to deal with. [The letter goes on to describe the proposals in complete detail.]
>
> I am writing down the draft of this letter during the negotiations in Moscow and after they have been broken off only to be resumed again. I write to ask you a difficult question of conscience: Is there any chance that Sweden, particularly since Hanko Cape is at issue, will intervene in this matter by giving Finland effective military assistance?
>
> I think I know Swedish opinion on this matter. Consequently, I am also aware that my question is a difficult one … I am not asking for anything. I do not even call for a reply if giving it would cause you difficulty. But if you have any chance of helping us, discussion will be necessary.
>
> I should like to emphasise further that for the time being the Soviet demands must be regarded as confidential. For the moment we have not informed the Finnish people of them, as we have not wished to make the negotiations more difficult through public discussion.[42]

The letter was dispatched in the care of a Finnish Cabinet minister who was going to Stockholm and Tanner received his reply from Per-Albin Hansson, the Swedish prime minister (and, for now, a close friend) the next day. At least Hansson had not dodged the issue, but the letter was, from the outset, unpromising:

Brother,
Your letter, which Fagerholm gave me personally yesterday evening, brought upon me that state of depression which arises when a person finds himself obliged to say something different from what he would wish to say.

After some more verbiage, Hansson reaches the key, depressing point:

Here, then is also the answer to the question you have asked: 'Is there any chance that Sweden, particularly since Hanko Cape is at issue, will intervene in this matter by giving Finland effective military assistance?' You must not reckon with any such possibility.[43]

Tanner was not remotely surprised by Hansson's answer, but now that the temperature was clearly rising, it was vital to know whether there was any state upon which Finland could now rely in any constructive or material way. Others were watching, too.

Outside Scandinavia, the progress of this shuttle diplomacy was followed with some interest. Of particular moment were the views of Germany. One Scandinavian who enjoyed total access to the rulers of the Reich was the Swedish writer and explorer Sven Hedin, very much a friend of the German regime. As the first delegation was plodding back to Helsinki, Hedin had conducted an interesting pair of interviews, the first, on 15th October, with his old friend Hermann Göring, who was crisp and authoritative:

If the war turns into a trial of strength in which life and liberty are at stake, I fear the neutrals will have cause for grief. The fate of the small Baltic States is already sealed. Finland will be attached to Russia, which will also occupy Rumania. Yugoslavia will be split up. Turkey's position is ticklish, because Stalin, like all Russian statesmen before him, wants the Dardanelles.

The second interview, with Adolf Hitler, took place the next day. If Göring was breezily practical, then the Führer was positively petulant:

HITLER: It is my conviction that neither Finland nor Sweden need fear that any major quarrel will break out between Russia and Finland. I believe this because the demands Russia has made upon Finland, so far as we are aware, are reasonable and do not, in any case, go so far as those presented to the states of the Baltic littoral.

HEDIN: But if Finland, contrary to expectations, is attacked from the East, what will your position then be, Herr Reichskanzler?

HITLER: In that event, Germany will steadfastly maintain a position of strict neutrality. But I do not believe such a situation will arise.

HEDIN: But if Sweden, by reasons of its relationship with Finland extending over six hundred years, should either officially or through the medium of volunteers come to the aid of that country in its desperate plight, how would you react to such an intervention?

HITLER: I would still remain neutral. But I do not believe that Swedish aid would mean much in a really serious conflict. I have no great regard for your countries of the North.[44] Ever since I came to power, the papers of Sweden, Norway and Finland have vied with one another in insulting me personally and my work and in calumniating it. Nothing has been too vile and scandalous to accuse me of. I have truly no reason to feel any friendship towards countries whose press has treated me with such indignity. As for Finland, seeing that Germany in 1918, through von der Goltz's expedition, helped Finland out of a difficult spot, I should think that we are entitled to expect greater gratitude and consideration than we have been accorded.[45]

An interesting illustration, as if one were needed, of the delicate sensitivities of politicians of all types to the media, but this from the man who, less than two months previously, had coolly consigned Finland and the Baltic states to the tender care, however temporarily, of the USSR.

IN WASHINGTON, the potential crisis energized the already energetic and enterprising Finnish minister Hjalmar Procopé, who, like his counterparts in London and Paris (not to mention Berlin) had been attempting to garner support for his cause. In Washington, though, relations with the Soviet Union, at best lukewarm, were now in the process of rapidly chilling to sub-zero. The reason was another test of Russo-German friendship now taking place. The American freighter *City of Flint* had been ordered to heave to and had been captured by the pocket battleship *Deutschland* while en route to Britain carrying allegedly contraband cargo. The ship had been sailed to Tromsö in Norway by a German prize crew. Technically, Norway, as a neutral country, should have interned the German prize crew and released the vessel Instead, the *City of Flint* was ordered out of harbour after two hours, before setting out for Murmansk, where she now remained in complete contravention of the laws of the sea. The American ambassador in Moscow, Steinhardt, was not even permitted to assure himself as to the welfare of the crew. This provocation, arm in arm with Germany, was a clear and public statement of Soviet hostility and, as such, made it extremely difficult for the USA to undertake any *démarche* on their own behalf, let alone Finland's. It is not impossible that the *City of Flint* affair was a deliberate provocation in the light of what was planned in Finland: the respect in which the country was held – particularly by its creditors, of which America was the largest – was well known.

Not that America tried very hard. After meeting with the Swedish minister in Washington (who delivered a personal appeal from the Swedish Crown Prince) as well as a highly agitated Procopé, President Roosevelt, despite his misgivings that his influence in Moscow was 'just about zero', agreed to draft a telegram to be dispatched to Steinhardt in which it was stated that it was his hope that Russia would not make war on Finland. This was done without the knowledge of Cordell Hull, the secretary of state, who was less than pleased when he learned of it.[46] Reactively, Hull watered it down to:

> While the United States is taking no part in existing controversies in Europe, the President wishes to call attention to the long-standing and deep friendship which exists between the United States and Finland ...
>
> Such being the case, the President expresses the earnest hope that the Soviet Union will make no demands on Finland which are

inconsistent with the maintenance of amicable and peaceful relations between the two countries, and the independence of each.[47]

This message, delivered by Steinhardt to Soviet President Kalinin, certainly ticked the box marked Concerned Friend (and creditor) and may even have helped Roosevelt's cause in the isolationist Midwest, where much of Scandinavian America chose to live, but it cut little ice in Moscow, as Ambassador Steinhardt would shortly discover. In fact, it had little effect in the Midwest either; if Americans of Finnish origin were to make a contribution to this crisis, then they would have to do it themselves – and they did.

At least Procopé had done something; his next task was to close a $60 million loan, an undertaking which he had been essaying for some time, but would now bring him to the edge of a nervous breakdown.

IN LONDON, G. A. Gripenberg, the Finnish minister plenipotentiary, was meeting with whoever would talk to him. He had already complained to an apparently disinterested Lord Halifax concerning the glacial pace of the progress of existing Finnish armament orders, which were so slow that many of the articles ordered were – literally – obsolete. Halifax conceded that Finland 'had every reason to be dissatisfied and promised to do what he could'.[48]

Gripenberg also saw the leaders of the opposition parties, Greenwood and Attlee, both of whom were pessimistic, using almost exactly the same form of words as each other, that: 'England would not forget Finland'.[49] This was less than cheering. Gripenberg himself was getting very little information from Helsinki and worked very much as his title suggested, taking matters into his own hands. On 13 October, he saw R. A. Butler (Undersecretary of State, Foreign Office) who was calming, if somewhat elliptic: 'If, during your conversation with the Foreign Secretary, you got the impression that the British Government was not interested in your country and it is not following with great interest the development of relations between Finland and the Soviet Union, then I only wish to say you are mistaken.'

The Soviet ambassador, Ivan Maisky, was at the end of October on the receiving end of a very pointed statement from the languid but disapproving Halifax, who informed him that while the British government was anxious to improve Anglo-Soviet relations, that would be impossible if 'anything happened to Finland'.[50] Maisky assured him that 'under no circumstances could the Russo-Finnish negotiations lead to a serious conflict'.[51]

Matters remained tense and uncertain until the Finnish delegation prepared to return once again to Moscow armed with no major concessions, but determined to continue with the dialogue. If anyone broke these talks off, it was not going to be them. But as their train pulled into Viipuri station at 6.30 in the morning, it became clear that there had been a development: the previous evening, in a speech to the Supreme Soviet that Moscow had thoughtfully broadcast, Molotov had put the whole matter into the public domain. This was no longer confidential; the stakes had been raised.

With the effect of Molotov's keynote speech to the Supreme Soviet, the pressure on the Finns was now intense, as it was clear that the Soviet Union was not going to back down. The Red Army, massed in the Leningrad *oblast* (surrounding district) and positioned all the way up to the northernmost border opposite Petsamo, settled down to await the outcome.

CHAPTER THREE

Questions of Command

War is not merely a political act, but also a political instrument,
a continuation of political relations, a carrying out of the
same by other means.

Karl Maria von Clausewitz, On War

DESPITE THE APPARENT willingness of Stalin to negotiate through October, there were already contingency plans afoot to invade Finland. That these might have existed as a matter of basic Russian outlook is quite natural – what was perhaps not was the sheer scale of them. The Chief of the General Staff had indeed drafted a plan in the summer – that is to say as the Anglo-French-Soviet talks had been taking place – which advocated a full assault on the most strategically important part of the country, the Karelian Isthmus. In a spirit of 'Socialist competition' Stalin had already instructed the commander of the Leningrad Military District to draw up an alternative, grander scheme, at the heart of which was the destruction of the Finnish Army and the suppression of the entire country. According to one authority: 'Stalin was "impressed by the rapidity of the Red Army's victories against Poland that Autumn" and was "convinced that the class antagonisms that had made those victories possible also existed in Finland"'.[1] This was no doubt due to a report sent by Deravianski in the wake of the Russo-German pact, which reflected more wishful thinking than anything else: 'Finland now stands at a distinctive cross-roads. Always inclined to side with the enemies of the Soviet Union, they do not know exactly where to go or what to do.'

The issue of which Red Army commander would have the honour of managing this possible invasion – migration, really, given its eventual scale – was relatively easy to settle. Almost certainly the lucky candidate would be a crony from the First Cavalry Army, a unit which had served without distinction but with great brutality at Tsaritsyn (by now Stalingrad), as well as being roundly beaten in Poland in 1920. It was this force, around which a curiously inflated mythology had grown up (mainly due to the fact that Stalin had been its political commissar), that had provided a higher number of senior commanders than any other in the wake of the Russian Civil War. Further, these men seemed fireproof when it came to the ferocious blood-letting that had commenced in June 1937, when the Party finally turned on the armed forces.

Kirill Afanasievich Meretskov, 42, had been for the previous few months commander of the Leningrad Military District, after an undemanding posting to the Volga Military District. He had, during a peripatetic career, served in Spain as an adviser to the Republicans, as well as a spell as military liaison officer in Czechoslovakia, which was of course now a redundant task. He was an early graduate of the Frunze military academy and laid claim to a properly politically correct peasant origin (which may or may not have been strictly true).[2]

Meretskov's career progression had been, up to this point, relatively smooth. He had made himself sensibly agreeable to all who mattered and, as a result, was on something of a fast track. As the competition for senior command started to disappear when the purge turned its attention to the Red Army, he was thus well placed to benefit from the resultant command vacuum which had been the most observable result. The privilege of steamrollering the recalcitrant and impertinent 'White Finns' was by any measure his most significant achievement to date. Or so it must have seemed.

Politically, Meretskov fell within the ambit of Andrei Zhdanov,

Party Secretary in Leningrad and a prime mover in taking a hard line with the Finns. Zhdanov viewed Finland in its 'proper' historical context, as being merely part of the political hinterland of Leningrad itself. Helsinki, by this analysis, was thus merely a wayward provincial capital and Zhdanov clearly looked forward to his role as neo-Imperial satrap once the matter in hand was settled, and in the judgement of many, that would not take very long.

Zhdanov had been preparing his ground for some time. His attitude to Finland had been made clear as far back as November 1936:

> We people of Leningrad sit at our windows looking out at the world. Right around us lie small countries who dream of great adventures or permit great adventurers [3] to scheme within their borders. We are not afraid of these small nations. But if they are not satisfied to mind only their own business, we may feel forced to open our windows a bit wider, and they might find it disagreeable if we have to call upon our Red Army to defend our country.

NOT ALL WERE as confident as Zhdanov. In the spirit of 'socialist competition', two war plans were given an audition. The first contribution was penned by the Chief of the General Staff, Commander (First Rank) Boris Mikhailovich Shaposhnikov, and drawn up in the summer, during the aborted three-power talks in Moscow. It was a purely military effort, and carried with it no glib assumptions regarding political conditions in Finland. Shaposhnikov's view was that this invasion was no small matter, and he had set aside several months in which to achieve his objective. In his view, the key task was possession of the Karelian Isthmus, allowing penetration into the heartland of Finland and a quick route to Helsinki via Vyborg (Viipuri). That fighting would occur he was sure; that it would be fierce he only suspected, but the Shaposhnikov plan focused almost entirely upon the crossing of that vital land-bridge which separated the Ladoga from the Gulf of Finland. To achieve the border rectification and the acquisition of Hanko were the political drivers; after all, the neutralization of the Finnish Army was a natural concomitant of that, and all else, he reasoned, was merely a distraction.

Shaposhnikov's early writings reveal an innate conservatism, which was rather at odds with the modernizing tendency as expressed by such advanced thinkers as Tukhachevski, and although his work concentrated mainly on the historical aspects of the contemporary character of the Red Army, he managed to appear more or less agnostic on the subject of mechanization over cavalry. In doing this, he had managed to avoid engagement in the wrong-headed and sentimental squabbling which had taken place between the modernizers (led by Tukhachevski) and the flat-earthers, as represented by Voroshilov and Budenny, for whom a horse was as vital a piece of military equipment as a field gun.

As chief of staff, Boris Shaposhnikov was perhaps, at this distance at least, something of an anomaly. Of undisguised bourgeois origins (his father had been a brewery manager) he was a career officer in the Imperial Army, and had been since 1910. He was scrupulously courteous – even courtly – and had adjusted his personal outlook (and therefore his conduct) very little in the light of the obvious socio-political developments since the Revolution.[4] He had only joined the CPSU (Communist Party of the Soviet Union) in the spring of 1939, the year he was 57. He was by no means unusual in being an ex-Tsarist officer, but with such a background, to hold a senior military rank bespeaks a certain personal authority, which even the most rabid political correctness could not crush.[5] Had he not been a soldier, perhaps we can imagine B. M. Shaposhnikov as a senior central banker: polite, even cultured, but professionally gloomy. Many wondered why Stalin offered him such powerful patronage. According to one estimate, this revolved around his 'lack of character': he was more than able, but clearly harmless, an unthreatening antique to the placemen around the central circle, a useful and qualified technician.

Shaposhnikov had also, perforce, hedged his bets politically. As the author of several learned (if rather impenetrable) tracts concerning Soviet military theory and Tsarist military history, he had come down firmly on the other side of the Polish argument from his rival Tukhachevski.[6] It is perhaps sobering to realize that this gentle and gifted man's signature appears on the charge sheet, and death sentence, which was handed down to that unfortunate in June 1937. As well as being chief of staff, Shaposhnikov was also a reserve judge in the Supreme Court.

So, a very powerful man indeed, and not one stupid enough to contest the issue when his meticulous, but narrow plan was rejected in favour of Meretskov's grander scheme, with its none too subtle overtones of 'liberation'. The Leningrad Military District Commander took a rather more political view of the Finland problem, and we can see the hand of Zhdanov behind its core assumptions. It was held, in the light of the successful agitprop that had attended the September invasion of eastern Poland (and transformed it – instantly – into western Ukraine) that Finland would present a similar opportunity, so the military execution of the plan, a vast, broad-shouldered lunge across the entire length of the border, would be married to a political initiative which would be part terror and part propaganda. It was widely held (based on assumptions faithfully reported) that Finland was ripe for a popular uprising; a senior proponent of this view was the commissar for defence, Voroshilov. In his view, the Red Army was unbeatable. Indeed, had that not just been proved?

It is hard to identify a more overrated figure in military history that Kliment Yefremovich Voroshilov. A year older than Shaposhnikov, he had, in a long and undistinguished career, progressed from semi-literate roustabout to marshal of the Soviet Union without delivering a single example of leadership or military vision, instead taking the easier route of becoming a symbol of rugged Bolshevik 'soundness'.[7] The journalist Joan 'Rosita' Forbes (no particular friend of this regime), who met him in the late 1930s, described him as a 'kind, loyal and honest' figure; Nikita Khrushchev, who knew him rather better, opted for an earthier description: 'the biggest bag of shit in the army'. Events would suggest that Khrushchev perhaps had the better measure of his man. But, whatever his faults, Voroshilov had physical courage, if only due to his lack of imagination, particularly in dealing with Stalin.

Voroshilov had, along with the other cronies from the First Cavalry Army, risen effortlessly to the top; untainted by any association with Léon Trotsky who, very practically, had welcomed all-comers into the officer cadres of the Red Army, even men who held the Tsar's commission and fought with the Whites during the civil war. Voroshilov and Budenny carried no such dubious political baggage with them, hence their insulation from the catastrophe that had befallen Tukhachevski. But unhappily for the Finns, Budenny would not be involved in this scheme.

THERE WAS, of course, one other Red Army commander who had already placed himself in a Universe of One by his actions, and that was Georgi Zhukov, whose masterly thrashing of the Japanese Kwantung Army at Nomonhan on the Khalkin-Gol River in September had ensured two things; first, that he had set a standard by which all Red Army commanders would be measured from now on and second, that he himself would be safe from the depredations of the NKVD, which, by its conduct, had started to behave by any rational measure with complete insanity. If Meretskov was nervous at being asked to match Zhukov's exacting standards, he seemed not to show it. His plan, after all, had the official sanction of the Kremlin as well as the full support of Andrei Zhdanov. He had air cover, both literal and metaphorical.

SO, BY THE END of October 1939, the contingency plan, such as it was, awaited its trigger. As Finnish students had spent the late summer making good some of the deficiencies in the defensive line across the Isthmus, so on the Soviet side of the border, battalions of hapless *Zeks*[8] laboured even harder in order to add some density to the otherwise rather sparse road and rail networks for the task which now awaited completion. The sheer scale of the enterprise in hand mandated a large-scale upgrade to the existing transport facilities, at least on the Soviet side of the border.

Molotov pulled the trigger on 31 October in his speech to the Supreme Soviet. In extracts, which were thoughtfully broadcast on Radio Moscow that evening, he revealed the full range and scope of the Russo-Finnish negotiations. The whole matter now being public, the Finns' room for manoeuvre was curtailed dramatically, as the two sides of the argument lurched, blinkingly, into the broader public spotlight. As a wider Scandinavia woke up to the crisis developing in the east, the opportunity for deals in smoke-filled rooms rapidly evaporated and an embarrassed Finnish Cabinet was obliged to consider the issue in the full glare of the resultant publicity. Europe was at war, but only technically, and here was a fine distraction. Having attempted to keep their ghastly secret *sub rosa*, the pressure upon the Finnish government was now intense; they did not rise to the occasion.

The timetable of the Russian contingent plan was neat, tidy and unimaginative, with little or no margin for error. The key date was 21 December, Stalin's sixtieth birthday. By then, it was imagined, the marching bands of the Red Army would be swinging through the centre of Helsinki (or at least, for the pessimists, Vyborg), cheered on by hordes of liberated and breathlessly happy Finns, freed from the yoke of Fascist oppression. Zhdanov had even commissioned a celebratory piece from Dmitri Shostakovitch (to be ready no later than 2 December) entitled *A Suite on Finnish Themes* and to be performed in Helsinki for the amusement of the *Vozhd* (supreme leader). For reasons which will become clear, the 'Composer of the Revolution' would never lay claim to the authorship of this trite little work.[9] Clearly intended to counter and supplant the broader influence in Finland of Jean Sibelius – definitely *not* a composer of the Revolution – it would not be performed until 2002.

Inside the north-western border of the Soviet Union, events acquired a peculiar momentum of their own. In Leningrad, the press-gangs were out in force, as the topping-up of under-strength units gathered pace. Anyone would do, it seemed, as no military experience was deemed necessary: 'Visit Finland before Finland visits you' ran the orthodox propaganda. In workers' Soviets all over the country, but particularly within the orbit of the Leningrad Military District, the carefully orchestrated call went out for

Foreign Commissar Molotov to get tough with the Finns. *Pravda* matched the tone of injured innocence, and Zhdanov's utterances on the subject of the awkward neighbour waxed frothier by the day. Moscow Radio followed suit, and sundry political assets in the west, either consciously or not, took their cues from there.

Illustrative of the total lack of useful communication at any level between the two countries, let alone the diplomatic one, was an atmosphere of eerie calm on the Finnish side of the border; the only sign of animation being that which emanated from Mannerheim, who was becoming extremely worried. Even without detailed knowledge of the level of Soviet activity, he had the imagination to realize that these tangential diplomatic contacts, which had some of the formality of a Versailles levee, would give way very quickly to something much more robust; after fifty years as a soldier, the very least he could do was read a map.

DESPITE THE NAZI leaders' apparent acceptance of the fate of Finland, as revealed to Hedin, there now occurred a strange episode, which has never been satisfactorily explained. A Swedish relative of Hermann Göring's late wife, Count Armfeld, appeared to see Erkko and Mannerheim at the end of October, apparently bearing an undertaking of assistance should Finland's relations with the USSR break down terminally. Further, he revealed that German battleships were on station in the Gulf of Riga and the mouth of the Gulf of Finland and that the Finns should 'hold firm' in their negotiations with Moscow.[10] Interestingly, Mannerheim makes no mention of this occasion in his memoirs, but if he was unmoved by this apparent suggestion of German help, Erkko chose to remain confident.[11]

The public announcements by Foreign Commissar Molotov that the Soviet-Finnish talks were no longer a matter of confidentiality sent a frisson of unease through the rest of the Finnish Cabinet, as Moscow had predicted. Ever since Yartsev's initial approach, Stein's mission and Litvinov's courteous murmurings to Yrjö-Koskinen, it had been tacitly assumed that the negotiations were essentially a private matter. The Cabinet entirely failed to appreciate the strategic importance of Finland in the event of Soviet-German hostilities, choosing to assume that the Nazi-Bolshevik pact would preserve peace in the area, rather than destabilize it. Even with the evidence of Poland and the Baltic states, the Cabinet failed to identify the clear agenda – was not Finland's independence protected by the Tartu treaty, and the 1932 bilateral non-aggression pact, the like of which Finland had just rejected when approached by Germany?

The evening before the delegates' departure, Mannerheim had, rather unusually for him, urgently buttonholed Paasikivi: 'You absolutely *must* come to an agreement. The Army cannot fight'.[12]

IN MOSCOW MATTERS resumed on 3 November. A *Pravda* editorial that day read: 'We shall pursue our course, let it lead where it may. We will defend the security of the Soviet Union regardless, breaking down all obstacles of whatever character, in order to reach our goal.' There was no appreciable change in the Finnish counter-proposals, merely small matters of emphasis. Importantly, Hanko was still not up for negotiation, although the islands in the Gulf of Finland (including half of Suursaari) now were. Molotov was unmoved, and while the tone of the meeting was for a while relatively cordial, the more so when Stalin arrived, nothing was accomplished. As the Finns took their leave, Molotov's parting words were: 'We civilians can see no further in the matter; now is the turn of the military to have their say.'

On the anniversary of the Revolution, 7 November, Tanner (Paasikivi claimed illness) attended a gala dinner in the evening, where the German minister, von der Schulenberg, introduced himself; Tanner was given something of the true flavour of the Russo-German relationship when Schulenberg, casting a dismissive eye over the drunken assembled Soviet *prominenti*, sneered, in parting: 'Und mit diesen Menschen mussen wir zusammenarbeiten!' [And we have to work with these people!][13] Rather like Drax's previous remark to Erkko, perhaps Schulenberg's comment (certainly not a reflection of official policy) created a rather false impression for Tanner.

The next day attitudes in Helsinki had clearly hardened. In a telegram deciphered mid morning new instructions were received, which served to take even the islands in the Gulf of Finland off the agenda. Disbelievingly, Tanner cabled urgently: 'Instructions received. If no agreement on this basis, may we let the negotiations break off?' At midnight, the response came back: 'You are aware our concessions have gone as far as our security and independence permit. If no agreement on the basis proposed, you are free to break off negotiations.' Erkko Paasikivi was predictably furious, venting his spleen on the nearest culprit, the hapless Colonel Paasonen. He spat: 'Now, if ever, would be the time to fight. But since you of the army can do nothing, it is necessary to avoid war and back up. None of the army people except Mannerheim understands anything!'. This new initiative ran counter to everything which Paasikivi and Mannerheim believed about Russian intentions, and the change of tack in Helsinki almost guaranteed an escalation of a situation about which neither Paasikivi nor Tanner could do anything.

The meetings resumed at 6 p.m. on 9 November. As feared, the conversation was a short one. Tanner presented a memorandum: 'Finland cannot grant to a foreign state military bases on its own territory and within its own boundaries.' The looks of disbelief on the faces of both Stalin and Molotov were memorable indeed, and after half an hour of desultory haggling, Stalin commented, slightly disbelievingly: 'Then it doesn't look as if anything will come of it. Nothing doing? [*Nichevo ne boudet*?]'

It was the last meeting. After a final attempt to keep the negotiations going with a dramatic midnight note to the Finnish legation – an attempt by Molotov to redefine what was meant by 'Finnish territory' from the memorandum: if Hanko was *sold*, then surely it would be *Russian* territory? – the Finnish delegates prepared to leave for home.

In Helsinki the Soviet chargé d'affaires had paid a call on Erkko, attempting to short-cut the apparent deadlock, to no effect. In Moscow the delegates, unaware of this last-minute initiative, waited for a subsequent approach, but nothing was forthcoming save an ominous silence. Except in the press. The editorial of *Krasnyi Flot*'s 10 November issue read:[14]

> Provocateurs, warmongers and their henchmen are trying to represent the Soviet proposals as a threat not only to the independence of Finland, but also to the security of Scandinavia, particularly Sweden. The Soviet people repudiates with loathing these filthy insults of the international political sharpers. We know that our government's sole motive is and has ever been a concern to restrict the war zone and to underwrite the life and peaceful work of the states which are neighbours of the Soviet peoples. Unshakeably faithful to the principles of its pacific policy, the Soviet government will find ways and means to guarantee the security of the extreme northwestern land and sea frontiers of our fatherland.[15]

In fact, the Soviet government had already started to secure its frontiers, as the delegates had noted on the Isthmus. But that editorial, and a host of others like it, rather served notice that the time for talking was over.

If the tone of this and other editorials signalled, with a sinister finality, that the issue was now perhaps a military one, as Molotov had already hinted on 3 November, the atmosphere in Helsinki seemed strangely and inexplicably euphoric when the small delegation returned on the 15th. The schools, having been shut since October, reopened. The banks started to fill up with deposits once more, and a measure of commercial and social confidence appeared to have returned, outside Mannerheim's circle, at least. To his dismay, a partial demobilization was even suggested.

IN THE BRITISH War Cabinet there was a current acceptance of the Soviet point of view, which was rather at odds with the evolution of future policy. Churchill, whose interest in the Baltic area was not only well known but also unique in this body of faintly disinterested men, had been setting the agenda. On 27 October, he had written that it was 'quite natural' for the Russians to require bases to secure the future of Leningrad. When the talks in Moscow seemed to be at a standstill, he further added in Cabinet on 16 November, that it was in British interests that the USSR should 'increase their strength in the Baltic'. Given that, he felt it was an obvious error to stiffen Finnish resistance to Russian demands.[16] But, unhappily, it was by then too late. The myth would emerge, reinforced by his pronouncements of January 1940, that he was in favour of supporting Finland come what may. He wasn't, but this emerging crisis would be useful to him.

GIVEN THAT RELATIONS with Moscow were suddenly very chilly indeed, Prime Minister Cajander availed himself of the opportunity to deliver what he thought would be a calming, resolute address to the nation, which he did after a concert at the Helsinki Fair Hall on 23 November. After a brief (and more or less accurate) assessment of the previous two months, he went on to comment on the situation of Finland's southern friends and neighbours:

> When Poland was near to collapse the Soviet Union marched its troops into Eastern Poland and occupied it. Simultaneously, the Soviet People's Commissar for Foreign Affairs made it known to the governments of Finland and the Baltic countries, as well as others, that it would conduct a policy of neutrality towards them.
>
> The defection of a Polish submarine to Tallinn was at first brought out as an excuse for proposals made by the Soviet Union to Estonia, which then finally resulted in allocating important military bases to the Soviet Union in Baltischport, Ösel and Dagö. In quick succession, similar events followed in Latvia and Lithuania. These three vigorous Baltic countries with their own characteristic old cultures and a splendid future ahead were overnight turned into more or less dependencies of the Soviet Union. Especially depressing for us, the Finns, is the fact that among these countries faced by this unfavourable fate is the State of Estonia, our dear fraternal Nation.[17] A follow-up was also the mass departure of Germans from the Baltic where they, over a period of 600 years, have made history and loftily carried the flag of German culture.

Finland's view, Cajander continued, was that:

> Finland will not submit herself to the role of a vassal country. We will not yield to this by someone waging a war of words or trying to exhaust us, or

the opposite; by offering us temptations. Finland will, with her eyes open and with determination, now observe the events in the West and in the East, and as a peace-loving country (which always appreciates good neighbourly relations) is at all times ready to continue the negotiations on a basis which does not risk the vital of Finland or her National values. No further concessions can be attained, especially now that Finland herself can gain nothing from these territorial exchanges.

After a brief disquisition about the economic and social impact of the recent tension (the runs on the banks) he concluded:

We must learn to plough carrying rifles on our backs ... There are certain elements in society who try to sow the seeds of dissention among us, especially at the grass roots level. Beware of these elements! Their real effects are so insignificant that no factual relevance can be attributed to them. But abroad, their significance can be exaggerated and thus be used to harm our country.

Every Finnish citizen has his own guard post and everyone is expected to stay alert at his post without defying anyone but firmly defending the rights of the Finnish Nation. We are obliged to this because of our history; we are obliged to this because of our Nation's future.[18]

It was a calm speech, but firmly defiant. Cajander got his reply, and not the one he was hoping for, three days later.

A 'Buffoon Holding the Post of Prime Minister!' shrieked the *Pravda* headline of 26 November.[19] It is fair to say that the rest of the piece (which may have been penned by Kuusinen himself) was complete and utter gibberish, and need not detain us overlong. But the Finnish Prime Minister was likened to assorted circus performers as well as wildlife. So badly written was it that it caused some real amusement in Finland, but what happened later that day did not.

The adoption of the military solution, only hinted at by Molotov's speech on 31 October, served to set events in motion that, given the emerging intransigence in Helsinki, as well as Soviet perceptions of discontent in Finland, made a confrontation now more than likely. But, in keeping with the tradition of legalism to which the Soviet government attempted to adhere, a *casus belli* was required. 'Indirect aggression' was not enough. Something rather more direct was called for.

When the Wehrmacht had launched its attack on Poland on 1 September, the excuse had been an incursion by 'Polish troops' (in fact, Germans in Polish uniforms) upon a radio station at Gleiwicz. The Russians had come up with something not far from this: a Finnish attack on their border.

The village of Mainila, 1,000 yards over the Russian side of the border on the Karelian Isthmus, was quiet at 2.30 p.m. on 26 November. A Finnish border guard, Urbo Sundvall, was on duty. He related to H. B. Elliston what happened next:

> I saw eleven Russians in the field sloping down in front of the foremost building in Mainila. A horseman came riding up. He stopped for a moment to talk to them, then all twelve went away in a westerly direction. The horseman went a short distance with them, then wheeled around and disappeared at a gallop in an easterly direction. Ten minutes later [I] heard a shot fired crosswise from the East and in a matter of twenty seconds a shell exploded just where the men had been. It was a loud explosion, and seemed to make a big hole, because a lot of earth was thrown into the air. The shot was succeeded by six more, all the shells exploding in the same field. The last shell exploded at 3.05 p.m. Ten minutes later six men arrived on the spot where the shells had fallen, stayed three minutes in inspecting the ground, then went back. No dead or wounded were taken away, the spot being deserted at the time.

Sundvall and two of his colleagues, Hänninen and Savolainen, confirmed the story, even down to the type of weapon used, a high-trajectory Stokes trench mortar (this would account for the twenty-second delay). All went quiet again, then the guards observed a smoke-screen going up behind the village, behind which little could be seen.

AT 9 P.M. MOSCOW TIME (10 p.m. in Helsinki) Baron Yrjö-Koskinen was summoned to the Kremlin. It was to receive a note, in which Molotov stated that Soviet border guards stationed at Mainila had been fired upon by Finnish artillery. Three privates and an NCO had died, and two officers and seven soldiers were wounded:

> The Soviet government brings this to your attention and considers it necessary to emphasise the fact that during the negotiations recently held with your Messrs. Tanner and Paasikivi the Soviet government remarked upon the danger to which the concentration of numerous forces in the immediate neighbourhood of the frontier close to Leningrad give rise…
>
> On this account the Soviet government, protesting emphatically against the deed [elsewhere described as a 'deplorable act of aggression'] proposes that the Finnish government withdraw without delay its forces on the Karelian Isthmus … twenty to twenty-five kilometres, thus eliminating the possibility of fresh provocations.[20]

Yrjö-Koskinen recalled that even Molotov appeared to believe this utter nonsense: 'He seemed to be carrying out orders like an automaton.'[21]

Naively, the Finns were tempted to deal with this latest pressure in the same serious vein in which it had been put to them. Accordingly a reply was drafted, which stated that the shots had come from the Russian side, but despite this Finland was prepared to put into place the protocols relating to border incidents that were a part of the existing non-aggression pact. Further, it suggested that perhaps both sides should withdraw the same recommended distance.

This elicited the following response: '[The Finnish reply typified] the deep hostility of the Finnish government toward the Soviet Union [and] forcing the relations between the two countries to a point of extreme tension.' And, 'The fact that the Finnish government denies that Finnish forces fired upon Soviet forces with artillery and inflicted casualties, can be explained only as a device to mislead public opinion and as an affront to the victims of the shooting.'

By way of complete clarification the Soviets added:

> By reason of all these circumstances the Soviet Government considers itself obliged to declare that from the date of the delivery of the note it

regarded itself as free of the obligations which had bound it under the non-aggression pact ... now systematically violated by the Finnish government.

...As is well known, the attacks by units of the Finnish armed forces against Soviet forces continue not only on the Karelian Isthmus but also at other points on the Soviet-Finnish frontier.[22] The Soviet Union can no longer tolerate this situation. By reason of the situation which has arisen, for which the Finnish government alone bears responsibility, the Soviet government can no longer maintain normal relations with Finland, and is obliged to recall from Finland its political and economic representatives.[23]

Most of them, of course, had departed already.

This sudden and obvious collapse in the situation prompted an exhausted Mannerheim to tender his resignation, to make room for a younger man:

In recent years I have found it difficult to understand the attitude of the government as well as of parliament towards the danger which a European general war would mean to the independence of our country. While everything has pointed to a gigantic conflict approaching, the indispensable demands of our defence have been treated with little understanding and with a parsimony which left a great deal neglected ...[24]

His resignation was accepted.

MOLOTOV ANNOUNCED at midnight on 29 November that the Red Army and the northern and Baltic fleets should commence operations. Shortly afterwards, Commander Meretskov addressed his giant army:

Comrades, soldiers of the Red Army, officers, commissars and political workers! To fulfill the Soviet Government's and our great Fatherland's will, I hereby order: The troops in Leningrad Military District are to march over the frontier, crush the Finnish forces, and once and for all secure the Soviet Union's Northwestern borders and Lenin's city, the crib of the revolution of the proletariat.[25]

CHAPTER FOUR

The Assault on the Isthmus

Generally in war the best policy is to take a state intact.
To ruin it is inferior to this.

Sun Tzu

SPRAWLING AND POLITICALLY skewed though Meretskov's plan
was, if there was one area where military failure was not an option,
it was on the Karelian Isthmus. Although a superficial glance at the
map would indicate that it was a wide enough neck of land to
allow a broad-fronted assault along its entire width, in reality it
presented a rather more problematic prospect.

An accident of geology had created a land front of rather less
than a third of its width. From the shore of the Ladoga on the
north-eastern side, the ground was scoured by an extension of the
filigree of lakes that, broadly running north-west to south-east
and linked by the Taipale River, characterized the entire southern
portion of the country. Thus, the only accessible route through
the Isthmus to the vulnerable Finnish interior followed the path of
the Leningrad–Viipuri railway in the south, which ran along the
main stretch of dry land; the further network of lakes in the centre
of the Isthmus caused this to narrow to a practicable corridor of
roughly 12 miles in width, centred on the little village of Summa.[1]

It was across this well-surveyed southern passage that the Finns
had placed their most ambitious and costliest obstacles. Whereas
the defences to the northern flank of the Isthmus utilized almost
every puddle behind which to build bunkers and dig trenches,

here, in front of the 'Viipuri gateway', nature had provided a dearth of natural obstacles, so the Finns had built their own. They were, at best, modest; Offa would have recognized parts of them, Hadrian would have thought them inadequate, the architects of the Maginot Line would have considered them laughable.

A great mythology was to emerge concerning these defences; the creative imaginations of frustrated journalists penned up in the bar of the Kämp Hotel in Helsinki came up with 'the Man-nerheim Line' as an appropriate title, and it stuck. Other reasons for its apparent impregnability will become clear. Further, the role of Soviet propagandists after the event, both within the USSR and outside, was to present the Mannerheim Line as an immovable and mighty obstacle, the storming of which was to offer the world a feat of arms unparalleled in military history.

In a singularly disreputable book published in November 1941 (that, in the light of the Nazi invasion of Russia, was clearly expected to fly off the shelves) the authors described Finnish defences thus: 'There is no doubt that this fortified zone, chris-tened after Baron Mannerheim, included a number of improve-ments over both the Maginot Line and the German West Wall [Seigfield Line].'[2] It is extremely hard to believe this.[3] The Maginot Line, with its extravagant fire control systems (essentially naval in their sophistication and mindset), armoured underground magazines, dormitories, sun-ray equipment, air-conditioning, proper catering and, above all, the terrifying destructive power of the large calibre rifles safe in their radiused, revolving cupolas atop it, marked the acme of fixed defensive military architecture, however conceptually redundant it later proved to be.

The Finnish defensive line (we shall call it the Mannerheim Line) on the other hand, was rather different. Given the onerous constraints of the Finnish military budget estimates it was not, with certain exceptions,[4] constructed at great expense. It was certainly practical, as was its purpose – to delay, rather than repel, a Russian invasion, in order that diplomacy might prosper. It used predominantly local materials – the same unyielding, ore-streaked granite from which generations of farmers had scratched a meagre

Intended assault on the Isthmus

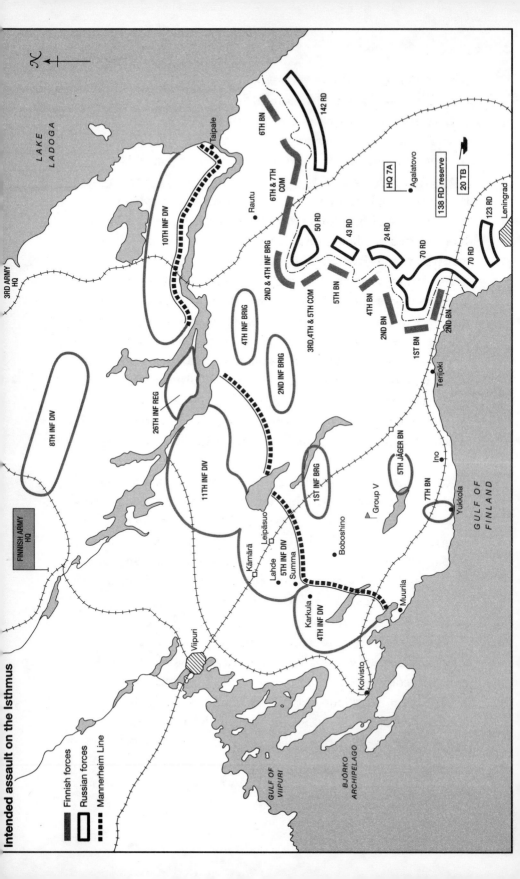

Legend:
- Finnish forces
- Russian forces
- Mannerheim Line

Map labels:

LAKE LADOGA

GULF OF FINLAND

GULF OF VIIPURI

BJÖRKÖ ARCHIPELAGO

3RD ARMY HQ

FINNISH ARMY HQ

HQ 7A

138 RD reserve

20 TB

142 RD

6TH BN

6TH & 7TH COM

50 RD

43 RD

24 RD

70 RD

70 RD

123 RD

Leningrad

Agalatovo

Rautu

Taipale

10TH INF DIV

8TH INF DIV

26TH INF REG

11TH INF DIV

4TH INF BRIG

2ND INF BRIG

2ND & 4TH INF BRG

3RD, 4TH & 5TH COM

5TH BN

4TH BN

2ND BN

1ST BN

2ND BN

Terijoki

Ino

Yukkola

1ST INF BRG

5TH JÄGER BN

7TH BN

Group V

Boboshino

Kämärä

Lahde

Summa

5TH INF DIV

Leipäsuo

Karkula

4TH INF DIV

Muurila

Koivisto

Viipuri

living, leavened with ferro-concrete when affordable – but more often than not the 'forts' were little more than timber and earth embrasures, built from the ubiquitous birch and pine logs that provided the bulk of the harvest in this unpromising piece of real estate. If connected at all, they were linked by simple trench works. Along the whole line were placed a series of purpose-built 'hard points', which had some element of proper protection for the soldiers manning them. The bulk of them were little more than fortified pill-boxes or machine-gun nests, which whenever possible offered mutually supporting fire.

Construction of the line had commenced in 1919 under the orders of Major General Enckell, then Chief of the Finnish General Staff in the wake of Mannerheim's resignation (he had been appointed regent in December 1918). The purpose was simple; to provide an economical method of defence against the Russians, who it was assumed (prior to the Treaty of Tartu) would be back soon, and probably across the Isthmus. At that time, the Finnish Army could dispose of perhaps three divisions. The original plan, a network of flank-firing bunkers that would decimate approaching infantry, was costed but abandoned as too expensive – instead, a series of compromises was reached, whereby the defences would be built when affordable. As a result, the whole defence line was constructed piecemeal, using mainly French and German consulting engineers. For reasons of cost, the bulk of the hard fortifications (until 1936) were of unreinforced concrete,[5] which provided only modest protection at best – the compression density of the concrete was too low to offer resistance to anything but medium artillery. The hasty addition of steel plates to some of the bunkers (during refurbishment) improved matters somewhat, but again, the cost was high. By November 1939, the line was by no means completed.

With great irony (and not a little sloppiness at the Red Army intelligence level) the USSR had already been provided with a detailed map of the defences on the Isthmus. According to one report, the person responsible, Wehrmacht General Arniké, who had worked in the office of the Reich's military attaché in Helsinki, handed it over in Moscow in September 1939, perhaps on his own initiative, perhaps as part of the secret protocol.[6] Either way, while his map may have been neglected, gathering dust on some functionary's desk, his conduct was not. Upon his return to Germany, according to the same account, he was wordlessly offered a loaded pistol by a band of his brother officers and, without demur, used it upon himself. This sentiment certainly reflected the general opinion of the Ribbentrop pact among the German officer corps.

THE FINNS COULD NOT afford emplaced heavy ordnance except at the extreme ends of the line. The coastal batteries on the Gulf of Finland and the Ladoga shore were ageing but serviceable, and were of calibres of up to 10 inches (254 mm). In support of the defensive positions, the Finnish Army had a limited amount of field artillery of a bewildering variety of ages and calibres. Along the length of the line itself, though, there was an observable dearth of any ordnance heavier than the Maxim gun.[7]

However, what the Finnish artillery park lacked was in part compensated by ingenuity and thorough preparation. In front of the line (and in particular density in front of the Summa corridor) lay a primary level of defence in modest depth, which was both unsuspected and unwelcome when it was tested. Extensive minefields, protected by anti-tank obstacles (mainly granite or concrete blocks) and a lattice of tautly strung barbed wire, were laid in front of the fixed defences. Further, the forest and woodland which characterized the gently undulating terrain was selectively cleared, which would have the effect of corralling the approaching enemy into carefully calculated (and measured) fields of fire. Each yard of ground had been plotted, with accurate distances marked on the defenders' artillery maps; thus the modest contribution of the Finnish artillery to the fragile defences would be made to punch above its weight. Every round would count.

This was just as well for the Finns, as Mannerheim's own inventory revealed that reserves of field artillery rounds were few enough – sufficient for perhaps twenty-one days of fighting. Given the antiquity of some of these weapons (and their Imperial

Russian origin) it had not been possible to replenish ammunition supplies outside the country, even if there had been any spare manufacturing capacity available, which outside the United States there was not.

Of anti-tank ordnance there was little; more critically, neither was there any experience in armoured warfare. The benchmark weapon of Europe was the 37 mm Bofors gun, manufactured in Sweden.[8] The order book of that company was obviously fuller than it had ever been and, despite the fact that the Finns had facilities to manufacture this and other weapons under licence, this was a process difficult to accelerate. The 37 mm cannon could, it was later discovered, punch an armour-piercing round through most light-to-medium Russian tanks.

THE RED ARMY order of battle was, on the face of it, formidable. On the Karelian Isthmus itself waited the Seventh Army, under the order of Commander (Second Rank) Yakovlev. At his disposal, this hastily promoted officer had no less than twelve divisions of infantry, supported by the same number of artillery regiments and three brigades of tanks, together with a host of specialists. The total number of Red Army soldiers, therefore, on the Isthmus alone, approached 200,000, or just over 40 per cent of the Leningrad Military District's manpower. Six divisions would undertake the initial assault.

Against this, the Finns could also offer six divisions, and a scattering of units in battalion and company strength, amounting to perhaps one more. In total, a little more than 125,000 men. Critically, they had no tanks to speak of and, on the Karelian front, sixty-seven of the valued Bofors guns.[9]

The commander of the Finnish Army of the Isthmus – the Kannas Army – was Lieutenant General Hugo Östermann. It consisted of Army Corps II and III, the former commanded by Lieutenant General Harald Öhqvist and disposing of four divisions. III Corps was commanded by Major General Erik Heinrichs and comprised two divisions and responsibility for the covering forces.

BEHIND THE RUSSIAN lines, away from these enormous troop concentrations, Otto Ville Kuusinen was very busy indeed. Part and parcel of the plan was the simultaneous launching of a pseudo-political initiative that had been tried before (by Lenin) and which, humiliatingly, had been sent packing from Poland, along with the Red Army, twenty years before. Now, here was the same strategy being dusted off again.

The 'Provisional Revolutionary Soviet Government' of Julian Markhlevski, established during the Russo-Polish War of 1919–20, had been a manoeuvre such as this, a shaky and illegal structure whose only purpose had been to call for liberation, albeit amid an utterly chaotic situation, for Poland had also been involved in no less than four other contiguous conflicts at the same time. The Poles, having inflicted the first and only serious defeat that the Red Army had experienced, had thus set themselves up as natural targets for pitiless destruction, which, as the Leningrad Military District massed itself behind the borders of Finland, had been bloodily proceeding for over two months already.

However, the political 'success' of the September occupation of Poland, accompanied as it was by hordes of imported, cheering proletarians (and, it also must be allowed, many Poles of Ukrainian origin) had allowed Moscow to believe that a similar propaganda exercise could succeed in Finland. The responsibility for this extraordinary error of judgement must lie with Stalin and Zhdanov, who were eagerly advised by Kuusinen.[10] Molotov's view on the subject, with his thinly veiled references to military action since the outset of the diplomatic encounters, was probably more realistic.

Kuusinen had run into some early difficulties in terms of re-cruiting Finland's new government, not the least of which was the reluctance of Arvo Tuominen to act as prime minister. It had been taken as read that this zealous Communist, who had served a lengthy prison sentence for his political beliefs, would share a similar set of motivations as Kuusinen when the proposal of a complete takeover of Finland was put to him; not so. Tuominen later recalled in a letter:

The longer my conscience-struggle continued, the clearer I realised that was not a question of the liberation of the working people of Finland. Instead it was a matter of an unprecedented crime, which I could not go along with...

I should rather stay in prison for ten years more or live the remainder of my life in exile than lend myself to such a dirty and criminal action.[11]

As is clear from the foregoing, Tuominen honourably refused the kind offer extended to him by Kuusinen, on 13 November, to return to the Soviet Union before assuming his post in Helsinki. He also turned down, by degrees more brusquely, subsequent preremptory demands to do the same.[12] Unhappily, despite his foreknowledge of what was to happen, he neglected to warn Helsinki of Moscow's clear plans.

The People's Revolutionary Government was possessed, eventually, of a Cabinet, a proposed seat of government – symbolically the coastal resort village of Terijoki (the first Finnish settlement to be seized) – a newspaper and even an army, the First Finnish Corps. All this was designed to allow the wider far left in the rest of Europe, as well as the citizens of the Soviet Union, the illusion that there was a fig-leaf of quasi-legal respectability in this operation – something upon which the intellectual bowel, if challenged by this action, could grip. The entire Soviet policy during this 'phoney war' period – the propaganda, the smashing of Poland, the enforced bilateral boiler-plate treaties of mutual assistance, the hurried strapping together of Kuusinen's puppet government, the Mainila incident and the official announcements – all belonged, taxonomically, to the same disreputable genus: barefaced fraud. Despite this, Moscow would still wince somewhat at the world's jeering response.

The First Finnish Corps was, of course, effectively a Red Army unit commanded by Leningrad Military District line officers and leavened with NKVD soldiers, under the overall control of Aksel Antilla, a Red Army officer of Finnish origin, who was Kuusinen's 'minister of defence'. The corps would take no actual part in the fighting, being used mainly as a militia force behind the line (and, it was hoped and assumed, a recruiting magnet) while enforcing the activities of the Popular Front committees that would inevitably appear, like bacteria, confiscating and reallocating property and convening kangaroo courts – in all ways, a Polish model. Kuusinen himself would be eagerly present at both prisoner interrogations and the sniffing-out of what were already being referred to as 'Tannerite agents'. But first, there was the matter of the invasion.

AT TEN MINUTES before seven on the morning of 30 November the Red Army artillery barrage opened up on the Isthmus. It lasted until 8 a.m., whereupon the first elements of Yakovlev's Seventh Army, all rifle divisions, moved forward. They were accompanied by renditions of the *Marseillaise* and the *Internationale*, blasted out of loudspeakers already hung in the trees, punctuated by tediously interminable recorded speeches by Kuusinen. To the Ladoga side of the Isthmus, the L Rifle Corps under Commander Gorolenko advanced between the shore of the Ladoga itself and the small town of Lipola along the path of the Leningrad–Kekisalmi (Kexholm) railway. Immediately, the L Corps encountered stiff resistance from two covering formations of Finnish border guards (in little more than battalion strength), Groups 'L' and 'R', who were positioned behind minefields and anti-tank obstacles, which had been further reinforced during the late summer.

To the south-west, the XIX Rifle Corps under Starikov attempted to take Terijoki, and the 70th Rifle Division, commanded by Kirponos and supported by the 20th Tank Brigade, were tasked with the job. They found to their dismay that not only was the Finnish Army still present in apparent strength, but that the town itself had been systematically evacuated, barricaded, booby-trapped and mined, which caused heavy casualties among the inexperienced Russian troops. In fact, there were far fewer Finns than it appeared; present were merely the forward elements (1st and 2nd cover battalions) of Group 'U', which had orders to delay and harry the approaching enemy rather than engage them in open battle. Finnish snipers in the higher buildings and the church tower commenced picking off officers. At ground level, the combat was hand to hand – street fighting of the most savage and costly type: grenades, rifles, knives and fists. The Russian tanks, scattered piecemeal through the attacking force, found themselves powerless to attack an enemy they could not see, and vehicle-to-vehicle communication was still a thing of the future. The situation was further complicated by the efforts of gunboats of the Baltic fleet to offer (inaccurate) fire support, as perilous to the Red Army as it was to the Finns.

The two battalions of Group 'U', against all rational expectations, held up the 70th Rifle Division for 24 hours; only on the morning of 1 December was Terijoki finally declared captured, although the pipe bombs, mines and sundry booby traps left behind continued to claim victims for several days. Those elements of Group 'U' who were still alive fell back, blowing up the Leningrad–Viipuri railway bridge in the process, and already, the Seventh Army, which had hoped to be approaching the main defensive line by now, was a whole day behind its schedule. Terijoki was hardly itself a useful prize; the entire town, not pristine before, was now a corpse-strewn, smoking ruin. Worse for the Russians internationally, the delay had caused a fatal flaw of logic in Kuusinen's squalid propaganda exercise.

So, in the orotund tones to which its listeners had become accustomed, on 1 December Moscow Radio announced solemnly that an 'unknown radio station somewhere in Finland' had been detected, broadcasting an urgent appeal for help from the Red Army. To be sure, thanks to the efforts of Group 'U', the announcement actually came after the Red Army had already invaded the country, but a plan was a plan, and it was the only one Moscow had. A day into the invasion, this was a political embarrassment.

North of Terijoki, the remains of XIX Corps, particularly the 24th Rifle Division, experienced similar difficulties as the Russian policy of advancing en masse into the thickly sewn minefields while under flank attack from mobile groups of snipers paid few dividends. Rapidly the soldiery developed a morbid fear of the hidden enemy and particularly its minefields, as the Red Army lacked any sort of workable mine-detecting apparatus. The solution was simple – soldiers would clear the mines with their own bodies. Safe behind them were ranked the political officers, the *politruki*,[13] whose task it was to urge the soldiers forward, with chanted Party slogans, or if those failed, with plaited leather whips, cruelly strung with ball bearings.

Reports at the time suggested that the Russians were using Polish prisoners of war, now dressed in Red Army uniforms and driven at gunpoint in front of the main body of soldiers, in order to find the mines. The veracity of this cannot be established, but the experience of these operations has been left to us in a grim account:

> Of the more than 100 men of my company who went into the first attack, only 38 returned after the second one had failed...The rest I remember through a fog. One of the wounded, among whom we advanced, grabbed at my leg and I pushed him away. When I noticed I was ahead of my men, I lay down in the snow and waited for the line to catch up with me. There was no fear ... This time the Finns let us approach to within 100 feet of their positions before opening fire.[14]

TO THE NORTH, on the Ladoga end of the Isthmus, Gorolenko's L Corps was experiencing similar problems. On the evening of 30 November the 142nd Rifle Division, supported by medium tanks, succeeded in advancing 6 miles and capturing the wrecked hamlet of Metsapirrti, which was found to be in a similar state to Terijoki and thus of little strategic importance. It was, however, within sight of the Taipale River, behind which the north-western end of the main Finnish defences, manned by the 10th Infantry Division of the Finnish III Corps, began. Again, the toll exacted by snipers and mines was heavy and morale-sapping; the Red Army had advanced in close order, as if merely on a march, and had already started to pay a high price. Bizarrely, some Red Army units were already reporting ammunition shortages. Given the expectations, driven home by leaden indoctrination, that the people of Finland would welcome this liberation, the reality of pitiless fighting and of 'barbaric and filthy tricks',[15] – perpetrated by an enemy that, according to the official, orthodox view was whipped, starving and on the very edge of spontaneous revolution – was a shock.

THUS, THE FIRST DAY of the battle for the Karelian Isthmus had been one of profound bloodiness for the Red Army and, despite the initial success of their covering units, profound gloom for the Finns. The reason was simple – the defenders had encountered massed armour for the first time and there was little obvious defence against it. The lighter Russian tank models[16] were vulnerable to the scarce and precious anti-tank ordnance, but the heavier ones, as encountered at Metsapirrti, were not. Further, despite the fact that the Russian armour was not acting in the organized, disciplined way that would three years later make it famous, the effect was the same. As the Red Army soldiers swiftly developed a terror of the minefield, so the Finns developed an equally morbid dread of the clatter of approaching caterpillar treads.

The 'armour problem' was later addressed in a brutally practical manner. Given the 'road strategy' that was clearly being applied by the Russians, the Finnish solution, which would prove costly in terms of men, was to form special squads of volunteers to attack the Red Army with whatever fell to hand. Initially, satchel charges were used to cripple the enemy armour, but quite soon the use of fire bombs became the norm; the state liquor board provided the containers and the contents, potassium chloride and coal oil, mixed with a blend of petrol and kerosene (or sometimes merely whatever flammable fluid was available) proved devastating, as Soviet tank tactics rapidly revealed severe shortcomings. The policy of scattering armour piecemeal throughout the army made organized infantry support for the vulnerable vehicles almost impossible; once their defensive weaknesses were discovered, the death toll among Red Army tank crews rose exponentially. But meanwhile, before these *ad hoc* arrangements were put in place, the covering troops of the Army of the Isthmus acquitted themselves superbly, crippling or destroying eighty Russian tanks in the first week of the war.

ON THE LADOGA itself, the lake flotilla under the command of Captain Kobylski had been tasked with supporting the advance toward Taipale, the lakeside town which marked the extreme north-eastern end of the main Finnish defence line. With Taipale pressured, the Finns would be forced to weaken their defences in front of Viipuri to relieve it, allowing the left wing of the Seventh Army to punch through to Finland's second city, the ancient capital of Karelia. Conversely, if on the off-chance that Taipale could actually be taken, the defence line could, it was felt, be rolled up with comparative ease. To support the offensive, the 1st Detachment (actually the only detachment as it tran-spired) under a Captain Trainin, set off on 30 November, heading towards the mouth of the Taipale River where it emptied into the lake. His force consisted of two cutters, two minesweepers and the battleship *Orangenbaum*. On 1 December, Trainin was about to commence his barrage against the Finnish coastal defences at Jarisevänniemi, when the Finns fired first. Both cutters swiftly withdrew, damaging themselves in the process on submerged rocks. As for the *Orangenbaum* itself, Trainin managed to ground it on the outflow sandbar of the Taipale River, where it would remain, undamaged but tactically useless, for several weeks.

Given that the main defence line was already manned, and had been for several weeks, the planned role of the covering units was now severely limited by military possibility. The Finnish Army had performed quite brilliantly, even in the face of the dismaying amounts of tanks (let alone infantry) arrayed against them, but even more was to be demanded of them now. In this, Manner-heim, whose basic defence doctrine was the possession of ground, would be brought into sharp conflict with his General Staff.

IN HELSINKI, the Soviet attack was airborne. An hour after the opening movements on the Isthmus medium SB2 bombers of the Baltic fleet, stationed at their newly acquired bases in Estonia, attacked the Finnish capital and other targets in the south of the country. The shock at this was profound and, far from representing a lack of Soviet coordination, was timed (however unwisely) to coincide with a Cabinet meeting, at which the first news of the Red Army attack on the Isthmus (and shortly afterwards, elsewhere) was already coming in. As well as bombs, the Russians dropped leaflets, of which the following is an example:

TO THE FINNISH PEOPLE!

The dastardly provocation of the military clique in Finland has aroused anger in our country and in the Red Army. Our patience is utterly exhausted. We are compelled to take up arms, but we are not waging war against the Finnish people, but against the government of Cajander and Erkko, who oppress the Finnish people and have provoked this war. We come to Finland not as conquerors, but as liberators of the Finnish people from the oppression of the Capitalists and landlords. Therefore let us not fight each other, but end the war and turn our weapons against our common enemies – against the government of Cajander, Erkko, Tanner, Mannerheim, and others.

Another read:

The Finnish government represented by Cajander, Kallio and Mannerheim has embarked on a military adventure against the Soviet Union. At the behest of the imperialists[17], Messrs. Cajander, etc., have broken off the peaceful negotiations with the Soviet Union and have transformed Finland into an armed camp, subjecting the Finnish people to incredible suffering. The provocations carried out from Finland against the Soviet Union were made in the interests of military imperialism. Down with the anti-popular Government of Cajander and Mannerheim! Long live the alliance of the people of Finland and the Soviet Union![18]

There were others, all in a depressingly similar vein: 'Don't starve! We have bread!', and so on. These leaflets, very clearly penned by Kuusinen himself, were taken by their recipients, (accompanied as they were by 500 lb bombs and incendiaries) as merely a black joke, doubly ironic due to the appalling quality of the paper upon which they were printed.[19] However, behind the injured innocence of these risible texts, we can see that Kuusinen,[20] stuck in a deluded time warp, clearly believed (or at least claimed to) in what he had been telling the USSR for years. As a job application his approach was, to say the least, flawed.

MANNERHEIM WAS now made commander-in-chief; his previous tactical resignation offer was accordingly withdrawn. President Kallio announced that the country was in a state of war and the issue immediately arose of a profound reshuffling of responsibilities. Mannerheim had well-developed views on this – the previous day he had been overheard (by his deputy, General Oesch) on the telephone to Cajander, expressing, very pungently, his opinion of the hapless Prime Minister. Assuming that he was on the point of 'retirement' Mannerheim evidently felt justified in clearly expressing himself: 'I had never heard anyone berated as the Marshal berated Cajander.'[21]

Given that Mannerheim (who could be profoundly grand, even stuffy at times) was not a man known for using the language of the barrack-room, it would be interesting to know the exact form of words used. This was one of the few moments in his career to date when he can legitimately be said to have lost control. There would be others though, and quite soon.

Any reservations Mannerheim might have felt concerning Tanner were pragmatically swept aside – the importance of the Social Democrat Party, however much he might have privately disapproved of its policies, was primary if the government was to have the support of the whole country. Tanner, who now acted with a merciless swiftness, was to be the mainspring of the reorganization of that government. After the interrupted Cabinet meeting, Tanner took soundings among his Social Democrat colleagues, and all agreed that both Cajander and Erkko had to go; what was now clearly needed was a government that might make peace; the Cajander/Erkko policy line had obviously failed – aural (and printed) evidence of that fact could now be found all too easily in the streets outside. Bluntly, Tanner made his view clear to a depressed Kallio, who unsurprisingly concurred that the pair should go, but only after a rushed vote of confidence was passed. Mannerheim, meanwhile, only tangentially interested in the party political process, set to in order to draft his first order of the day, in which he managed to cover much ground. Finland was at war, he announced. It was the 'continuation and final act of our war of liberation' against 'the traditional enemy'. And, 'We fight for our homes, our faith, and our fatherland.'[22]

Over two hundred Finnish civilians were killed in those first Soviet air raids, and tales that the Russian aircraft, which flew in at below 1,000 feet, had also strafed the city, deliberately targeting civilian workers' housing rather than military or political targets (the Foreign Ministry, for example, was untouched) later proved to be not so very wide of the mark. One piece of collateral damage which did cause some wry amusement, however, was that which hit the Soviet legation, which sustained quite serious harm. The building itself was almost empty; those few staff who had not already quietly slipped away were now awaiting a German merchant ship, the *Donau*, which would collect them on 2 December.

The new Finnish government was announced on the evening of 1 December, and held its first meeting the next morning. The new prime minister was Risto Ryti; the foreign minister, Tanner; and minister without portfolio, Paasikivi. Upon Mannerheim's insistence, the trusted (by the Marshal himself, which now mattered) General Rudolf Walden was appointed assistant defence minister under Niukkanen, with a watching brief in Cabinet as Mannerheim's personal representative. Mannerheim, therefore, finally had a man on the inside. However, there was already elsewhere a completely new administration.

As the last few Finnish soldiers, their ammunition spent, were blasted out of the church tower at Terijoki, Radio Moscow announced with a straight face the creation of the Finnish Peoples' Republic under President Otto Kuusinen. The new President was to fly the next day, from his temporary seat of government at the now almost flattened, smoking border village, to Moscow, where he now would conclude an 'historic treaty' with the Soviet government. The sneering derision with which this momentous news was greeted (both inside Finland and in the wider world) was quite deafening and served, more than any other single event of the first few days of the war, to bind the disparate political and social interests of the whole country even more closely together than the actual invasion had already done. Tactically, like the ridiculous leaflets, Kuusinen represented a colossal blunder.

AS THE NORTH EAST wing of the Red Army felt its way forward, coming to a halt in front of the Taipale River, it kept moving forward to the south-west. The fighting started to even out somewhat. A successfully planted rumour, suggesting that the Red Army had leapfrogged the Finnish covering units on the Gulf coast and landed at Ino, caused a rapid, pell-mell fallback on the part of Group 'U', on the orders of the commander of II Corps, Öhqvist. When it proved to be false, Mannerheim was infuriated as even now, emergency last-minute preparation of the line in front of the Viipuri gateway was still under way. Similarly, rumours of a strong Red Army tank force arriving at Sormula[23] caused General Östermann to direct Heinrichs (III Corps) to withdraw Group 'R' from its engagement with the Red Army's L Corps all the way back to the main defence perimeter at Lake Suvanto. Despite orders from Mannerheim himself, issued on 2 December, that the covering forces should regroup and, reinforced, take back the initiative, they did not – Östermann chose to ignore the instruction. Thus, by either disinformation or confusion, 15 miles of precious ground on the vital and vulnerable south-west of the Isthmus was surrendered without a fight and the only element of the defending army that had been battle-seasoned, (albeit only by a matter of hours) was now withdrawing from the field, destroying every scrap of shelter in the process; the Red Army did not lay waste to the Karelian Isthmus – that job had already been accomplished by the time it arrived.

The opportunity offered the Russians by this unforced error was significant, and they attempted to seize it. The most forward element of the Seventh Army was Grendal's L Corps, which had harried the withdrawing Finnish border units as far back as the Taipale River. But the Russian corps was overextended already, with insufficient artillery support within range quickly enough to stage a successful river crossing in hot pursuit. Further, it emerged that there was a simple lack of pontoons (Finnish fire destroyed dozens) with which to effect a crossing, an undertaking that was apparently quite new to the Russians. The absence of Yakovlev who (suspiciously) remained safely behind the lines at Aglotovo (the Seventh Army headquarters) added little insight or weight to the operation. His orders to Grendal were both imprecise and ill-informed, a fact which Shaposhnikov was quick to spot. The Chief of Staff penned a sulphurous memorandum to Yakovlev, pointing out, with a ponderous formality, that: 'You are a front Commander and do not have the right to leave the command of your army for an entire 24 hour period. This is the last time I warn Commander Yakovlev about the purposeful negligence of his staff concerning the actions of his own troops.'[24]

It certainly was. Unsurprisingly, Yakovlev was removed from command of his army a week later and returned in disgrace to Leningrad.[25] Meretskov himself was then placed in direct command of the Seventh Army, but the overall control of the campaign now passed to the General Staff Supreme Command (later known as *Stavka*), directly under Stalin and Voroshilov, eagerly but ineffectively assisted by Lev Mekhlis, the Director General of the Red Army Political Directorate.

Meanwhile, Grendal's attempts to cross the Taipale River had not prospered. It was 200 yards wide and, this being early December, with temperatures hovering around 0°C, flowed fast, cold and deep. It was a formidable natural barrier made more effective by the Finnish emplacements on the far shore and up to a mile behind it. Grendal was thus the first Russian commander actually to come up against the fortified line, and the experience was sobering. Of particular note was the astonishing accuracy of the

Finnish gunners, firing from a network of well-concealed nests and gun-pits. L Corps's failure to cross the river was to have a profound effect. In essence, it represented the first and last opportunity to maintain the schedule that had been so optimistically laid down in Meretskov's plan.

THERE IS NO DOUBT that the Finnish Army was jumpy, and likewise that the Red Army was vast and the situation uncertain, but as the possibility arose in Mannerheim's mind of attempting to retake the lost ground, he ran into further serious opposition from his field commanders. He was briefly at risk of losing that vital attribute of a commander-in-chief, unflappability. Thus only days into the war, a command crisis was only narrowly averted as the generals, now relocated to the standing General Headquarters at Mikkeli (St Michael) calmed and reviewed the unfolding situation.

It was not good. Not only had the Russians attacked in vast strength on the Isthmus itself in numbers that could not be accurately ascertained, but also north of the Ladoga, indeed along the whole frontier, reports had been arriving of vast Red Army formations, accompanied by armour, artillery and cavalry, plodding along the scanty road network. Of particular concern was the vast pressure being experienced directly to the north, along the far shore of the lake itself. This could only mean one thing – that the Russians were planning to attack the main defence line not only from the front, but from the north as well. This contingency had been already thought through, more unwelcome was the sheer scale of the second invading army.

IN THE GULF OF FINLAND itself, the Russian Baltic fleet attacked during the morning of 1 December. The heavy cruiser *Kirov*, escorted by two gunboats, commenced shelling the coastal batteries near Hanko Cape, with no particular accuracy. This was certainly not the case when the Finns returned fire. The *Kirov*, lightly damaged, was forced to sheer off and promptly strayed into a minefield (of which the captain had not been informed) sustaining enough further damage to be put out of effective commission. Humiliatingly, the pride of the Baltic fleet limped away, to be taken under tow and escorted back to safety. As we shall see again, the Russian fleet did not acquit itself well.

Farther out into the Baltic Sea itself, the Russian submarine fleet was on station in an attempt to blockade southern Finland from outside assistance. There was immediate tension as the Swedish Navy, fully mobilized (along with the other armed services), heightened its patrol activities in the waters off the Åland archipelago and out into the Gulf of Bothnia, laying mines as they went.

CHAPTER FIVE

Responses

Finland ... should have been a sensible neighbour.

G. B. Shaw[1]

TO DIGNIFY THE RESPONSE OF the Anglo-French alliance to Stalin's actions with the description 'chaotic' would be perhaps to imply, relative to what happened, that there was some non-linear but nevertheless ordered structure to the process. While there had been disquiet in all the capitals of Europe and America at the rapidly deteriorating situation between Helsinki and Moscow, no-one had calculated that the USSR would take the extraordinary step of actually attempting the full-blown invasion of what was essentially a neutral and pacific (if uncooperative) neighbour.

That the Anglo-French position on Finland led to such chaos had in its root cause a fatal lack of coordination between London and Paris. The chain of command was both vague and subject to wide interpretation. Even as the first element of the British Expeditionary Force had alighted in France, for example, it was not even clear to whom its commander, Lord Gort, should report. Was it General Georges, the local area commander, or his superior General Gamelin? Georges thought he knew, but was reluctant to press the point for fear of upsetting Gamelin.

The evolution of British policy in the event of an expansive and hostile Germany had been governed by a set of tensions that were by no means unique, but which had been further complicated by the clear politico-military agenda that was the result; it all boiled down to the future role of technology and, more critically, the affordability of that technology.

LESLIE HORE-BELISHA, the British War Minister since 1937, had never really comprehended why so many influential people hated him. Until the outbreak of war he had enjoyed a relationship with the media that both he and they had sought and he had become a national figure as a direct result of his sponsorship of the pedestrian road-crossing beacon that bears his name even today, but his agenda, which included a massive self-regard (which was notable even in a profession not short of examples), caused him to clash serially with the higher reaches of the Army Command. A particular irritant was Hore-Belisha's apparent dependence upon the military advice of Basil Liddell Hart, who had not had a 'good war' first time around, in 1914–18. Further (and clearly connected with this in the minds of his critics, at least), he was a mere *captain*, a rank that he should by custom have dropped upon retirement.[2] The constant presence (perceived or real) of 'that damn'd writin' feller' at Hore-Belisha's elbow cannot have helped matters, particularly not for Lord Gort, who was a viscount, a general and a Victoria Cross holder from the Great War.

With the rank and file, however (and their newspapers), the energetic Hore-Belisha was extraordinarily popular; his stated mission, to 'democratize' the army, had led to him being adopted by certain quarters of the press as, predictably enough, 'a breath of fresh air.' His policy of large-scale officer promotion from the ranks won him many friends outside the army, despite the irritation it caused among the General Staff, but his attempt to abolish such distinctions of rank as the Sam Browne belt for officers was seen as trivial and petty, particularly by those who wore it. This was less for the sake of the appurtenance itself, far more for the attention-seeking (and diversionary) micro-management that it represented, for in truth the British Army was beset with far more problems of a manpower and technical nature than it was with sartorial ones. But it was not the matter of officers' kit which would cause the fall of Leslie Hore-Belisha; indirectly, it would be the matter of Finland.

AS THE FINNISH CRISIS erupted into war on 30 November, it became obvious that the meaning of 'indirect aggression' was now well and truly defined. Indeed, what had been feared and many of the essential mistrusts of the Soviet regime that had been felt and expressed in the prior months seemed to have been proved correct. Few drew comfort from this, but the tone of opinion is well summed up by the diary entry of John Colville, private secretary to Neville Chamberlain, for that day: 'Evidently, the Russian threats were not bluff. Using the same technique as Hitler, a technique which does not gain in dignity for being second-hand, they invaded Finland this morning.'[3]

To a distracted Europe, already busy attempting to second-guess Nazi intentions in the West, the Soviet attack on Finland came as something of a shock. As the news filtered through that this was no minor escalation of a rather technical border squabble, but rather a full-fledged invasion, mild alarm turned to a collective outrage, albeit one tinged with a certain hopeless *naïveté*. An indignant Beatrice Webb confided to her diary:

> 'Another shock for the friends of the Soviet Union! The March of the Red Army into Finland and the bombing of the towns by a Red Air Fleet. As before, it is the manner of doing it – the working up of hard hatred and parrot-like repetition of false – glaringly false – accusations against poor little Finland, which is so depressing.'[4]

Poor Little Finland. Webb did not make clear her view for posterity as to what might have been an acceptable approach – but she was clearly upset by the bad manners.

The outrage felt across Britain at Russia's action simply cannot be overstated. At this distance, with Norway, the fall of France, the 'Miracle of Dunkirk' and the Battle of Britain rather serving to obscure what went before, the simple impact of this unexpected and unwelcome attack gave notice to the Western Allies what the Royal Navy already knew – that this was a real war, not a 'phoney' one.

The initial response, of the media at least, was to opine, optimistically, that the invasion would serve to drive a wedge between the USSR and Germany. Correspondents who should have known better were moved to write: 'Russia's invasion, I learn, is causing consternation in orthodox Nazi party circles. Army circles agree with party men that the Russian attack is scandalous.'[5] And, in tones suspiciously redolent of First Lord of the Admiralty. Churchill, *The Times* said:

> '...another setback to Germany. To the control of the lower Baltic, Russia would add that of the Gulf of Bothnia and the iron ores of Sweden could not be transported to Germany without Stalin's leave. It would be a sorry day for the German surface navy, whose chief role in time of war may be said to be that of assuring the safe arrival of these ores.'[6]

These opinions were further spiced by detailed descriptions of the instant and massive schism which had 'clearly emerged' in the Nazi hierarchy. The major source of these seems to have been Amsterdam, where Reuters were reporting, for general circulation, that: 'Furious quarrels are reported to have broken out among Hitler's lieutenants. Even General von Brauchitsch, hitherto regarded as an extreme 'yes man', is stated to have attacked Ribbentrop in Hitler's presence.'[7]

And so on. Göring furious, Ribbentrop isolated, the German General Staff frothing in a condition of barratry. These wishful fantasies would continue, until it became clear that the attack on Finland, as a unilateral Russian effort, was the second (but most important) test of the August pact, and it would hold, in the letter at least. Glib assumptions concerning the strain that this war would put upon the non-aggression pact were to give way to a collective unease at its apparent solidity as the weeks went by.

In Poland, through which he was travelling, Josef Goebbels gleefully confided to his diary on 1 December: 'Russia has crossed the Finnish border. Thus the war has broken out. This is useful from our point of view. These days, the more instability, the better!'[8] A week later, however, the minister for propaganda and popular entertainment was more circumspect: 'Brauweiler [a Propaganda Ministry official] reports on his trip in Scandinavia. There is not much more we can do there. A very anti-German mood, which has only been strengthened by the events in Finland. The German people is also absolutely pro-Finnish. We must not let that get too far out of hand...'[9]

IN ROME, the public response was less restrained than it clearly was in Germany. Mussolini's Foreign Minister (and son-in-law) Count Galeazzo Ciano reported in his own diary that same week: 'In reality, the whole of Italy is indignant about Russian aggression against Finland, and it is only a sense of discipline that checks public demonstrations.'[10] This state did not persist for long. Two days later he recorded: 'In all Italian cities there are sporadic demonstrations by students in favour of Finland and against Russia. But we must not forget that the people say "Death to Russia" and really mean "Death to Germany"'[11]

In fact, Mussolini's government was one of the first to attempt any kind of concrete assistance to the Finns. On 8 December, Ciano noted:

> I receive the Finnish Minister, who thanks me for the moral assistance given to his country and who asks for arms, and possibly specialists. No objection on our part to the sending of arms; some 'planes have already been sent.[12] This however, is possible only so long as Germany will permit the traffic. But how much longer will Germany consent? The Minister replies that that side of the question is settled, and confides to me that Germany herself has supplied arms to Finland, turning over to her certain stocks, especially from the Polish war booty.[13] This proves that the German-Bolshevist understanding is not so complete as they would have us believe in Berlin and in Moscow. In reality, distrust, contempt and hatred dominate.

The next day, in an exchange that was of itself a microcosm of the August pact (and also revealed some of the clear operational shortcomings of the Baltic fleet), Moscow requested assistance from Berlin in the matter of the submarine blockade of Finland. Could German steamers on the regular route to northern Sweden undertake to supply Baltic fleet submarines at sea? The very same day, Hitler approved the suggestion. With great irony, those very steamers were delivering arms to Sweden that were immediately trans-shipped to Finland. It is hard to see otherwise how the official Finnish-announced figures of Swedish supplies – including no less than 77,000 rifles and 17 million cartridges for them – could have been found from that country's modest reserves.

Sweden was highly active in the first ten days of December 1939 in arms procurement, particularly from Germany – there was, in effect, nowhere else to go. A memorandum exists, over the signature of Emil Weihl, director of the Economic Policy Department of the German Foreign Ministry, which puts the scale of the Swedish orders and enquiries into some perspective:

> During the last few days the Swedish government has been trying very hard to get large quantities of arms delivered as soon as possible. It has approached the Rheinmetall Borsig firm with regard to delivery of anti-aircraft and anti-tank guns and 105 mm. field howitzers, together with ammunition for them, if possible within three months. Furthermore, the Swedish Military Attaché … asked that the following *matériel* (around 100 million RM in value[14]) be relinquished, if possible at once, from Army stocks:
>
> > 32 anti-tank guns, 54 field howitzers, 350 (20 mm.) anti-aircraft guns, 18 (37 mm.) anti-aircraft guns, 30 (20 mm.) anti-tank rifles, 500 sub-machine guns, 10,000 hand grenades and 100 armoured cars.
> >
> > According to information … the Führer, after a preliminary report by General Keitel, agreed to arms deliveries to Sweden in so far as we do not deprive ourselves thereby… Probably only part of the requested arms can be delivered, at most about 60 million RM in value.
> >
> > Considering the arms deliveries which, according to press reports, Sweden has recently made to Finland, it is important [to note] that the Swedes have, on their own initiative, proposed a clause in the contract in which they obligate themselves not to sell to third parties the arms which they obtain from Germany.[15]

Clearly, that was a particular clause the Swedish government was quite happy to radically bend, as quantities (and calibres) of arms not dissimilar to the Berlin enquiry did, in fact, arrive in Finland later with a stated origin of Sweden. Officially, 25 million Reichmarks of weaponry was contracted for delivery to Sweden on 27 January 1940,[16] but the exact calculation of value is hard to determine – the weapons were bartered for gold and raw materials, and the price of raw materials was going up rather faster than the price of weapons.

An encounter between the Swedish Count von Rosen[17] and Hermann Göring on 6 December had rather set the scene for this. The agenda had been prepared in advance, so that when Göring spoke, Rosen knew (or thought he knew) that he had already talked to the Führer:

ROSEN: If Sweden becomes involved in an armed conflict with Russia, may Sweden be assured that Germany will not, through armed force or otherwise, help Russia against Sweden?

GÖRING: Sweden may be entirely at ease in this respect, as I continue to be Sweden's friend.

ROSEN: May I consider this reply as meaning that it is quite sure that Germany, in the event of a possible armed conflict between Sweden and Russia, will not assist Russia against Sweden?

GÖRING: Yes. It is absolutely certain, provided that Sweden, in other respects maintains a position of neutrality with regard to the struggle between Germany and the Western powers. I cannot even understand how there can have cropped up in Sweden the notion that Germany might attack Sweden if Sweden were to become involved in a dispute with Russia.[18]

This casts an interesting light in which to look at Russo-German relations, and which is presumably why the arms supplies were made so readily available, despite the obvious possibility of their going to Finland.

Another nation concerned at the fate of Finland was, for cultural reasons, Hungary.[19] Count Csáky, the Hungarian foreign minister, had instructed the minister in Berlin, General Döme Sztójay, in the first week of December, to request that Germany intercede on Finland's behalf. The fact that the Hungarians had been agitating for three months for fresh arms supplies from the Reich, as well as fortifying their frontiers in the east, meant that they had a long and complex set of agendas, but Finland now assumed huge importance for them; despite their own critical hardware shortages, the Hungarians managed to supply an impressive arsenal to Finland, but little diplomatic help.[20] Ribbentrop's negative reply to Csáky's démarche went out on 13 December.

The Hungarian Regent, Admiral Horthy (with whom Mannerheim had much in common), had been swift to establish a Volunteer Corps upon the outbreak of war – according to Mannerheim,[21] Horthy had raised a force of 25,000 men, all eager to fight Russians, but wiser heads prevailed; some 5,000 were earmarked for service in Finland, of whom 10 per cent actually arrived, the rest making it as far as London.

The huge risk, that the August pact would break down under the weight of the war in Finland, was evident. The constant Russian pressure on Germany, whether for naval assistance in the Baltic, or the pained accusations of infidelity with regard to third party war supplies (see page 144) were unceasing, putting a huge strain on German patience, as Stalin and Molotov tested the accord again and again, apparently unable to believe their luck, as the Finns proved so stubborn and the Germans so apparently cooperative. Publicly, the pact did hold, but clearly, only by the letter.

THE INITIAL REACTION of the British government was, in the person of Neville Chamberlain, coolly realistic, at least in private. He wrote (with an almost cavalier disregard for such imperatives as security) to his sister on 3 December:

> The situation is complicated by Stalin's latest performance, which seems to have provoked more indignation than Hitler's attack on Poland, though it is no worse morally, and in its developments is likely to be much less brutal. I am as indignant as anyone at the Russians' behaviour, but I am bound to say that I don't think the Allied cause is likely to suffer thereby. It

has added a great deal to the general feeling that the ways of dictators make things impossible for the rest of the world, and in particular it has infuriated the Americans, who have a sentimental regard for the Finns because they paid off their war debt.[sic [22]] [23]

Chamberlain rather underestimated the popular reaction in Britain, as he rather overestimated the reaction in American official circles. He was certainly to be winded by developments in France. But these were early days; the general and logical assumption was that the Red Army would roll over the Finns in a vast khaki tide, and present the impotent Allied cause (which certainly did not yet include America) with yet another fait accompli. That this was not to be would be the cause of some extraordinary and unforeseen developments.

THE FIRST DIPLOMATIC initiatives to Moscow came, unsurprisingly, from Helsinki on 3 December, in an appeal to the League of Nations, literally a wake-up call. The *démarche* was unilateral, and made without the knowledge of the other Scandinavian states, which caused some friction; none of the other three were happy that this 'local difficulty' should be opened to global inspection, as it was hoped that the matter could be settled quietly and bilaterally. The next day the Swedish minister in Moscow, Winter (who had been so rudely rebuffed before), called on Molotov to confirm that Sweden was now responsible for Finnish interests (Baron Yrjö-Koskinen having requested his passports), and to bear a message – that the Finnish government wished to reopen negotiations. He was rebuffed again, for ploddingly legalistic reasons that would emerge shortly.

To a Europe that seemed to be only technically at war, the events of 30 November 1939 had come as a colossal shock. Here, suddenly, was an event so unexpected in most quarters that commentators were lost for words, but not for long. Of course, the Comintern's own assets seemed a little less confused: 'Heroic Red Army throws back marauding Finns!' trumpeted the *Daily Worker*.[24]

For those of the 'progressive left' who were not drawing salaries in Moscow, the Russian invasion was intellectually and politically quite catastrophic; Europe's *bien-pensants*, already on their back foot in the wake of the Russo-German non-aggression pact and the partition of Poland, were now utterly discredited. All the carefully built constructions, the closely worded opinion pieces that had striven since the first Moscow show trials to lend some moral legitimacy (and distinction from the Nazis) to a regime that was already and now attacking its defenceless neighbour, were dust. The liberal left was pole-axed as Russia, having already clearly acquiesced to Nazi attitudes in private, now started to use Nazi methods in public. At one stroke, the hard work of the Spanish Civil War, which had served to bring many members of the general public closer to the cause, was abruptly cancelled out.

And this revulsion went bone-deep. A previously optimistic *Daily Worker* seller was actually chased out of the East End pub where he had every reason to expect a decent trade, and pursued down the street by outraged drinkers, many of them women. Transport House was utterly aghast, but Labour Party leader Clement Attlee was thoughtful; Soviet action would soon present him with some interesting stable-cleaning possibilities as the right wing of the Labour Party now rounded savagely on the left. Attlee did not know it then, but – indirectly – the Soviet invasion would now provide him with a unique political opportunity as Conservative interests started quickly to apply a prism through which to regard the left; the litmus test of political 'soundness' now became, overnight, one's views on Finland. Any residual sympathy for the Soviet cause, at least if publicly stated, would be punished by expulsion into the outer darkness; Stafford Cripps had already been denied the whip in September as a result of his response to the Polish debacle. The organized far left, save those who would support the USSR whatever it did, thus fell into an embarrassed and agonized silence, saving their instantly recovered optimism for a role for the League of Nations, which was by then quietly expiring unnoticed (and not much loved) in Geneva. The Finnish initiative jerked it, briefly, into life.

Policy documents came thick and fast from Transport House. Due to the imaginative nature of the reporting press, the TUC resolved to send a fact-finding mission at the earliest opportunity.[25] The news that civilians were being bombed was a particularly disturbing issue, given that a major platform of the anti-Fascist movement was a collective howl of disgust, recalling events from Guernica to Warsaw, at the heartless Nazi tactics of total war. Even worse, the reports that Russian aircraft were strafing the general population as it fled the bombs by road and rail was a huge political embarrassment.[26] These, surely, were the rantings of a right-wing press? Sadly not, as it turned out.

BUT IF POPULAR OPINION was inflamed in London, both official and popular opinion in Paris (moving towards a condition of rare unity for once), seized upon Finland as a *deus ex machina*, a potential salvation from the prospect of having actually to fight Germany at or near the Maginot Line. In this matter, policy instantly diverged between Britain and France, cracking even wider the gap between French assessments of what was possible at the moment and British attempts to control the pace of events, to which now had to be added this apparently baffling development.

French policy, particularly with regard to the Alliance itself, included a determination to wrest back the moral leadership in the light of the humiliation of Munich and the resultant destruction of Czechoslovakia, which, when all was said and done, had been largely the work of Neville Chamberlain, with French diplomacy in mute support. It was, after all, the French Army that would bear the weight of any German assault in the West, and thus it was this contingency that Paris was most keen to avoid. Edouard Daladier, mindful of the splintered state of public opinion, was quick to exploit the first consensus that seemed to emerge (in the media at least), which was that something must be done about Russia's action in Finland.

The hostility between left and right in France was of an altogether more sulphurous order than that in Britain. The failure of the Popular Front government, with accusations of fellow-travelling levelled at it from all sides right of centre, had led to a fracturing of normal political relations, which the cause of Finland did much to unite; the Finnish League of Nations initiative granted common cause to those of the left, embarrassed for the Soviet Union, and those of the right who, reluctant to engage with Germany, viewed this as a splendid displacement activity, whatever their reflexive disdain for the moribund League. As the cynical and well-informed commentator Pertinax put it: 'Calcul politique à droite, movement sentimentale à gauche.'[27]

Daladier was disliked by both left and right. The far right disliked being at war with Germany, the centre right disliked being at war with anyone, the mild left felt his conduct of the war was lily-livered and the far left loathed him whatever he did. The opportunity to finally hammer the coffin closed on the fellow-travelling community was a hard one for him to resist.[28]

It was Daladier's analysis of the relationship between Germany and the Soviet Union, which was shared by many others in both Allied governments, that governed his view of this new crisis in Finland. The August pact, it was claimed, had created Teutoslavia, an unholy totalitarian alliance of the two states. Certainly, by the volume of trade between the two states, together with clear evidence of the Soviet Union enquiring on behalf of Germany for the purchase of embargoed goods, it was easy to assume that this was the case, particularly because in public at least, neither side denied it.

THE LEAGUE OF NATIONS, dozing in Geneva like some Paris-dwelling Tsarist exile, was briefly energized by Holsti's initiative. The ex-Foreign Minister buttonholed Joseph Avenol, the Secretary General, and urged him to convene both the Council[29] and the Assembly in order to air the problem. Otherwise depressingly unemployed, Avenol seized upon the opportunity, the invitational cables being sent out the next day, just as Molotov was rebuffing Winter in Moscow. The cables proposed a Council Assembly for 9 December, with a full Assembly two days later. Molotov replied promptly; his statement was, on the face of it, breathtaking:

> The Soviet Union is not at war with Finland, nor does it threaten the people of Finland with war. Consequently, appeal to Article 11, paragraph 1, is out of place. The Soviet Union maintains peaceful relations with the Finnish Democratic Republic, whose government on December 2nd concluded with the Soviet Union a treaty of friendship and mutual assistance. This treaty settles all the questions with regard to which the Soviet government had negotiated fruitlessly with the representatives of the former government of Finland, now ejected from office.

The telegram finished with a highly colourful account of how the Finnish Democratic Republic had approached the Soviet Union to request armed assistance. On this basis there really was nothing to discuss, and Moscow declined to send a representative.

The oratory that was the result of the rather truncated League session (three others apart from the USSR did not attend) was vaulting in its eloquence in criticizing Soviet conduct, but curiously softly spoken when it came to hard action. Holsti's production of sufficient documentary evidence – not for nothing had he been a newspaperman – to support his case was skillfully done, and the responses to it were almost unanimous[30], but when it came to a Council vote, on 14 December, to expel the Soviet Union from the League, the result was half-hearted at best. Of the fifteen delegates who were present, only seven – France, Britain, Belgium, South Africa, Egypt, Bolivia and the Dominican Republic – voted for expulsion; the rest abstained. The motion was carried, despite the fact that according to the constitution of the League, a quorum (at least sixteen) did not exist.

The Finland matter was the League's last act, if this fiasco can be characterized as such. The expulsion of its largest member country (and only totalitarian one) under such dubious constitutional conditions, amidst a general and clearly escalating state of war, rather summed up the inglorious evolution of this uniquely toothless institution. There had, however, been a subsidiary resolution, urging members: 'to furnish Finland in the measure of their ability material and humanitarian aid and to refrain from any action which would be calculated to reduce Finland's ability to resist.' There were some who were to rather hang on to this notion. Meanwhile, the League of Nations itself gently sank back into its coma. TASS reported on 16 December that news of the resolution had been greeted by 'authoritative circles' in the Soviet Union with 'ironic smiles'.

As well they might; others may have recalled the words of Maksim Litvinov at Geneva nearly two years earlier:

> It is quite clear that under international law no assistance is to be given to those who are in revolt against a lawful government; any assistance given to rebels in the form of war materials and particularly in the form of men would be a gross violation of international law; the recognition of the ringleader of the revolt as chief of state in the government does not improve the position, since in this way it would be possible to legitimise any revolt or revolution whatsoever through a simple declaration of the rebels as the lawful government in itself constitutes intervention.[31]

Within a week of the resolution, the broad sweep of French press opinion was urging at least some political action, the most preferred line being a suspension of diplomatic relations. As it became clear (from the inconsistent accounts emerging from the bar of the Hotel Kämp) that the Finns were giving a good account of themselves, the pressure was to mount something more than that, initially as a displacement activity, and later as something rather more.

DALADIER HAD HAD in his possession for some time a report, penned by Fritz Thyssen the German industrialist (who had reassessed the Führer's policies and decamped to France on the outbreak of war), which concluded that without access to the massive amounts of iron ore available in Sweden, Germany would simply lose the war.[32] This matter had also been raised in Britain as far back as 18 September, after a meeting at the Admiralty, during which Admiral Drax had discussed the simple importance of the ore traffic to Germany. The next day, Winston Churchill raised the subject in Cabinet, so that by the time war broke out in Finland, there was already a Scandinavian agenda in both

London and Paris. Indeed, Churchill already had a plan for naval activity in the Baltic, to commence on 31 March 1940, the objective of which would be to isolate Germany from Scandinavia. It was code-named 'Catherine'; its development was the responsibility of Admiral of the Fleet Lord Cork and Orrery.

The 'iron mountain' of ore was concentrated at Gällivare, in northern Sweden. It was of the highest grade (up to 50 per cent pure metal) found in nature and therefore easily extracted, simply dumped into trucks, and sent on its way. During most of the year, exports were shipped via Lulea, safely down the Gulf of Bothnia and towards the Baltic, but from December to March, the delivery route was changed; the vital material was then sent down the narrow-gauge electric railway link which connected Gällivare to the Norwegian port of Narvik, where, in time of war, the shipping which carried it down the ice-free Norwegian coast was vulnerable from the open sea. It is important to note that there was no road between the two towns.

Churchill, Drax and Daladier were not alone in estimating the importance of the Swedish ore. Wipert von Blücher used it as a pretext (one of very many) for urging action in Berlin to stop the Finnish war. On 7 December he wrote privately to Baron Ernst von Weizsäcker, reflecting his concerns. Clearly, his close relations with the State Secretary allowed him a certain personal latitude, which he was quick to exploit:

> Thank you … for the understanding – I should almost like to say consoling – words[33] which you find for the unpleasant position into which circumstances have forced me.
>
> …It can with no wisdom be predicted how far the conflagration in the north will extend now that Russia has hurled the torch of war into Finnish territory. Questions such as the ore supply from Sweden arise inevitably.[34]

Despite the fact that the same day a circular telegram went out, over Ribbentrop's signature, saying: 'England's guilt in the Russo-Finnish conflict should be especially emphasised. Germany is not involved in these events. In conversation, sympathy with the Russian standpoint should be expressed. Please refrain from any expression of sympathy for the Finnish position,'[35] Blücher's position on this would not change. He maintained a constant pressure on Berlin to act, and was certainly not alone in this attitude. Public German policy, though, was neutrality on the side of Russia. Swedish tankers were soon ordered to heave to by German warships, their captains being told that this was to 'stop supplies of oil from reaching Finland'. Clearly, as Göring's emissary had indicated, the *Kreigsmarine* was on station, but not, apparently, for the purpose of aiding Finland.

AMERICAN PUBLIC OPINION was, of course, outraged at the Soviet action. The *New York Herald Tribune* took the view that: 'In bold, crude, barefaced mendacity, the government of the Soviet Union ... has no peer in history.' President Roosevelt, contemplating the election pending in 1940, had to act but was constrained somewhat, not only by the large isolationist lobby but also by, as importantly, his secretary of state, whose finest hour this was not. Publicly, Roosevelt asserted: 'All peace-loving peoples in those Nations that are still hoping for the continuance of relations throughout the world on the basis of law and order will unanimously condemn this new resort to military force as the arbiter of international differences.'[36] Which was then, ludicrously, followed by an appeal to *both* sides not to bomb civilian targets, to which Molotov responded indignantly that the Soviet Union had not, and would not, do so.[37] An offer of mediation also contained in the appeal was brushed aside by Moscow.

The matter of Procopé's loan was to drag on until the end of February and so hedged about with restrictive clauses did the issue become (and, critically, so reduced in size[38]) that Procopé nearly reached his wits' end, particularly as the needs of his country now became the subject of a bewildering flurry of buck-passing between the White House, the Treasury, Senate committees and the Department of Defence. Roosevelt was happy to align himself with Finland on an *emotional* basis, but refused to push the matter through to the point of a confrontation with Congress. Accordingly, he stayed in the background and followed the advice of Hull.

Elsewhere, Roosevelt extended the moral embargo already in place upon Japan (as a result of the bombing of civilians in China) to include the Soviet Union. This was done on 2 December:

> This government hopes ... that American manufacturers and exporters of airplanes, aeronautical equipment and material essential to airplane manufacture will bear this in mind before negotiating contracts for the exportation of these articles to Nations obviously guilty of such unprovoked bombing.

Well, they certainly did bear it in mind – at the end of February the Treasury provided details of American exports to the Soviet Union for the November to January period – they had nearly doubled, to $29 million.[39]

AS THE SOVIET initiative concerning submarine resupply was being unquestioningly approved by Hitler, leaks concerning the arrival of the Italian aircraft reached the Swedish press and were, unsurprisingly picked up by TASS in Moscow; the resultant complaint from Molotov unsettled the Germans somewhat. A brusque exchange followed, complicated by 'extensive' Russian requests for weapons from Germany, which were politely refused, not on the grounds of non-cooperation, but simply because Germany was in a state of war. Carefully worded German assurances concerning a virtual embargo of traffic to Finland (but not Sweden) were made in order to reassure Moscow's growing sense of paranoia as, throughout December, the Red Army began to be comprehensively slaughtered, first on the Isthmus at Taipale, and then further north.

IN LONDON, the differences of opinion amongst the senior staff had already begun to make themselves clear. On 5 December, Lord Cork wrote to Churchill that the Russian invasion: '...affords us a wonderful chance – and perhaps the last – of mobilising the anti-Bolshevik forces of the world on our side.'[40] In common with Drax, who had made his unfortunate statement to Erkko at the end of August, it was clear that certain senior members of the

Admiralty had an agenda which differed somewhat from that held by the First Lord. Churchill responded: 'I still hope that war with Russia may be avoided and it is my policy to try to avoid it.'[41] But only directly – on 11 December, Churchill opined to the War Cabinet that it would be to Britain's advantage if Norway and Sweden, forced by the 'trend of events' in Scandinavia, found themselves at war with Russia: 'We would then be able to gain a foothold in Scandinavia with the object of helping them but without having to go to the extent of ourselves declaring war on Russia.'[42]

Despite the massive turmoil which would take place in the War Councils of Europe over the coming weeks and months, this would remain Churchill's policy. For the present, however, he was neither a maker of high policy nor even a member of the Supreme War Council, which was scheduled to meet on 19 December in Paris. It was here that Edouard Daladier, armed with the questionable authority of the League, would unveil (to his French colleagues at least) his grandstanding plan for seizing back the political initiative and perhaps saving France from disaster in the process.

In this, he was cheered on by the French media, who were resolutely pushing for a severance of diplomatic relations with Moscow. In an unusual display of solidarity (the far left being in a state of suppression) the Fourth Estate obligingly lined up behind Daladier's circle, even the usually temporizing *Temps* opining vigorously that: 'A breach with Moscow would allow us to consider new possibilities of manœuvre.'[43]

It was against this uncompromising background of undisguised hostility to Moscow that Daladier set out his stall on 19 December. Tellingly, those members of the General Staff and British War Cabinet who attended had not had a chance to review the paper that Churchill had produced on December 16, again on the subject of the Swedish ore. When Daladier introduced his plan to create linkage between Finland's problems and the issue of the Swedish ore, the British delegates to the Supreme War Council, unbriefed as to Churchill's strategy, were fascinated. Here it seemed, despite their lack of knowledge of the technicalities involved, was common ground, this French identification of Swedish ore as a potential weapon in the war, an economic solution to an embarrassingly one-sided military problem, which can only have been attractive – and an obvious role for the navy.

Daladier's premise was that the ore fields were now in direct danger – if the Finnish Army were to be swept aside (as it was generally assumed it would be) then the entire interior of the Scandinavian peninsula would be under Soviet hegemony, to be invaded at will or, worse, that both Norway and Sweden would be simply handed over to Hitler – the two tyrants carving up Scandinavia between them, as they had already done so recently to Poland. He did not say (but must have recalled) that Napoleon I and Alexander I had contrived a similar arrangement in 1807 at the Treaty of Tilsit.

It was to take some time for the truth to sink in: that the Daladier initiative (it was as yet too Delphically phrased to be called a plan), however much it emphasized the importance of iron-ore supplies, had a rather different motivation – to export the front to Scandinavia and aid Finland in the process. Whereas Churchill's limited initiative (about which the British War Cabinet would learn in detail upon its return to London) mainly concerned the throttling of German war-making ability from an industrial point of view, the French solution, as it would emerge, was rather more straightforward and reflected as much a desire to protect the soil of France as it did to deliver a mortal blow to Moscow. A grander scheme altogether; although this plan was to deliver the ultimate iteration of the appeasement of Hitler, by risking the opening of hostilities with the Soviet Union.

The military coordination Committee of the War Cabinet met the next day in London, and the matter was top of the agenda. But at the full Cabinet two days later, the French plan was put forward, not by a politician but by a senior Foreign Office official, Orme Sargent, who read out a draft of the outline discussion which had taken place at the Supreme War Council on the 19th. The draft referred to the decision to cooperate with Norway and Sweden:

'[This] might be developed with the despatch of an expeditionary force, which in that case would be able to occupy Narvik and the Swedish iron ore fields as part of the process of assisting Finland and defending Sweden.' Even better, there was a League of Nations resolution to justify this. Churchill rather leaped at it: 'The new plan was worth all the rest of the blockade … a great chance of shortening the war and possibly saving immeasurable bloodshed on the Western front.'[44]

The issue, of course, was one of timing. Finland was, against all reason, holding – indeed, would launch a major counter-offensive the next day – but as to how long the country could stand, there was no way of telling.

Halifax took the view that it was 'very doubtful' whether Norway or Sweden would exactly leap for joy at the prospect of Allied help against the German invasion that would surely follow the seizure of the iron-ore fields, 'whatever might be their attitude to an offer of assistance against Russia'. Neville Chamberlain was initially unpersuaded, too, sensibly uncertain about risking a ground war with the Soviet Union. But shortly, he addressed a dinner at the Mansion House, where Gripenberg (a very sought-after guest by now) was present: 'Today, just like ourselves, Finland is fighting the forces of conscience-less power. It is fighting for the same goals, for freedom and justice. Since it needs our sympathy and help this brave people can be sure that our answer to the statement recently approved by the League of Nations will not only be a formality.'[45]

Gripenberg had had no inkling of the musings of the Supreme War Council or the War Cabinet, so he was now startled to hear reports, coming from both Helsinki and Paris (where the energetic Finnish minister, Harri Holma, now ably assisted by Colonel Paasonen, had been very active) that Allied military intervention in Scandinavia was rather a foregone conclusion. Daladier's policy had clearly segued from merely hijacking the agenda to one of promptly jumping the gun with it. Paris, not London, was now the powerhouse of decision-making.

Events now moved very quickly. Bemused by this intelligence

(and the polite disbelief in Helsinki) Gripenberg went to see the Foreign Office. Cadogan assured him (he obviously believed it, too) that the only conclusion that had been arrived at was that the Scandinavian countries would be sounded out as to their view of receiving Allied help in the event that they, too, were to be involved in the general war, the spectre of Soviet occupation being presumably as horrible to contemplate for them as it was for the Finns. Gripenberg was really left none the wiser and wired Tanner that: '…the Allies had decided in Paris to urge Sweden and Norway to assist us in every way but that they themselves were not planning to send troops to Finland.'[46]

DIPLOMATICALLY, the heat was now intense for the Russians. Ivan Maisky was in a particularly difficult position in London and clearly, by his memoirs and diary, upset by the abrupt collapse of Soviet relations with the Western Allies over the issue of Finland. Molotov, according to the official Soviet account, sent him a message (clearly intended to stiffen his spine somewhat) on Christmas Day, 1939:

> We have decided to put an end to this situation and we will liquidate it by any means in spite of everything. Secondly, rumours about some political, or even military agreement of the Soviet Union with Germany against the Anglo-French do not correspond with reality. Third, if they calculate on weakening the Soviet Union by supporting Finnish resistance, nothing will come of it. We will liquidate the Mannerheim-Tanner gang and we will not be stopped by it in spite of its accomplices and well-wishers.[47]

The day before, Maisky had had a fruitful conversation (that he had immediately reflected back to the Soviet Foreign Office) with one of the relatively few senior British political figures who would still speak to him, albeit one who was out of office, David Lloyd George, who had urged him to 'end the Finnish war as soon as possible'.

One who was in office, R. A. Butler, had in fact maintained contact with Maisky throughout the whole crisis, and as the undersecretary of state was able to act as a useful go-between in order to save Lord Halifax's blushes.[48] It was not long before Butler laid out the precise risks that the Soviet Union was running – the news of a great French enthusiasm for bombing the Russian oilfields at Baku from General Weygand's bases in Syria was a piece of information that he delivered in late December with particular care.

As for Lord Halifax himself, he was by the end of the year as well briefed as he needed to be about the existence of both initiatives: Churchill's, which was, and would remain, entirely focused on the matter of the iron-ore fields, and the French *Dessin Grand*, which was still evolving consistently becoming more ambitious, even Napoleonic and would shape-shift between Scandinavia, the Balkans and the Caucasus, but all to one constant purpose – a giant distraction operation. Lord Halifax didn't like either of them, his stated concern being the obvious infringements of Norwegian and Swedish neutrality, either tangentially, in the case of the Churchill plan, or totally, in the case of the French one.

But Churchill's original plan – to mine the Leads and drive the German ore-ships out to sea where they could be seized or sunk – was strictly limited in its objectives, and a mere litmus test of Norwegian neutrality.[49] The Norwegians might lift the mines – which could be replaced – but if they did, then surely that implied, at least, that they were neutral on the side of Germany? Further, the Churchill plan had called for no occupation of territory or seizing of the ore fields – it was in all ways an economic interdiction, purely by the navy. Daladier's stated concern (and his hidden agenda) about Russo-German control of the ore fields rather pushed the matter towards a more territorial, intimate outcome.

Here then was a chance to do something; the lack of activity that was fraying the nerves of all concerned now had a solution and French diplomacy suddenly took the lead. Regardless of the hesitation expressed by Chamberlain concerning war with the Soviet Union, or the concerns of Halifax about Scandinavian neutrality, Paris, brandishing the League resolution, started to set the pace.

Halifax, it transpired, was correct about the Scandinavians, but for the wrong reasons. In Stockholm in the last week of December, the Swedes made it clear that to give more extensive aid to Finland (as Halifax had been urging them to do) would be 'national suicide'. Further, the Swedish king himself was noted to say that he desired 'peace with Germany', adding that it might be possible to engage with Göring (for a general peace conference) who was less 'untrustworthy' than Hitler.

And, over the matter of Finland, the Swedish king was right. Hermann Göring was, by virtue of his marriage to Carin von Kantzow (he had been widowed in 1931), closely linked to the Swedish establishment, which tended toward a resolutely pro-German sentiment. And, by and large, he was well liked. Further, Göring's stepson, Thomas, was in the process of enlisting to join the Swedish volunteers in Finland, which makes Göring's apparently maverick activities in the field of arms supplies to Finland, now and later, perhaps easier to grasp. That by doing so he broke both the spirit and the letter of the August pact is clear; he gave both Ribbentrop and Schulenberg (even if they realized it) much to lie about to Moscow.

This reluctance of the Swedes to permit escalation of their role gave Halifax ammunition to head off Churchill's plans at a Cabinet meeting on 27 December, but not as forcefully (if such a word can be used) as he had before, as he must have calculated that if Scandinavian timidity was that extensive, then it would only withstand one test, if that. Why risk upsetting the northern neutrals twice, when something far more interesting had now presented itself – the larger plan.

WHILE EUROPE SPECULATED as to the true nature of the relationship between Berlin and Moscow, one who had thought he understood his own position with Berlin very well indeed, was moved to write to Adolf Hitler:

> Finland. Fascist Italy is favourably disposed toward this brave little nation, in spite of the sanctions which the Government voted for at Geneva but which the better part of the people did not accept.[50] There

has been talk of immense aid given by Italy to Finland. That is a matter of 25 [sic] fighter planes ordered before the war and nothing else. Thousands of volunteers have presented themselves at the Finnish Legation in Rome and at the Consulates but these offers have to date been declined by the Finns.

No one knows better than I, that politics has to admit the demands of expediency. This is true even of revolutionary politics … nonetheless, the fact is that in Poland and the Baltic it is Russia which has been the great beneficiary of the war – without firing a shot. I, who was born a revolutionary and have never changed, I say to you that you cannot sacrifice the permanent principles of your revolution to the tactical needs of a passing phase of policy. I am sure you cannot abandon the anti-Bolshevik and anti-Semitic banner you have brandished for twenty years … and I have a duty to perform in adding that one step further in your relations with Moscow would have catastrophic results in Italy.[51]

Mussolini would not receive a reply to his letter for three months.

CHAPTER SIX

The Ordeal of Ninth Army

When troops flee, are insubordinate, distressed, collapse in disorder
or are routed, it is the fault of the General. None of these disasters can be
attributed to natural causes.

Sun Tzu

IT WAS CLEAR TO THE FINNS that the disposition and direction
of the Soviet Ninth Army (part of the XLVII Army Corps) so far
to the north of Lake Ladoga indicated one objective: to bisect
Finland at its waistline, by seizing the port of Oulu in the armpit
of the Gulf of Bothnia.[1] This would have the effect of cutting off
southern Finland from its land border (and only railway link) with
Sweden. The lessons of the civil war had not been forgotten. With
the Gulf of Bothnia frozen solid, as it would be by the New Year,
southern Finland would thus be totally isolated from potential
foreign resupply. The Ninth Army, commanded (initially) by Corps
Commander V. Dukhanov, consisted of five divisions; the 44th,
the 54th, the 88th, the 122nd and the 163rd – and elements of this
army were now moving towards the vital intermediate rail
junction of Puolanka, albeit in a somewhat circuitous fashion.
Before Puolanka could be seized, the village of Suomussalmi,
which commanded the only major road in from the USSR, would
first have to be subdued. This was, by its heading, clearly the task
of the 163rd (Tula) Motor Rifle Division.

Suomussalmi had been a village of 4,000, built largely of wood
and a local hub for logging, fishing, hunting and, in better times,

tourism. It was poorly defended; the only Finnish presence consisting of a single border police unit of fifty-eight men, ROII, commanded by a Civil Guard reservist, Lieutenant Elo. At 22 years of age, his peacetime occupation was that of a local primary school teacher. This would be his first and last battle.

Despite the unpromising odds, it was clear from even a rudimentary analysis of the radio traffic of the 163rd Division that its commander, one Zelentsev, was perhaps not quite the master of his subject. Firstly, he had divided his force in the midst of hostile territory that was totally unfamiliar to him.[2] Second, the forward element of that force, the 662nd Regiment, was clearly having particular problems of its own. Not only was it reduced to two battalions (Zelentsev had retained the third as a commander's reserve) but there was clear evidence of insubordination, even mutiny, among the 2,000 men who now comprised the effective regimental combat strength. The 81st and the 662nd Regiments of the 163rd Division had crossed the border together, north of Raate at Juntusranta, and the former drove south to Suomussalmi, while the 662nd Regiment had unexpectedly swung north to Haapavaraa on the shore of Lake Piispajärvi. There, they were halted by the hastily deployed independent 16th Battalion, under the command of Major I. Pallari.

Despite being outnumbered by more than two to one, Pallari's battalion staged a counter-attack on 8 December and managed to throw the 662nd on the defensive at very modest cost, although a significant casualty was Pallari himself, who was badly wounded. Lieutenant Colonel Paavo Susitaival, who also took command of all the disparate forces scattered north of the secondary road junction of Palovaara and regrouped them into Task Force 'Susi', replaced him. Susitaival, as both a Member of Parliament and a reservist officer (and yet another Great War veteran of the Jäger 27th Battalion) had presented himself for service before the outbreak of war. He had been informed, with the scrupulous *punctilio* that affected all matters to do with democracy, that he would need a special dispensation in order to be absent from the Diet. Without delay, he had got one.

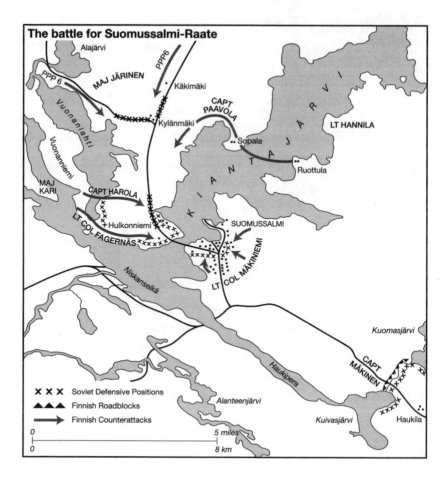

The battle for Suomussalmi-Raate

Alajärvi

Käkimäki

PPP6

MAJ JÄRINEN

PPP 6

Vuonanlahti

Vuonanniemi

MAJ KARI

CAPT HAROLA

LT COL FAGERNÄS

Hulkonniemi

Kylänmäki

CAPT PAAVOLA

Sopala

Ruottula

LT HANNILA

K I A N T A J Ä R V I

SUOMUSSALMI

LT COL MÄKINIEMI

Niskanselkä

Haukipera

Kuomasjärvi

CAPT MÄKINEN

Alanteenjärvi

Kuivasjärvi

Haukila

✗ ✗ ✗   Soviet Defensive Positions

▲ ▲ ▲   Finnish Roadblocks

➤   Finnish Counterattacks

0   5 miles
0   8 km

On 11 December, the Finns intercepted an *en clair* radio transmission from the commander of the 662nd Regiment, Colonel Sharov, in which he declared that not only had a political commissar, one Boevski, attached to Sharov's artillery contingent, been murdered the previous week, but that he himself had also been forced to send forty-eight frostbite victims to the rear as a result of his soldiers not being equipped with either suitably warm clothes or felt boots (*valenki*). Worse was the fact that he had received no replacements for his 160 other (combat) casualties, which rather suggests that Lieutenant Elo's efforts had not been in vain. Significantly, Sharov made his remarks not to Zelentsev's headquarters, but to the XLVII Army Corps, commanded by Dashichev. So Sharov revealed to anyone who was listening (and there were, naturally, very many) that he had already taken unrecoverable casualties in the order of 10 per cent of his total force, his immediate commander could not or would not help, and the fighting had barely started. The further news that 'the reserve officers cannot handle their men' was merely the icing on the cake for the Finns. Clearly, the time was ripe to exploit this chaotic (and clearly mutinous) situation. The opportunity was offered on the night of 14 December, when Sharov launched an aggressive but ill-advised attack towards Ketola village. Mortar and automatic fire reduced his force by another 150 men, which served to make the 662nd Regiment an even more marginal asset.

Further south, the regiments of the 163rd Division's left wing, the 759th Regiment and the 81st, had managed to link up with each other and occupy Suomussalmi itself. They had not been materially opposed, and had taken over the town on the evening of 7 December. Given that Colonel Susitaival was occupied in suppressing Sharov's regiment, Mannerheim instructed Colonel Hjalmar Siilasvuo, presently stationed at Kemi near Tornio, to head south by train to retake Suomussalmi.[3] His unit, the 27th Infantry Regiment (JR27[4]) was severely under-equipped, with no anti-tank or anti-aircraft ordnance and not a single piece of field artillery of any calibre whatever.[5] He reported to General Tuompo (who had only just arrived himself) at Kajaani on 8 December. The

Finns moved with remarkable speed in fact, and Siilasvuo, his regiment to be reinforced by two local units already present, was within 25 miles of Suomussalmi on the evening of 10 December. His force, by now just over 4,500 men, would be ready to attack the following day.

Siilasvuo, despite his role in the Civil Guard, carried with him no political baggage, unlike certain of his colleagues; given that he was in command of a section of the Finnish population whose attitude to the USSR was something of an unknown quantity, Mannerheim had chosen him with care. Not only had northern-central Finland been under more of a battery of wearisome and crude cross-border propaganda than anywhere else, but this also seemed to have had some effect – at the previous general election, nearly 40 per cent of the locals had voted as far left as they were permitted. In fact, Mannerheim need not have worried; events would show that almost without exception, whatever the political complexion of the population, the Soviet invasion drove such considerations firmly into the background.

Siilasvuo had complete surprise on his side, but this fact had an unfortunate downside to it. Not only did the Russians not know he was coming, nor did the beleaguered Finnish border units who had been fighting the 163rd Division for over a week, and with which his unit would combine. Lieutenant Elo, in charge of a small detachment that had taken appalling (50 per cent) casualties, had shot himself on the 10th. His desperation rather echoed the general level of morale. The fact that his two meagre companies, isolated and hungry, had failed to halt the occupation of Suomussalmi by the best part of an enemy division was not itself unremarkable (although ROII had managed to burn much of it) but communications were so fragmented in this early phase of the war that it was impossible to alert the local Finnish forces on the ground either that the Soviet division was having its problems, or, more critically, that help was at hand. ROII, in common with other, similar scratch units, had no radios; they were forced to rely entirely on the civilian telephone net, itself vulnerable to sabotage and enemy action. It had been a traumatic few days for them, fighting an undirected, piecemeal action against an enemy that appeared to be of inexhaustible size. Critically, neither ROII nor any other unit of the Finnish Army had ever faced tanks before. Even those officers of the First World War Jäger battalion who had served on the Eastern front had no first-hand knowledge of armoured warfare; the tank had been unique to the Western front. It was this traumatized state that Colonel Siilasvuo had to reverse, and quickly. Artfully, the rumour was then spread that JR27 was merely the vanguard of an entire Finnish division, the 9th, which was approaching from the south and this gross (but necessary) exaggeration served to stiffen the resolve of the hard-pressed, exhausted and depressed border units.

Before first light on 11 December, JR27 moved to a position 5 miles south of the Raate–Suomussalmi road, south-east of the village. They skied silently through the forest and, after a savage firefight, managed to sever the only direct connection between Suomussalmi and the Russian border. In effect, the village was now cut off, with Finnish forces occupying over 2 miles of road to the east of it. JR27 then pushed back westward as far as it could go, and two companies under Captain J. A. Mäkinen then headed back to the east, to form a roadblock on a small ridge between lakes Kuivasjärvi and Kuomasjärvi. They dug in as best they could and awaited developments, while Siilasvuo now turned to the matter in hand.[6]

The by now hysterical radio traffic between Zelentsev, Sharov and XLVII Army Corps headquarters had its desired effect, and the 44th (Ukrainian) Motor Rifle Division, under the command of Commander (Second Rank) A. Vinogradov, was dispatched from the border up the Raate road to rescue them. They were spotted by Finnish aerial reconnaissance on 13 December. Thus the only Finnish forces facing the entire 44th Division were Captain Mäkinen's two infantry companies at the roadblock; less than 300 men against over 17,000.

The morale of the 44th, despite its reputation as an elite unit, was low. Ismael Akhmedov, a GRU captain attached to the division recalled arriving for duty, transferred from the Isthmus:

> North of Raate, we overtook elements of the Forty-fourth moving towards
> headquarters and the front. Some were resting, others were on the
> march. I checked the schedule of each unit we passed, and whenever
> possible I talked to individual officers and men. Some of those we passed
> were pretty young girls, part of the medical and signal units. None of
> these hundreds seemed in the least bit enthusiastic about the campaign,
> as Party papers we had at headquarters had reported. Their faces were
> sullen, their bodies tired, their spirits low. Men, machines, artillery, tanks,
> horses, all moving towards Suomussalmi; most of them, it proved, to
> destruction and death.
>
> At one stop among those troops, a soldier, a simple Ukrainian peasant
> from the Poltava area, asked me a question. 'Comrade Commander' he
> said 'tell me, why do we fight this war? Did not Comrade Voroshilov
> declare at the Party Congress that we don't want an inch of other people's
> land and we will not surrender an inch of ours? Now we are going to fight.
> For what? I do not understand.' Nikolayev[7] gave me no chance to reply,
> butted in to tell the soldier about the Finnish danger to Leningrad.[8]

Around Suomussalmi, Siilasvuo settled in; his objective was
to tighten, by degrees, the garrotte that he had thrown around the
neck of the 163rd Division. He was aware, after the aerial reconnaissance reports on 13 December, that the 44th Division was on
the way, but he could ill spare any reinforcements for Mäkinen's
modest roadblock. What he did do was to construct an ice road[9]
which paralleled the path of the Raate road, but 5 miles to the
south of it. This would allow swift and hidden movement when it
came to engaging with Vinogradov's approaching force. Meanwhile,
he set about ejecting the Russians from Suomussalmi. The street
fighting was bitter; house to wrecked house, room by scorched
room. After three days, the Russians broke out to the north-west
and what was left of Suomussalmi was back in Finnish hands –
although the village could be rebuilt, not so the road junction.

AT GENERAL HEADQUARTERS in Mikkeli, Mannerheim was as
concerned as Siilasvu at the news of the approaching division.
The 44th was, by reputation at least, an elite unit, and fully

equipped with its own artillery and a brigade of forty-three T-28 tanks; JR27, despite its heroic efforts, was simply not a match for it. Accordingly, on 20 December, Siilasvuo's command was gathered up, reinforced and renamed the 9th Division. On the same day, a further Russian radio message was intercepted, revealing that the 44th Division would reach the area of Mäkinen's roadblock two days later. The message was again sent *en clair*, unencoded, by the communications department of the Ninth Army, which possibly reflects the organizational dysfunction of that body, or at best, its total lack of experience and training – to the Red Army, this was still fundamentally a political operation, merely handicapped by climate.

On the day of his estimated arrival, *Stavka* issued specific instructions to Vinogradov, ordering him to fortify the Raate road as he went along it. For reasons which will become clear, he did not receive the message, and thus proceeded cautiously towards Mäkinen's modest position, of which he had no knowledge.

To compound the misery of what was now about to happen, Commander Vinogradov himself had also made an unforced but critical error; due to a shortage of transportation, the lightly armed but more mobile reconnaissance elements of his division reached their point of departure, Vazhenvaara, on foot and behind the armour and artillery that had gone on ahead by rail. Thus, as the 44th Division started up the Raate road, it was in effect back to front and completely unable, such was the narrowness of the road, to carry out any investigation of what might be ahead of the column; it was, almost literally, at risk of falling over itself.

This fact was not lost on Mäkinen; on the morning of 23 December, he abandoned his roadblock and threw his tiny force against the forward element of the Russian division, which, it transpired, was the 25th Regiment. The entire 44th Division, uncertain as to the strength of this Finnish attack, (or, as significantly, the politically correct response to it) promptly ground to a halt, all momentum lost. Almost instantly a vast traffic jam was formed, consisting of thousands of vehicles, horses and men packed onto a single carriageway of unmetalled road, the surface of which, already wrecked by tracked vehicles, was now also marred by frozen iron-hard ruts; less of a road than an assault course. The weather was closing in.

Because of the projected speed of the Soviet campaign, neither the 163rd nor the 44th were equipped with anything like enough *matériel*. In the case of the 163rd, penned up around Suomussalmi and constantly harassed by increasingly aggressive Finnish attacks, the food situation was already becoming critical; it was, after all, supposed to be 'liberating' Oulu by now.[10] In temperatures which now plunged to as low as –25°C, the soldiers were starting to go hungry. The remnants of the main body of the division were, as Christmas approached, split in two either side of the southern end of the frozen lake Kiantajärvi; the 662nd Regiment was still pinned down further north by Task Force Susi and thus quite unable to make any contact with Zelentsev's two other regiments.

By now, Siilasvuo had finally received the artillery which his new status as a division commander merited. There were four model 1902 76 mm cannon, together with two precious Bofors 37 mm anti-tank weapons. With all his reinforcements deployed, Siilasvuo could now call upon a force of no less than 11,500 men, in theory the thick end of a whole division, albeit one deprived of all the supporting units of his enemy. For the first time since engaging with the Russians, there was something like parity of manpower, if not equipment. Siilasvuo started to plan for the ambitious knockout blow.

But not before desperation forced Zelentsev to attempt a breakout on 24 December. He had with him two regiments of artillery, the 86th and the 356th. He unleashed them at 11 a.m., which at least succeeded in damaging Finnish telephone lines, and started to move south at noon. He was contained by Colonel Mäkiniemi's two cover battalions and withdrew. The next day the Russians tried again, but to little avail. Elements of the 759th Regiment even attempted a breakout to the west, deeper into Finland, which was halted as they crossed the ice of Lake Vuonanlahti.[11] Given that the soldiers were not wearing snow

Mannerheim as Chairman of the Defence Council, 1937.

ABOVE King Gustav of Sweden (left), Erkko and President Kallio at the Stockholm Conference, 1939 (IWM).

RIGHT Väinö Tanner, Paasikivi and Baron Yrjo Koskinen depart for Moscow, October 1939 (IWM).

OPPOSITE LEFT A 'Lotta' unit preparing food at a Finnish reservist camp,
October 1939 (IWM).

ABOVE A passenger bus takes a direct hit, Helsinki, December 1939
(Photo Pressens Bild, Stockholm).

BELOW A Red Baltic Fleet bomber, one of many downed over the Isthmus.
It would be recycled very soon (IWM).

OPPOSITE TOP Life on the Mannerheim Line (IWM).

OPPOSITE BELOW Morning prayers (IWM).

ABOVE The northern front at Salla, where Wallenius had, early in the war, distinguished himself (IWM).

BELOW The terrain at Tolvajärvi.

ABOVE The monochrome landscape of the Winter War.

BELOW A Finnish machine-gun crew on the Karelian Isthmus, January 1940 (IWM).

OPPOSITE TOP A Finnish mobile kitchen (IWM).

OPPOSITE BELOW A column of Red Army POWs after Suomussalmi, January 1940 (IWM).

TOP Two Finns walk past some of the remnants of the Red Army's 44th Division after retaking the field. Suomussalmi, January 1940 (IWM).

ABOVE Karelian refugees prepare to leave their homes, March 1940 (IWM).

capes, they stood out as easy targets for Task Force 'Kari', by then approaching from the north-west.[12]

One of the reasons for the Finns' consistent ability to outreach their numbers in terms of total effect was their possession of automatic weapons, with which their opponents were simply not equipped. The standard Red Army long-arm (with which the Finns were also equipped) was a fine weapon; well balanced and well made, it had a killing range that was at least the equal of the German Mauser, if not the Enfield. In a forest environment, however, it proved to be of severely limited use. Squads of Finnish skiers, if enough of them were equipped with the 9 mm Suomi machine pistol, could wreak terrible damage as they arrived – skiing silently and unheralded by artillery, upon a force of now beleaguered Red Army soldiers.

By now it seemed clear that the 163rd Division was no longer functioning as a cohesive unit. Accordingly, on 27 December, Siilasvuo launched his final attack. Quickly, though, it became clear that however chaotic the command and control of the division might have been, its soldiers could still fight. Time after time, the Russians held off determined attacks from an increasingly anxious 9th Division, nervous of the 44th on the far side of Suomussalmi, and for three days, the fight see-sawed. The Russians were hungry and cold, but they had tanks; they were appallingly badly led, but the tenacity of the individual Russian soldier seemed to know few bounds.[13]

Finally, at noon on New Year's Eve 1939, the 163rd Division broke. What had been characterized as a series of pockets of grim determination now became a disorganized free-for-all. The disparate force broke up and fled in all directions, but mainly across the ice of the frozen Lake Kiantajärvi, where, once again, they and their main supply dump made easy targets. Even the Finnish Air Force became involved, as a pair of Bristol Blenheim medium bombers added their payloads to the carnage, smashing the ice across which the demoralized Russians were fleeing. Men, tanks, horses and soft-skinned vehicles simply crashed through; they are still there.

The haul of useful booty from the rout of the 163rd Division was considerable, even allowing for how relatively poorly equipped it had been. Most prized were the small arms ammunition supplies,[14] but the thirty pieces of field artillery captured and some three dozen anti-tank weapons were to prove as immediately useful for Siilasvuo's next task. Of less utility were the cheap and shoddy cotton uniforms or the inadequate and unsuitable footwear, although the characteristic conical caps (*budenovka*), as worn by the Red Army since 1920, would prove useful in deception operations later on. What few rations were found proved to be almost inedible.[15]

We do not know exactly how many Russians died in this first phase of the battle of Suomussalmi, for the simple reason that there was no exact record of how many started out, but the Finns counted over 5,000 corpses (on dry land) and took 500 prisoners. For the men of the 9th Division, there was barely time to consider this as, after salvaging practically anything of use, they turned immediately east to engage with the Russian 44th Division, which had been inexplicably quiescent.

DESPITE THE FACT that Vinogradov and his staff were within earshot of the demise of the 163rd Division and could literally hear the men dying, the 44th had moved not an inch from where Mäkinen had stopped it with his handful of men. Later it would transpire that this was not necessarily the fault of Commander Vinogradov himself (although that fact would not save him) but rather the chief of the operations department of the Ninth Army, Commander Ermolaev, who took it upon himself to 'edit' radio messages to the 44th Division. If this was inexplicable, then it was also terminal to the fortunes of Vinogradov and his command.

The 44th had thus been stopped, but it had not yet been annihilated. The first efforts to chop it up into manageable sections took place on the night of 1/2 January 1940, when 1,000 men of the first battalion of JR27 under Lieutenant Lassila arrived 400 yards south of the Raate road at 11 p.m. They had eaten a hot meal and, although not rested, they were at least warm, inside

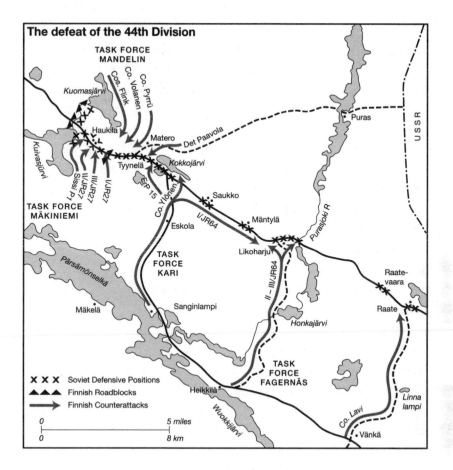

The defeat of the 44th Division

TASK FORCE MANDELIN

Kuomasjärvi

Cos. Flink

Co. Volanen

Co. Pyrrö

Haukila

Matero

Det Paavola

Puras

USSR

Kuivasjärvi

Tyynelä

Kokkojärvi

Sissi P.1

II/JR27

III/JR27

I/JR27

Co. Ylönen

EP 15

Saukko

I/JR64

Mäntylä

Purasjoki R

TASK FORCE MÄKINIEMI

Eskola

TASK FORCE KARI

Likoharju

II – III/JR64

Raate-vaara

Mäkelä

Pärsämönselkä

Sanginlampi

Honkajärvi

Raate

TASK FORCE FAGERNÄS

Heikkilä

Linna lampi

✕ ✕ ✕   Soviet Defensive Positions

▲▲▲   Finnish Roadblocks

➤   Finnish Counterattacks

Wuokkijärvi

Co. Lavi

Vänkä

0	5 miles
0	8 km

and out. From their vantage point, they could see the roaring log fires built by the miserable Ukrainian soldiers, haplessly heedless of their safety. It was now 30°C below zero.

These road-cutting exercises were remarkable enterprises. About ninety minutes were set aside for this one. Lassila set up two groups, each of six Vickers Maxim guns, about 500 yards apart, trained on the extremities of the gap that they wished to make. Two rifle companies advanced in close order, with instructions to separate, the one going east, the other west, to commence the cutting-out operation. In this case, it was realized that their navigation was marginally out; they had in fact arrived at a section of the road that contained a large part of the 44th Division's artillery park, which only served to make their task easier. At the signal, the infantry rushed the road, easily disposing of both sentries and gun crews with short, accurate bursts of Suomi sub-machine-gun fire. The engineers followed, blowing up trees and so creating roadblocks at either end of the gap that had been made. These were reinforced with the captured Soviet artillery tractors. Mines were then laid, and the position reinforced, in this case with the two precious 37 mm anti-tank guns, one for each side of the roadblock. Thus, when the Russians counter-attacked, tanks and armoured cars could be destroyed (or at least halted), adding to the quality and depth of the barriers.

By first light on 2 January, the first attack had succeeded and the 44th Division was now effectively decapitated. It stretched, from 2 miles east of Suomussalmi, all the way back to Raate, some 20 miles in all. Over the ensuing days, the road was cut and cut again, so that by the time the final phase of the battle started on 5 January, there were no less than seven separate detachments of what had once been calculated was one of the Red Army's finest divisions. The Finnish word for these dissected units was simple and evocative – *motti* (a pile of cut logs kept ready for use) – a rather suitable description, and one probably coined by the loggers and trappers who made up the bulk of Siilasvuo's 9th Division.

The state of the 44th Division rapidly deteriorated, despite reinforcement by units of the crack 3rd NKVD Regiment that had attempted, with only partial success, to link up along the Raate road on 3 January. Those elements that did get through only served to increase the vast log-jam of traffic, which was now in effect aiding the Finns in blocking the road; only three days after the first road-cutting operation, the Raate road was effectively impassable for most of its length.[16] The only further reinforcements that could have been provided would have to come on skis through the dense forest; basic to Siilasvuo's strategy was the core assumption that the Russians would not attempt this.[17] It was a gamble, but one supported by the analysis of Russian radio traffic. It worked.

Given that Vinogradov could not know the strength or disposition of the enemy that he faced, it became a straightforward matter for the Finns to keep the disparate elements of the stranded Russian division pinned down at very little cost to themselves. They learned quickly that a single burst of automatic fire would unleash a response entirely out of proportion, to the extent that quite soon a shortage of ammunition would add to the woes of the beleaguered Russian soldiers. The simple tactic of using mortars to disable the field kitchens further ensured that they would be deprived of hot food; given that the weather showed no sign of improving, the Finns could thus afford to let nature take its course. But not without some assistance. Akhmedov recalled: '...the battalion had been badly punished when the men had lit fires to warm themselves and heat food. From treetops the Finns had machine-gunned every fire, easily picking out the dark silhouettes of the men against the snow.'[18]

The effects of the weather on the Red Army and their weapons were catastrophic; the standard Red Army rifle, the model 1902 Moisin-Nagant, was a single shot bolt-action weapon of 7.62 mm calibre. In temperatures of lower than –15°,[19] the gun-oil with which it was lubricated simply froze, and the weapon became inoperable.[20] Likewise, the armoured vehicles trapped in the forest, although powered by sophisticated aluminium diesel engines, were uniquely vulnerable; the differential between the coefficients of expansion of the alloy engine blocks and the ferrous metal moving parts ensured that if the engine cooled below –10°C, the bearing clearance on the crankshafts closed up and would not permit them to turn over. Thus, the engines were left running constantly and as a result, used precious, irreplaceable fuel and lubricant. Further, the primitive (and very bulky) batteries required to maintain electrical power became less efficient as the temperature dropped, which is why the later iterations of the Russian tank instead employed massive pump-driven compressed air reservoirs with which to turn over their engines.[21]

So, for the Russian soldiers, these forests were very far from quiet. The constant rumble of tank and truck engines, the terrified whinnying of hungry horses,[22] the non-stop fusillades from Finnish snipers, the sharp reports from exploding trees as their very sap froze, all made for a further deprivation – sleep. Soldiers also discovered that to touch cold metal was to be instantly welded to it. With little or no hot food available from most of their sixty scattered and damaged field kitchens, constantly under suppressive fire, they resorted to the one sovereign remedy with which they were singularly well equipped – vodka. But a high alcohol consumption in cold weather merely produces the illusion of warmth and comfort; in reality, it has the effect of opening the pores of the skin and the consequent loss of body heat, with no reliable sources of external warmth save the suicidal log fires, can be terminal, even over as short a period as that endured by the 44th Division.

Panic fear, the ancients tell us, is the fear of the works of the woodland god Pan; whether these men were classically educated or no, that instinct was alive and well that winter in Finland, as the people of the Steppe discovered the forest for the first time: 'All was terribly unreal. I thought of the haunted forests of the fairy tales of boyhood. I was very nervous, but tried not to appear so. I looked at the faces of Nikolayev and the driver. They were ashen', observed Akhmedov.[23]

For the wounded in such conditions, even a comparatively trivial injury (frostbite was the commonest) could prove fatal; the Red Army medical experience in the whole campaign was one of a constant, unequal struggle against the toll exacted by gangrene.

Freezing wounds, however minor, mortified extraordinarily fast, leaving the hard-pressed medical staff with little option but to amputate limbs that, as curious Finns discovered later, appeared to be only marginally damaged. The sight, serially repeated as Finnish units retook the dismal battlefields, of these great piles, stacked like cordwood outside makeshift dressing stations, was a sobering one, the most compelling image of the frightful sordor under which these men had been fighting.[24] The great piles of frozen excrement, unburiable atop the permafrost, told a different tale.

Vinogradov, stranded in the middle of this freezing horror, assessed – correctly – that his division was probably doomed. On 4 January, he sent a message requesting the discretion to act upon his own initiative, which was curtly refused. Only two days later, after much lobbying, was he advised that he was permitted to make a 'tactical withdrawal', at which point the rout of the 44th was complete. The Finnish forces harried the demoralized remains of the division back over the border. One thousand prisoners were taken, 700 made it back – the rest died.[25]

TO SOVIET SUPREME COMMAND, a long way away, rather warmer and in the middle of a comprehensive review of this and other disasters, Vinogradov's conduct had seemed quite inexplicable. When the traumatized commander finally emerged at Vazhenvaara, having rather unwisely fled the battlefield in a commandeered T-26 tank, L. Z. Mekhlis was dispatched to conduct an investigation. There can be little doubt that Mekhlis was less interested in actually discovering the truth of what had gone wrong (given that he was politically responsible) than he was in making an example of the unfortunate Vinogradov together with anyone else who fell easily to hand. Eschewing the military procurator's token attempt to stage a formal hearing, Mekhlis pulled political rank and placed Vinogradov and his senior commissar, Gusev, under close arrest. A detailed and damning report was swiftly drawn up under the auspices of the GRU and the army, and Vinogradov and Gusev were publicly executed by the NKVD in front of the 700 survivors of the 44th Division who had made it back to

Raate, a suspiciously high number of whom were political officers and thus, embarrassingly, Mekhlis's responsibility. One of them was Akhmedov's old acquaintance Nikolayev: 'He had become a physical and mental wreck. He cried steadily, babbled incoherently, shot blindly at anybody, and was soon sent to an asylum.'[26]

Vinogradov's stated offence of record was 'the irrecoverable loss of 55 field kitchens'. Only later, at the end of January when a comprehensive audit of the staff work of the Ninth Army was carried out did the bewildering deceit of Ermolaev emerge, whereupon Mekhlis, not breaking step even to review the hastily considered fate of the hapless 44th divisional commander, had him arrested, too.[27]

Mekhlis attempted to bury the damning report, particularly the news that so many of his *politruki* had fled the field screaming, pulling rank but tearing off their insignia in the process. It was clear to those who debriefed the relatively few actual soldiers who survived that the overall conduct of the military rank and file had been generally exemplary, a view with which the Finns were to concur when they retook the icy battlefield. Thousands had fought to the last bullet, taking cover behind the stacked, frozen bodies and severed limbs of their dead comrades. The official GRU report concluded that 'more than seven hundred men overcame all difficulties'. A Finnish officer is said to have put it rather more laconically (and accurately): 'The wolves will eat well this winter.'

When the report fell into the hands of the NKVD and therefore the dreaded Lavrenty Beria,[28] Mekhlis, his position already questionable, panicked. 'You idiot!,' he is reported to have screamed at the culprit, 'I'm going to have you shot! Illegally, and probably intentionally, you let the NKVD have a copy of the inquiry. It's probably in Moscow, in Beria's hands by now!'[29]

The new Ninth Army Commander, Chuikov, who was present at this outburst and no doubt filled with a warm glow, stoked by the certain knowledge that this unprecedented disaster was none of his making, calmed him down. Chuikov did not in fact leave the matter there; shortly after the death of Vinogradov and his commissar, he instigated his own investigation in conjunction with his chief of staff, Nikishev, and outside the aegis of the NKVD, submitting it directly (and courageously) to Voroshilov.[30] It was blunt and to the point; after a general assessment of the unwisdom of 'road strategy' in a terrain which actually contained so few roads, the report went on:

> Our units, saturated by technology (especially artillery and transport vehicles), are incapable of manœuvre and combat in this theatre: they are burdened and chained down by technology which can only go by road. [And of the troops] Combat in special conditions is not studied – they are frightened of the forest and cannot ski.[31]

But by the time Chuikov's unwelcome report arrived at Voroshilov's office, it was irrelevant to the matter in hand. Given that the northern flank of the Ninth Army had ceased to exist, attention was turning to the prospects down on the Karelian Isthmus, which were dire indeed.

WELCOME THOUGH the captured booty was to Siilasvuo's men, much of it was a total mystery to them. Of particular curiosity were the plaited leather whips sewn with ball bearings and picked up by the dozen, with which the *politruki* apparently 'encouraged' their men. Some of the hardware was equally remarkable; the weird recoilless cannon, mounted on truck chassis, were certainly novel, but of no immediate or obvious value, as it was not clear quite how they worked. The captured tanks were pleasing, but shortages of trained crew and fuel rather militated against their widespread constructive use. Unhappily, their ammunition was not 'interoperable' with existing Finnish ordnance, but the modest artillery park benefited none the less.

Quite appalling, though, was the state of the captured Red Army soldiers. Aside from the ordeal through which they had passed, they appeared, almost to a man, to be barely up to their task. Undernourished, unfit and in many cases clearly middle-aged, many were totally unaware of where they were, indeed some assumed that they were already on the outskirts of Helsinki. They were, as well as being infested with body lice, also clearly under the impression that they would be shot after enduring blood-curdling torture. Swiftly, the Finns disabused them of that notion and they were deloused, reclothed (their noisome uniforms being ceremonially burned – a sound propaganda opportunity) and given a hot meal. As for the Russians themselves, most were genuinely surprised that there was even food to spare for them to eat, let alone hot and of this standard; they had been under the impression that Finland was, in the main, whipped and starving under the brutal heel of a Fascist tyranny.

Clearly, many of the captives were functionally untrained, an observation supported by later comments from defectors and the testament of letters recovered. One soldier, when questioned light-heartedly about a pair of women's shoes that he had in his kitbag, replied that he had been shopping in Leningrad on behalf of his wife when, literally, he had been press-ganged by a roving commissar, three days before the war started. This soldier, along with many others, was adopted by the unit that captured him as a mascot-cum-translator for the duration of the war. Given that it was not the habit of the Red Army to issue pay-books to even its regular soldiers, it is thus impossible to estimate accurately the overall level of casualties suffered by the Russians in this or any other action except by using basic arithmetic; the two Red Army divisions (not including specialist units) deployed and destroyed at the Suomussalmi–Raate road battles had totalled 35,000, suggesting that well over 30,000 perished.

There was a real sense in which the Finns actually felt rather sorry for the Red Army soldiers, at least at the individual level. If anything, this sentiment intensified as the Finns sorted through the dismal detritus that is the harvest of the battlefield; in particular, the letters from home as recovered from the corpses of the Ukrainian soldiers revealed something of the depressing conditions from whence they had come. Curiously, many of the letters retrieved (here and elsewhere) were found to be without any evidence of the military censor, which speaks volumes for the ingenuity of both sender and receiver alike.

Notwithstanding, full propaganda advantage was taken of the

piteous state of these prisoners of war.[32] The least attractive of them (the most Asiatic looking, in many cases, or even the ones with the worst teeth) were extensively photographed, the images being gleefully distributed among the impatient Press Corps in Helsinki. Obligingly, the Fourth Estate, penned up in the bar of the Hotel Kämp and subjected to strict (but scrupulously polite) Finnish censorship, started to introduce trite phrases into their largely fictive reports, of which 'cannon fodder' became a predictable favourite. Reports started to circulate concerning the appalling morale of the Red Army, the unfitness of the troops, their poor state of training, even that it was now clear that the attack on Finland had perhaps afforded the Politburo the opportunity to rid its huge army of 'undesirable elements'.[33] But this was nonsense; at an individual level, the Red Army soldiers had fought well, and wiser heads pointed out that it was not purely the presence of scattered NKVD 'blocking units' which prevented the 'Ivans' from retreating; it was simply not their instinct to do so and, more pointedly, never had been.

Generally, Finnish propaganda was crude in the extreme; there was simply not enough time to be subtle. The grisly photographs of frozen Russian soldiers, which were also distributed to the world's press, bordered (at the time) on the pornographic; those intended for purely Russian eyes bore a simple slogan – *Belaya Smert* (White Death).

Siilasvuo's 9th Division had performed magnificently; for a scratch unit, hastily assembled and critically short of equipment, to have routed and effectively annihilated two entire Soviet divisions was a feat of arms unparalleled in modern war, indeed it more properly belonged in the same order of importance as Thermopylae. But Siilasvuo had little time to rest on any laurels, as yet another opponent from a seemingly limitless inventory now hove into view.

FOR THE ORDEAL of the Ninth Army was not over yet. As the full calamity of the plight of the two doomed divisions had become clear, Corps Commander Dukhanov was reassigned to an administrative post at Leningrad Military District (alongside the incompetent Yakovlev[34]) where, it was reasoned, he, too, could do no more harm. His place had been taken by Corps Commander V. I. Chuikov, who would soon come to regret having volunteered his services so readily.

Chuikov's new command had not quite become neutralized. Further south lay Siilasvuo's third and latest target, the 54th Mountain Rifle Division, under the command of Commander (Second Rank) Gusevski. It was feeling its way along the road between the Soviet border and the village of Kuhmo, which, like Suomussalmi, commanded a rare strategic road junction. Siilasvuo received his orders to intercept Gusevski on 18 January, although the Russian unit had already been slowed down dramatically by the efforts of the scattered Finnish border units that found themselves in its way. By the time Siilasvuo made contact on 22 January, the 54th Division was only 15 miles from Kuhmo. And there, he stopped it.

The previous week had seen temperatures plunge yet again. According to records, the cold was of such a numbing quality that even reindeer were dying.[35] At Kajaani, the nearest weather measurement centre to Kuhmo, conditions were almost impossible with a temperature of –38°C.[36] On the Isthmus it was, suddenly, even colder. Under such conditions little is possible; men cannot breathe properly, let alone move about. All the 54th Division could do, its weapons frozen, its fuelless engines seized, its soldiers, staff and animals starving, was to cry for help, which it now started to do.

By now, it was clear to *Stavka* that this adventure to bisect Finland was an unrecoverable disaster, and the decision was taken to attempt to resupply the beleaguered units, but not to attempt to fight them as a cohesive army. Novel attempts would be made to relieve them, but the offensive towards the Gulf of Bothnia was over; the Russian objective here was now merely to stabilize a totally chaotic situation, as well as occupy the attention of the Finnish Army that, despite its signal success, was becoming ever more thinly stretched.

It must be said that the methods by which this was accomplished were little short of brilliant, even if they represented an expensive *ad hoc* improvisation. Taking advantage of the fact that the Soviet Union enjoyed total air superiority, at least numerically, it was decided to resupply the 54th Division by airdrop; the very first time that this tactic had been essayed under war conditions.[37] As an innovation it was highly successful and, coupled with another new initiative, offered one of the most potentially threatening situations for the Finns (away from the Isthmus) since the war started. A Siberian ski battalion, under Commander Dolin, was dispatched to attempt a link-up with the beleaguered 54th Division and fight the Finns on what had now become clear were their own terms; this effort would represent the only serious ground-based attempt to allow the survival of at least one element of the Ninth Army, the rest of which, due to the shambles which clearly characterized its staff work, had otherwise been completely edited out of the original order of battle.

As an example of the profligacy with which precious assets can be fed into a confused and collapsing situation, the waste of Dolin's battalion has few equals in modern war.[38] It is not a soldier's instinct to reinforce failure; that is the hard-wired response of the politician, but the haste with which this force was put into the battle (without any reconnaissance) reflected more a desire to be seen fighting the Finns on their own terms – that the Red Army was equal to the task – than a serious attempt to regain the initiative. In one savage engagement on the frozen bed of the Kesselinjöki River, Dolin's force, 2,000 strong, was annihilated, bar seventy who escaped and were rescued. The 54th Division was now completely encircled, and would remain so for the duration of the war.

But it was far from quiet; Gusevski defended his position with some flair and, with incessant pestering to his headquarters, managed to keep air supplies coming. These messages caused both disquiet and irritation to Moscow. After the war, Stalin made a particular point of deriding Gusevski's efforts to survive, his panicked telegrams and signals and, significantly, the sense of real fear which his messages expressed. Siilasvuo's commanding officer,

General Tuompo, on the other hand, was moved to pay tribute to the 54th Division's essential toughness.

Sensibly, Gusevski opted to keep his soldiers busy – their instinctive fear of the forest (as later pointed out by Nikishev) was a morale handicap that he was eager to redress and he had a practical solution – cut down the trees, enlarge the sky. Accordingly, a great swathe of timber was felled, the logs being dragged into laager fortifications. When the Finns retook the field in March 1940, a British reporter, John Langdon-Davies, was with them: 'The first victims we noticed were the trees. For ten miles and more the trees had been tormented; sometimes cut down to give a free view for killing, sometimes twisted into defence screens, with their stumps netted together with barbed wire...'[39]

THE NORTHERNMOST UNITS of the Ninth Army, the 88th and 122nd Divisions, had advanced from Kandalaskha towards Salla, 25 miles inside the Arctic Circle. Against them was a single battalion of covering troops who, while delaying the Soviet advance somewhat, was forced to fall back on, and then abandon Salla on 10 December. The 122nd Division's task was to link up with the 104th Division from the Fourteenth Army (which was driving hard down the Arctic highway) at the capital of Finnish Lapland, Rovaniemi, itself only 60 miles from the Swedish border. From there, the combined Russian force would drive to Kemi, on the Gulf of Bothnia, uncomfortably near the Swedish warm-weather ore export port of Lulea. Captured orders revealed, however, that Red Army commanders had strict orders not to violate the Swedish border, but merely to approach it and hold it.

In command of the Army of Lapland was the extraordinary General Kurt Wallenius. The territory was very familiar to him, as he had fought the Red Guards there during the civil war. He had also been the military face of the right-wing, demi-Fascist Lapua movement in the early 1930s, when he and his associates had botched a rather half-hearted *coup d'état*.[40] Wallenius was a swaggering roustabout of a man, a heavy drinker and something of a braggart – but he was a very good soldier.

CHAPTER SEVEN

In Ladoga-Karelia

In war, numbers alone confer no advantage. Do not advance
relying on sheer military power.

Sun Tzu

WHILE COMMANDER YAKOVLEV'S Seventh Army had been moving
up the Isthmus, the Eighth Army, under Corps Commander Khabarov, was cautiously probing along a 60-mile front on five (roughly)
parallel roads through the dense forests north of the Ladoga. His
force consisted of 130,000 men and no less than 400 tanks; in
manpower alone, let alone equipment, he commanded the equivalent of almost ten Finnish divisions that, like the Ninth Army
to the north, were tripping over themselves.

Against this, the Finnish IV Corps, under Major General Juho
Heiskanen, mustered two under-strength divisions, augmented
by three units of mobile covering troops, each of roughly battalion
strength. Khabarov's attack was not unexpected – his probable
path, to march around to the north of the Ladoga, capture Sortavala
and then proceed south down the single navigable road to turn
the defence line on the south-western shore of the lake, had already
been war-gamed (as extensively as budgets allowed) by Mannerheim and his staff. Unhappily the Finns, logically calculating the
road density as being capable of supporting perhaps three
motorized divisions at most, had underestimated the full scale of
Meretskov's plan and staffed the IV Corps appropriately, with the
bulk of the force defending the north shore of the Ladoga, between

175

the lake itself and a smaller one, Yanisjärvi, which was the obvious (indeed, the only) route of approach.

The Eighth Red Army was divided into five units. In the south, on the Ladoga shore, the 168th Division was heading initially for Salmi, to link up with the next force to the north, the 18th Division. Both would then head for Sortavala via Lemetti and Kitelä. Above them, the 56th Division was to take the railway line at Kollaa, just south of Suojärvi, which was itself the first objective of 139th Division. Finally, the northernmost division of the Eighth Army, the 155th, was to take Ilomantsi and then hold the ground between the Eighth and Ninth armies; this latter force was now starting to make its move due west across the 'waist' of Finland, set on capturing Oulu and thus cutting off potential aid from Sweden.

Aside from the Isthmus, where the defensive line had yet to be tested, the area north of the Ladoga offered the only opportunity to turn the defences on the Isthmus. Either the manoeuvre would draw reserves away from the Mannerheim Line to meet the northern threat, or it would provide the opportunity for a textbook pincer movement. Either way, Meretskov had assumed that to counter the threat from the Eighth Army, the Finns would have to compromise the defence of the Isthmus. A third possibilty, never to be tested, was for the Eighth Army to by-pass the Finnish defences altogether, leaving the Seventh Army to engage the main defence line, leaving Khabarov to drive straight for Helsinki.

But once again, the Russians found that the terrain was against them. The limited nature of the narrow forest tracks, the density of the trees and the unreliable nature of the rare patches of open ground, which were still waterlogged and yet to freeze, offered few opportunities for anything other than a 'road strategy'. Progress was thus very slow and, as early as 3 December, Meretskov, under pressure from the outset, was frustrated at the slow rate of movement, particularly given the proximity of the southern units' jumping-of points to the border. The Eighth Army plan called for a truly rapid rate of advance and it was becoming clear that the

Finns' resolution and flexible tactics (whatever their nervousness) were serving to hamper well the advance of this huge, well-equipped force, itself the same size as the entire Finnish Kannas Army of the Isthmus.

MANNERHEIM, perhaps expecting too much, and certainly nervous at the situation developing on the Isthmus, lost patience with Heiskanen and removed him from command after Suojärvi fell on 2 December, *pour encourager les autres*; his replacement was General Johan Woldemar Hägglund, whose exploits with IV Corps would make him the stuff of Finnish legend.

Hägglund, like all his senior colleagues, was a veteran of the Jäger 27th Battalion and found, as his colleagues had and would, that a certain stiffening of resolve was necessary as the Finnish troops, unaccustomed to the presence of armour and at best overawed at the apparently limitless numbers of the approaching enemy, started to lose composure. He needed to demonstrate that the Russians could be stopped.

In this, the terrain was in his favour. Dense forests, through which narrow tracks threaded their way, with sodden ground to the flanks preventing a broader advance, were perfect features for the plan that he now evolved, and which had been rehearsed extensively. As on the Isthmus, basic for a defensive strategy was an intimate knowledge of the ground. Further, for an army so badly equipped, an ability to utilize other, human resources was vital. Navigation, skiing, marksmanship and improvisation were all qualities that the Finnish Army had in abundance, and in the area defended by the IV Corps, there was now present that even more important factor; leadership, and at several levels.

As elsewhere, the Red Army's equipment was against them. The massive ChTZ caterpillar tractors (built in Chelyabinsk) and the STZs (built in Stalingrad)[1], both of which were used for towing heavy artillery, proved to be too weighty and unmanoeuvrable for the conditions; their tracks simply shredded the already weathered road surfaces and they guzzled fuel. The state of the roads once they and their attendant tanks and trucks had passed rendered them almost impassable, either for the purpose of reinforcement (not that this was considered necessary) or, more critically, resupply. The further these forces penetrated into Finland, the more logistically isolated they became.

Worse for them, the left wing of the Eighth Army (168th and 18th Divisions) soon came within the range of the Finnish coastal batteries of Mantsinsaari island. These guns, of between 152 mm and 254 mm calibre, were able to shell the Russians more or less at will, as the misfortunes of the Ladoga flotilla prevented their effective interdiction.

So, by the time the two Russian divisions arrived in the area of Kitelä on 10 December, almost a week behind schedule, Hägglund and his modest force were ready for them.

WITH THE FALL of Suojärvi, the position in the area of Tolvajärvi was even more perilous, the Finns' Task Force 'R', commanded by Colonel Räsänen, having been beaten back all the way to the Aittojoki River. With the Red Army now controlling the road between the two towns, with only weak and demoralized forces to stop them, urgent action was required if the invaders were to be stopped; there was a serious risk of a total collapse of the line if the transportation network was captured – the Finns knew their ground, but more importantly, knew their own operating capabilities very well, however much they appeared to have outreached themselves so far.

Two days after outbreak of war, another Jäger officer (and veteran of the civil war) had begged Mannerheim for a field command. He was Colonel Paavo Talvela, and was engaged in useful (but frustrating) work on the war *matériel* council. He had commanded in the Ladoga-Karelia region twenty years before and had war-gamed this invasion with particular care. He more than most realized that if the Russians were not stopped, and soon, then the position of not only the IV Corps but also the entire southern interior of the country would swiftly be at the mercy of the Red Army. He presented himself at the Hotel Helsinki (where Mannerheim was headquartered prior to the move to General

Headquarters at Mikkeli) on 2 December, the day the news came through of the fall of Suojärvi. Talvela not only requested a field command, but identified one particular unit that he felt was important to halt the crisis that was evidently emerging – JR16, an infantry regiment commanded by Talvela's old friend, Colonel Aaro Pajari. JR16 was, at present, attached to the 6th Division as part of Mannerheim's strategic reserve, and therefore something of a sacred cow.

Mannerheim and Talvela were old friends. Talvela, had he not resigned his commission in 1930 and become a businessman, would have already risen high in the General Staff; as it was, he was recalled to the colours (although he had remained a Civil Guard) on the outbreak of war. He felt, with justification, that he knew the area as well as anyone and proposed an aggressive plan. Initially Mannerheim kept his own counsel, but after relocating General Headquarters to Mikkeli, summoned Talvela there on 5 December to hear his plan in detail. He greeted him at 4 a.m. on the 6th in full uniform. As the news coming in became worse, he decided to separate the activities of the IV Corps into two commands. General Hägglund would contain the Soviet advance further south, in the area of Kitelä, and Colonel Talvela, with the units he requested from the commander-in-chief's reserve, would attempt to stop the Russians, who had so far swept all before them, in the area of Tolvajärvi.

For Mannerheim, this was a very big throw of the dice indeed. He assessed Talvela as: 'a fearless and strong-willed Commander, who possessed that degree of ruthlessness required in an offensive against a greatly superior adversary',[2] but was also acutely aware that by denuding his reserve division so early in the conflict, he was also running a huge risk, particularly as the news came through the next day of the first major assault on the defensive line at Taipale. But he had no choice. Hägglund had to hold near Kitelä and Talvela had to halt the Soviet incursion at or near Tolvajärvi and drive them back to retake Suojärvi, or quite simply, all would be lost – the Finnish defence, already dismayed by the size of the Soviet force and particularly unhappy at the vast size of the tank arm (nearly 200 in this sector alone) was now at risk of imploding.

Group Talvela was more or less in position by the late afternoon of 8 December. Pajari had arrived the previous day to take over command from Räsänen, and precious artillery units were already arriving, including the entire group's only anti-tank platoon. Task Force 'R' was retitled Task Force 'P' and Colonel Talvela himself arrived at Lake Tolvajärvi that evening in time to witness the 1st Battalion of JR16 retreating in disorder, their first encounter having been a sobering one. Calmly, Talvela ordered his officers to gather up the disparate units and lead them by example, at which Pajari, despite a serious heart condition (that he had concealed) and partial deafness (that he could not), would now prove himself to be an exceptionally gifted officer. Talvela's comment on this crisis certainly justified the regard in which Mannerheim held him: 'In situations like this, as in all confused and hopeless situations,' an energetic attack against the nearest enemy was and is the only way to improve the spirits of the men and to get control of the situation.'[3]

The temperature was by now dropping fast – in the area of Lake Tolvajärvi it was around –10°C, and the lake was frozen enough to undertake infantry counter-attacks across the ice, which the Finns carried out with great flair (but to little effect) until Pajari himself took on-the-spot command. In a series of savage firefights, Pajari and his two flanking forces to the north and south launched their attacks, which initially failed, particularly the northern one as the Finns had seriously underestimated Russian strength here. In this Tolvajärvi sector, it transpired that Pajari's regiment was against the entire Red Army's 139th Rifle Division, which had emplaced itself along the eastern shores of the two adjoining lakes.

Given the obvious size of the opposing force, Pajari had to husband his scarce resources very carefully. His men were extremely badly equipped, and many of them being townsfolk, were less used to the harsh conditions than certain other Finnish soldiers. They lacked uniforms, even appropriate boots, and were at risk of suffering from the deteriorating weather as much as their enemies were. Frostbite, rather than the hopelessly inaccurate Red Army artillery fire, was a particular threat.

The initial attacks had been expensive for the Finns. Of particular concern were the officer and NCO casualties who, given the rather thrown-together nature of this small battle group, did not necessarily know the rank and file of their fellow units. In a situation as chaotic as this, the loss of command and control would exacerbate an already dangerous state.

However, the Finns did serious damage, particularly to Russian morale, on the evening of 8 December. The 139th Division had become used to advancing in pursuit of a fleeing enemy; to experience a counter-attack, however disorganized, from an enemy they imagined was in complete rout was an unwelcome shock. Accordingly, as the first elements of the small Finnish force swept silently up to the sleeping Russians on skis, their Suomi pistols suddenly spitting out accurately placed short bursts of fire, the alarmed Red Army soldiers (of the 364th Rifle Regiment) responded somewhat wildly. As the Finns withdrew at 5 a.m. the Russian soldiers were heard to be shooting at each other, and were to do so for much of the rest of the long night.

Pajari, exhausted, was forced to rest the next day and command passed back briefly to Räsänen. There was a relative lull in the fighting around Tolvajärvi on the 9th and 10th, but further north, at Ilomantsi, an even smaller unit than Pajari's, Task Force 'E' under the command of Colonel Per Ekholm, had scored a major success, completely annihilating a battalion of the Red Army's 155th Rifle Division which had attempted a reconnaissance in strength during the night of the 9th. As important as the victory itself was the captured booty, particularly the much-prized Red Army felted boots; like Pajari's unit, Task Force 'E', which would never amount to more than four battalions, was appallingly badly equipped. Ekholm's artillery arm consisted of a single serviceable French '75' cannon from the Great War and four other field pieces that were of even earlier manufacture.

After visiting Ekholm and congratulating him on his efforts, Talvela returned to Tolvajärvi to plan a proper offensive for

11 December; this would be an encirclement attack. Pajari, rested after his ordeal, was then forced to fight an all-night battle against a Red Army battalion that had slipped through unnoticed, arriving north of Tolvajärvi itself on the evening of 10 December. They erupted from the forest in the vicinity of the General Headquarters of Pajari's main force, not to mention his few artillery assets. But quite by chance, the first thing the Russians saw was a field kitchen, on which bubbled that evening's meal – sausage stew – for the 3rd Machine Gun Company. In an error that revealed much, the Russian soldiers paused in their attack, and so hungry were they, they stopped to eat the food. This allowed Pajari to organize the rear echelon staff (of about 100) into an *ad hoc* fighting force, with which he launched an immediate attack, slaughtering almost all the Russian soldiers.[4] This, and other spoiling attacks, left Task Force 'P' quite exhausted and Talvela's attack plan was postponed until 12 December.

THE COMMANDER OF the 139th Division, Belaev, was under some pressure himself, unsurprisingly generated by his own superiors. Corps Commander Panin, rather like Yakovlev on the Isthmus, had received a stiff rebuke from Meretskov at the end of the first week of December, for lingering in the rear while the 139th had moved forward. Accordingly, he arrived at Belaev's headquarters on the morning of 12 December full of zeal and ardour, and anxious to redeem himself. In effect, he took over the command of the division, so although Belaev had forged through in the previous ten days to cover 30 miles of ground (the only element of the Eighth Army to actually stick to its timetable) it was Panin who would be in effective command of this exhausted (and clearly hungry) division when Pajari's men, presumably replete with nourishing sausage stew, attacked the next day.

Initially, Pajari's assault fared badly, as it had done a few days before. Prior to Panin's arrival, Belaev had ordered elements of the 718th Rifle Regiment to circle round to the north (it is rather unclear whether it was to forestall attack or to go on the offensive) and they were positioned at Hirvasvaara when the Finns encoun-

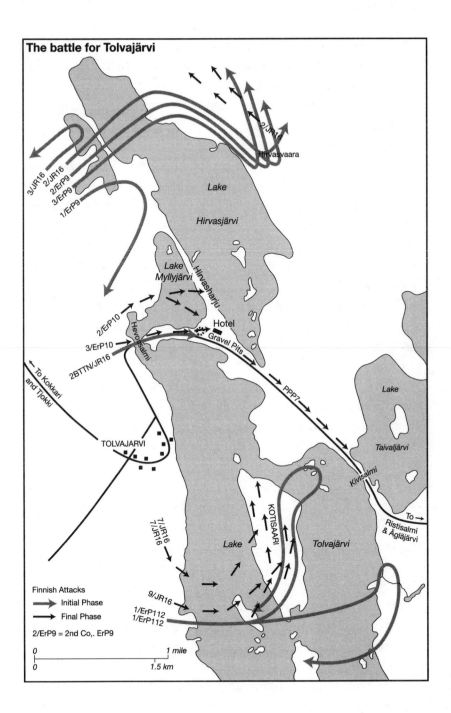

The battle for Tolvajärvi

Hirvasvaara

Lake Hirvasjärvi

3/JR16
2/JR16
2/ErP9
3/ErP9
1/ErP9

2/JR16

Lake Myllyjärvi

Hirvasharju

2/ErP10
3/ErP10
2BTTN/JR16

Hevossalmi

Hotel

Gravel Pits

PPP7

To Kokkari and Tjokki

Lake Taivaljärvi

TOLVAJARVI

Kivisalmi

KOTISAARI

7/JR16
7/JR16

Lake

Tolvajärvi

To Ristisalmi & Ägläjärvi

Finnish Attacks

→ Initial Phase

→ Final Phase

2/ErP9 = 2nd Co,. ErP9

9/JR16
1/ErP112
1/ErP112

0 — 1 mile
0 — 1.5 km

tered them. Similarly, in the south, the other leg of Task Force 'P' encountered the remaining elements of the 364th Regiment, who fought stubbornly.

Assuming that the northern approach had been defeated, Pajari had a difficult decision to make, which was in many ways a microcosm of the entire war. With his limited resources, and facing possible defeat, should he opt for a frontal assault on the Red Army regimental headquarters that lay in front of him? The 609th Regiment of what was now Panin's division had set up their base at a pleasant tourist hotel located on a terminal moraine that separated Lake Tolvajärvi from its northern neighbour, Lake Hirvasjärvi.

Better news from the northern flank decided him. At around midday, he ordered his centre force to attack the hotel, while throwing in the last of his reserves at the Red Army artillery batteries on Kotisaari island to the south, which had been bombarding Finnish positions since 10 a.m. The fight for the hotel was drawn-out, hand to hand and savage (it was not taken until the evening) although the assault on Kotisaari fared rather better; twenty heavy machine guns and two entire artillery batteries were captured. These were turned to threaten the 139th Division's only route out, the narrow moraine causeway that led back the way they had come towards Ägläjärvi, which Commander Balaev had captured only days before. Pajari did not know it, but Panin had ordered Belaev to launch an attack of his own that morning, hence the concentrated artillery salvos; when the remainder of the Russian infantry was ordered in to attack, they had, quite exhausted, simply refused to obey the order.

In one sudden attack on three pressure points the 139th Division had lost a regimental headquarters, a major part of its artillery and received a thorough mauling. Worse, a large element of the infantry, with few junior commanders left alive, was in a state of mutiny. Reports that the centre of the division had given way were thus all too easy to believe and encouraged Belaev and Panin to order a general retreat.

So, two weeks into the war, a Red Army division was withdrawing from the field, a thing unheard of in nearly twenty years. Naturally, the news spread quickly through a tired and depressed Finnish Army (and a startled Europe) and went a long way toward remotivating both. Talvela and Pajari's simple but imaginative aggression had accomplished the apparently impossible.

The battle of Tolvajärvi was by no means a massive engagement, but it served to demonstrate for the first time that the Red Army was not, despite its bulk, unstoppable. Coming as it did in succession after the small victory of Task Force 'E', not to mention the stalling of the L Corps attack at Taipale, the previously hopeless scenario seemed to Talvela to be now quite the opposite. Mannerheim agreed and ordered (not that he needed to) his aggressive field commander to pursue the fleeing enemy and to recapture Ägläjärvi and Suojärvi; in effect to re-establish the *status quo ante* in this part of Ladoga-Karelia.

In response to the collapse of the 139th Division, however, *Stavka* ordered another to advance in its place, at the same time removing Khabarov from the command of the Eighth Army. His replacement was Army Commander (Second Rank) Grigory Mikhailovich Shtern, 39, who seems to have been something of a favourite of Stalin's.[5] But as he took over, there was little Shtern could do about the crisis at Tolvajärvi, as something even worse was developing on the southern flank of the Eighth Army near the Ladoga shore.

Similarly equipped to the 139th, the 75th Rifle Division, under Commander Stepanov, had started to move up on 12 December as Belaev's ruined force moved back. The two divisions crossed each other at just west of Ägläjärvi itself, and the sight of the weary, starving and very heavily wounded, retreating soldiers cannot have done much to help the morale of the fresh (or at least untested) troops.

The replacement division, together with the surviving elements of the beaten one, made contact with Pajari's energized task force on the 16th and received a very bloody nose. As they had come in to Finland, in long, road-bound columns, so the Russians had to fall back along the same routes, harried by the pitiless guerrilla

The advance to the Aittojoki River

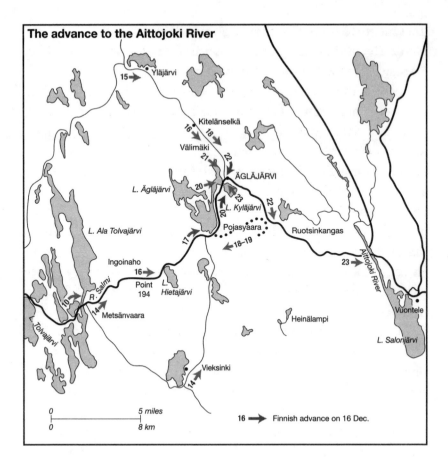

0 —————— 5 miles
0 —————— 8 km

16 ➡ Finnish advance on 16 Dec.

tactics of their enemy. Stepanov and Belaev reached Äglajärvi on 18 December, and almost disbelieving the ferocity of their opponents, now prepared to defend it.

In this, they had the assistance of air cover that, although it had been ineffective at the battle of Tolvajärvi itself, now began to inflict damage on the pursuing Finns. Further, Lieutenant Colonel Pajari was so exhausted that his heart condition was now life-threatening. He was promoted to full colonel by Mannerheim on the 18th and then ordered by Talvela (who was promoted to major general the next day) to rest for three days. His place was taken by another Jäger, Lieutenant Colonel Kaarlo Viljanen, whose task it now was to retake Äglajärvi.

By 20 December, the village was surrounded, save for a rather obvious escape route to the east. The first assault that afternoon was inconclusive, but Viljanen carefully built up the pressure before relaunching his attack on the afternoon of the 22nd. The fighting was bloody, again hand-to-hand, but by the evening of the 22nd, the 75th Division was in full retreat, out of the village and along the road to the Aittojoki River, the site of the first Finnish retreat from Suojärvi only twenty days before; for the Finns to be retaking this ground was not only symbolic – it was exhilarating.

Again, the Finns pursued the demoralized Russians with disciplined aggression, harrying them from the flanks with snipers, attempting to break up the straggling columns, so that by the time the 75th Division, with the traumatized remains of the 139th Division straggling along among them reached the Aittojoki River, it was utterly spent as a fighting force. But so was Task Force 'P'. The men were hungry, cold and tired. Their elation stemmed not only from a corporate pride in what they had done, but on an individual level, each soldier who had fled or fallen back in the face of the initial Soviet attack now regarded himself and his comrades with a certain justifiable pride. They felt seasoned, as well they might.

The exercise of routing two Russian divisions had been expensive, however. Casualties were alarmingly high, with over 30 per cent of Finnish officers and NCOs dead, and a quarter of the ranks.[6] With some reluctance, Mannerheim ordered Talvela to hold the Aittojoki River and prepare defences; the original plan was now reduced somewhat and no longer included the recapture of Suojärvi – the price paid for Aglajärvi had already been too high.

Over the entire action, from the first, tentative attacks by Pajari's task force to the triumphant retaking of Ägläjärvi, the small unit had lost 630 killed with 1,300 wounded, many of them seriously. That they had inflicted casualties on the Red Army of at least seven times that number was militarily remarkable, but Mannerheim realized full well that, whatever the significance of this achievement, the population of the Soviet Union was 40 times that of Finland.[7] This had been an important victory, but there were other theatres of war, one of which was a little further north, at Kollaa.

SOME EXTRAORDINARY weaknesses in the Red Army command structure had been revealed by what happened at Tolvajärvi, only one being the classic mistake of underestimating the enemy. Further, there was the vital issue of decision-making, or rather, the lack of it. We will see this time and again during the Winter War.

Those cadres of the Red Army who had seen service in the Imperial Army had become used to a flexible doctrine of information flow, both laterally and vertically, but one that was essentially class-ridden. The backbone of the Tsar's army had in fact been the senior sergeants, who had more or less run the affairs of the army at regimental level. The Revolution had swept all that away, to be replaced by an ideologically approved system of information management that comprised vertical flow upwards from the rank and file to the command level, in modern terms rather like a focus group, or at least a consensus view. It had been the role of a commander to interpret this information from the point of view of his own outlook or experience. Complementary to this was the doctrine known as *vzaimodeistvie* (interaction), which relied upon a horizontal transparency between different arms and units of the army, to be delivered by intensive briefings. It was a ramshackle, bottom-up and weirdly politically correct system (and most unmilitary), but given an energetic and intelligent commander, could be made to work.

The work carried out by Tukhachevski and others in the 1920s served to streamline this doctrine – the orthodoxies of deep battle demanded this – but the imposition of dual command by Stalin, resulting in all military decisions being ratified on their political merits by a unit commissar, ensured that the purely military commander was isolated from both his command and, by extension, his superiors. Dual command, at one stroke, destroyed the independence of a senior officer, indeed made the very idea of staff work itself – logistics, training and organization – almost completely redundant, which is why the quality of Red Army staff work was uniformly dreadful (with one or two exceptions) throughout the Finnish campaign. An illustration of the handicapping effect of this practice – which almost defined power without responsibility – was given directly to Stalin after the war by K. D. Mamsurov;[8] he is, as part of this statement, making an unashamed attack on the role of the political directorate:

> When carrying out ski missions I saw abnormal situations in the work of battalion commanders with my own eyes. Some ten men stood around and monitored the actions of the battalion commander and who were his subordinates. There was someone from the divisional headquarters, two or three from the corps headquarters, someone from the army's political directorate, a man from the army newspaper – a dozen besides the battalion commander. I remember two cases when the battalion commander stepped aside and said to me: 'I don't know what to do, shall I quit and let them run things themselves?'[9]

Further, the impact of the purges from 1937 – starting with Tukhachevski himself – had removed at one stroke that vital layer of command material without which no army can manage – hence Mannerheim's dismissive remark, that the Red Army was seen 'milling about like tourists' in front of the Finnish defences.

In no engagement of the Winter War were these inadequacies seen so effectively as at Kollaa. This epic encounter at no time developed into a pitched battle, rather it became a series of engagements of grinding attrition between an absurdly outnumbered Finnish unit and ever-larger Soviet ones, with the Russians hamstrung not by structure, but by process.

As Räsänen's task force was falling back after the loss of Suojärvi, another Finnish group, consisting of two infantry regiments, JR34 and 36, under Colonel Teittinen, was awaiting its fate. Against it was the Red Army's 56th Division. Forced into an attack under direct orders from Mannerheim, Teittinen did not relish his prospects, a sentiment confirmed when JR36 did not acquit itself well in the face of enemy armour. In fact, this unit, in common with others in the early phase of the Ladoga-Karelian theatre, broke. His second regiment (who witnessed the event) did not, and after gathering up the fleeing troops (none too gently) he organized a withdrawal to a semi-prepared defence line across the railway line at Kollaa, some 3 miles to the west. There, come what may, he resolved to make his stand. Teittinen knew that there was simply no one else to stop the enemy; failure here would be as catastrophic as anywhere else on the Ladoga-Karelia front.

These were the very nightmares which had kept Mannerheim awake at night for so long – lack of training, lack of equipment, lack of preparedness. Many of the weapons – even the aged rifles originally designated for Teittinen's command – were still in storage when the Red Army attacked.

CHAPTER EIGHT

Counter-attacks

If I am in good order and the enemy is in disarray, if I am energetic and he careless, then, even if he be numerically stronger, I can give battle

Sun Tzu

FINNISH TACTICAL DOCTRINE was sourced from *Basic Rules for Conducting Positional Warfare,* essentially the Reichswehr's field manual, and based upon German experiences in the Great War. Not unnaturally, this piece of work paid little regard to defence against armoured assault, of which there was much that December. There were two particular doctrines that were given emphasis – those of the reflexive counter-punch (*gegenstoss*) and the planned counter-attack (*gegenangriff*) – and these were the building blocks of *schlagfertigkeit,* or rapid response. Any boxer knows this.

The commander of the II Corps of the Army of the Isthmus, General Harald Öhqvist, had a prepared plan of the second category, which he had offered to Mannerheim (via his superior, General Hugo Östermann) on 11 December. His objective, to blunt the centre of the Russian line in order to relieve the pressure and break up the attack, was turned down. Mannerheim had read the book too, but reasoned that the critical shortage of anti-tank ordnance – the precious guns being generally held as a last line of defence – might well threaten the undertaking. He was right, as things turned out.

At the time Östermann submitted Öhqvist's plan, the Taipale

sector was still under immense pressure, the clear Russian intention being to draw forces away from the Viipuri gateway, which they failed to do. But as a feint attack, this sector was extraordinarily costly for the Russians, as they came up against murderously accurate Finnish machine-gun, mortar and field artillery fire on the carefully plotted ground of the Koukunniemi peninsula. The coastal batteries were also brought to bear on them, with catastrophic results for the Red Army infantry, as they were without cover and uncamouflaged. The losses they endured there, and further east when crossing the Suvanto waterway, were quite out of proportion to the expected results. The Finnish defenders, mainly men of the 10th Division of General Heinrichs' III Corps, defended this section of the Mannerheim Line more or less unrelieved throughout the entire conflict. Their resilience was astonishing.

The first phase of Meretskov's second attack, centred on Summa and launched on 17 December, was quite colossal, if uncoordinated. The pattern was becoming familiar; heavy (and ominously, increasingly accurate) artillery preparation,[1] followed by waves of infantry, with packets of armour scattered among them, but with the main armoured fist often unsupported and thus vulnerable to the increasingly ingenious (and kamikaze-brave) Finnish anti-tank cadres with their satchel charges and Molotov cocktails. The slaughter was frightful by any measure. Bizarrely, the Soviet armour relied upon the infantry opening up gaps, which it could then exploit and, as many of these attacks took place in poor light, the helpless Red Army soldiers, cleverly illuminated and dazzled by Finnish searchlights while crossing prepared ground, were mown down in droves by the terrifyingly accurate Finnish machine-gunners. When armour did break through (as it did at Summa on the 19th) it was either destroyed or withdrawn back from whence it came, any temporary advantage surrendered.

There was also ample evidence of weakness in the Soviet supply system, well illustrated by an entire battalion of tanks from the 138th Division grinding to an embarrassing halt in front of Summa on the 20th, their fuel tanks quite dry. A Red Army tank survivor,

Battalion Commander Yanov, recalled the chaos of that Summa offensive, revealing clearly that here and elsewhere, the Red Army was, almost literally, falling over itself. His testament, delivered in the cosy warmth of captivity to two British observers, Major Gatehouse and Captain Tamplin, is worth quoting at length – it clearly contains rather more than name, rank and number:

At 0600 hours, 17th December, the movements began to the jumping-off positions in the area of the village of Vosi. This presented incredible diffi-culties, since the roads were cluttered up with various units. I smashed my way through to Vosi ... On arrival at the jumping-off point I discovered a grim situation. Another battalion of tanks had crept into my area and a second battalion had also arrived there. All units were intermingled, and it was quite impossible to elucidate who, how, or in what order units were to carry out their duties. The regimental and light Divisional artillery [90th and 142nd Divisions] were, at that moment, also moving into that area, hours late, and the second line of infantry were also forcing their way into the crowd. In fact, there was incredible chaos. It was now about 1200 hours and the attack was timed for thirty minutes later, but so far nothing had been done for co-operation among [different] arms. I decided to contact the Commander of the 650th Rifle Regiment. He stated 'I do not know you. The 95th Tank Battalion is co-operating with me.' I explained that in accordance with instructions of Corps I was also acting with him, but only with the second wave of attack. He tried to sort out the orders, but giving no explanation, sent me to the chief of staff who could also make nothing out of the existing circumstances. He thrust at me the battle orders, which had apparently been written thoughtlessly and hurriedly. I offered to establish communication with the artillery, but nothing came of this, as his chief of communications was ... illiterate.

Yanov was also very clear regarding the complete lack of coor-dination of the command structure, and recalled that he did something quite unheard of (and very courageous) within the dual command system – he took his own initiative:

All those subordinate to this regimental Commander for the purpose of the action were piling up round the chief of staff for instructions, and everything was being rushed as the attack was due to take place in thirty minutes' time. Since everything was done in a hurry, he got tangled up in the wavelengths to several different units. Meanwhile, the diapason[2] of the waves was not suitable, since the radios were of different types and no communications were established. I decided to give it all up, as I could make no sense of it, and to await events and, on instruction to enter the action, to take independent personal decisions depending on the course of the battle.

There was further evidence of poor preparation two days later when the 138th Division (whose commander was described after the war as a 'boaster and a coward'[3]) was sent in without any artillery preparation whatsoever – until somebody changed their mind.

Commander Yanov, having survived the chaos of the 17th, also took part in the assault on the 20th, and afterwards related the terror of advancing unsupported into unknown territory. His account places him in the woods, 800 yards west of a freezing swamp, right in the teeth of the Mannerheim Line and heading for Summa. He was obviously a very lucky man:

I was again set the task at 10.00 hours to support infantry without artillery preparation, and to break through northwards for four or five kilometres. On our left, another tank battalion supported by infantry was to co-operate. At 10.30 hours, the battalion moved to the attack and at 11.30 I was ordered to retire, since there was to be ten minutes of intensive artillery fire. With great difficulty I withdrew the battalion and at 12.00 hours I received an order to attack again. I went through the second row of tank obstacles[4] and came up to the concrete fire-points. The infantry did not follow up the tanks, as it was separated from them by artillery fire and enfilade machine gun fire from the wood. I was thus stationary for about twenty minutes, but the infantry did not move forward. During this time a second battalion of tanks came up, and I informed the Commander that in accordance with my task I was leaving the concrete points and moving further since, some four or five kilometres further north we were to converge with him, as his task was to go through on our left and emerge at the crossroads north of Khotinen (Summa). Sending out a reconnaissance platoon (two machines) I moved forward about three kilometres when the leading tank was mined. The Commander of the reconnaissance platoon reported that on his left front was infantry. I shut off motors and listened. The infantry were Finns, obviously surrounding me in the woods. Becoming convinced that the other battalion had not come up level with me, I gave the order to retire. Having turned the column about, I became the last machine… On the way back, mines exploded under us twice and the gearbox was [damaged]. The tank in front of me caught fire and I was too close to pass and unable to use reverse gear. At that moment the motors died, the machine in front exploded, the crews of both jumped out and escaped into the wood; I remained.[5]

His crew had deserted him and he had received no infantry support. It is reasonable to suppose that the seventh Army, or at least part of it, was now in a state of near mutiny similar to that already discovered from radio intercepts between elements of the Ninth Army further north. The presence of NKVD 'blocking' units was also clear. Mannerheim recalled:

Letters found on fallen and captured Rusians spoke of the troops' exhaustion and it could be assumed that for a time the enemy would be short of ammunition and fuel. According to prisoners there had been cases of refusal to advance, both in the infantry and armoured units, and a number of death sentences had been carried out.[6]

An extract from one such letter, from a Red Army soldier to his brother-in-law (who had also been called up) reads: 'We have been sending tanks, artillery and infantry against the Finns, with no results – just killed comrades; sometimes as many as 300 after our attacks, and the Finns won't let us pick them up. Their fire is extremely accurate and they mow us down as with a sickle.' Another reported:

We marched for two days without food prepared in the mobile field kitchens …we have many sick and wounded. We are black like chimney sweeps from dirt, and completely tired out. The soldiers are again full of lice. Health is bad. Many soldiers have pneumonia. They promise that combat will end on the 21st of December, but who will believe it?[7]

Another factor at work on Finnish judgement was a touch of hubris – perhaps justifiable in the light of Group Talvela's astonishing success in Ladoga-Karelia, when outnumbered by over three to one, with no extensive prepared defences. The Finns had also counted the astonishing total of 239 destroyed, damaged or abandoned tanks on the Isthmus (most of them stopped by Finnish infantry), the crowded roads of which were now starting to resemble nothing so much as an improbably large military scrapyard.

When this second phase of Meretskov's attack on the Viipuri gateway started to lose pace, as it clearly had by the 21st (it was not lost on the Finns that this was Stalin's birthday), Östermann lobbied for Öhqvist's plan once again, and this time Mannerheim allowed himself to be persuaded.[8] It was an ambitious undertaking, a counter-attack on a 28-mile front, using selected elements from five divisions (including the impatient 6th Division, still largely in reserve apart from Pajari's regiment), which would attempt to drive south, either side of the Russian force in front of the Mannerheim Line and connect behind them, putting the Red Army 138th Division into a state of encirclement. There was something of a fait accompli about the presentation of the plan, as the situation had changed since its inception, but the potential effect on worsening Russian morale was clear; after three days of ferocious battle a determined Finnish counter-attack, even if only marginally successful, could be a shattering blow to the already fragile psyche of the enemy – soldiers, commanders and (hopefully) politicians alike.

For the Red Army was really supposed to be in Helsinki by now, parading itself, bands playing, past a gloating Otto Kuusinen and his puppet Cabinet; the fact that it was not, and had been beaten back and actually *lost* the battle for Summa, was a humiliation at every level, particularly internationally. Given the intense foreign interest in the war (especially the presumed curiosity of Germany, which would draw its own conclusions) the prestige of the Soviet Union was now at stake, and Summa itself would become for the Russians an even more particular, *political* objective.

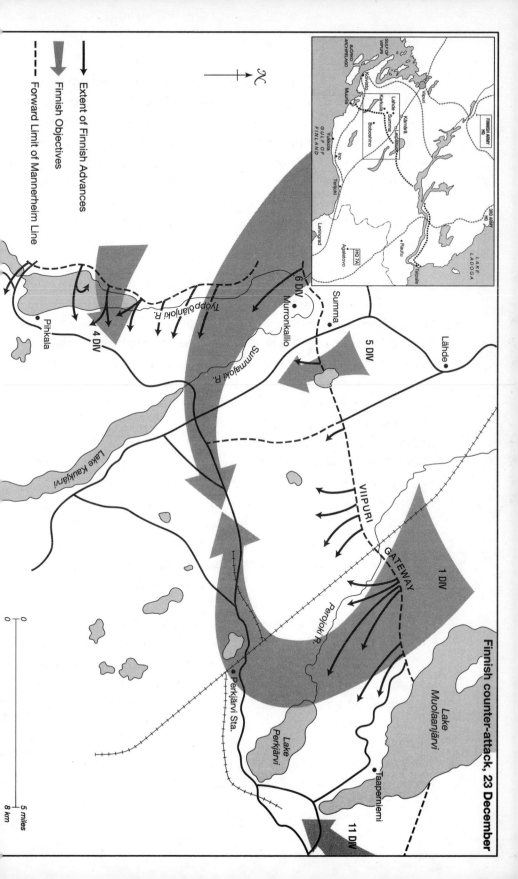

Finnish counter-attack, 23 December

Legend:

- Extent of Finnish Advances
- Finnish Objectives
- Forward Limit of Mannerheim Line

4 DIV

5 DIV

6 DIV

1 DIV

11 DIV

Pihkala

Murronkallio

Summa

Lähde

Summajoki R.

Tyoppolänjoki R.

Lake Kaukjärvi

VIIPURI GATEWAY

Perojoki R.

Perkjärvi Sta.

Lake Perkjärvi

Lake Muolaanjärvi

Lake Perojärvi

Taaperniemi

0 5 miles

0 8 km

Inset map:

FINNISH ARMY HQ

3RD ARMY HQ

HQ 7A

GULF OF VIPURI

SUOMI ARCHIPELAGO

Muurila

Koivisto

Lähde
Summa
Karhula

Kämärä

Vipuri

Leipäsuo

Bobashino

Yukola

Ino

Terijoki

Leningrad

Agalatovo

Raitu

Taipale

LAKE LADOGA

GULF OF FINLAND

The Finns' plan, an encirclement move, was scheduled to start at 6.30 p.m. on 23 December. Given that it was not finally approved – Mannerheim's misgivings not having been entirely dispelled – until the afternoon of the 22nd, there were some obvious gaps in it, particularly with regard to the exact whereabouts of the Red Army which, in large part having fallen back in some disarray, was now out of contact. Russian air superiority over the Isthmus making comprehensive reconnaissance impossible, the Finns were forced to make assumptions, many of which proved rather wide of the mark. Further, given that there were still isolated 'mopping up' operations going on to eject the last Russian soldiers still at or even behind the Mannerheim Line around Summa, there were difficulties in coordinating the disparate elements of the five separate Finnish divisions to be used, particularly the artillery and anti-tank arms. This would prove significant.

This would be the biggest offensive operation undertaken by the Finnish Army during the Winter War and given its simple importance (and the price that would attend its failure) it is perhaps surprising that it was not better prepared, as it could easily have met with disaster. Circumstances, however, seemed to call (shades of Suomussalmi) for a direct counter-punch and clearly, timing of this was of the essence, as the Finns had little idea of the complete organizational chaos behind the Russian lines as the chain of command started to collapse in upon itself.

In fact, the Russians were far closer than they seemed, not at all where they were assumed to be and – worse – still concentrated in great, if badly managed strength. The Finnish plan called for the 5th Division, from behind Summa, to strike directly south, supported by the untried 6th Division on its right flank, which would then swing round to the left and connect, behind the Russians, with the 1st Division, undertaking a mirror manoeuvre some 10 miles to the east. The outer movements of this ambitious exercise were the 4th and 11th Divisions, which would pressure the extreme limits of the opposing army from the flanks. The intention was to corral and encircle the Red Army forces into the area between the Perojoki and Summajoki rivers, where they then could be pounded by artillery. Important, therefore, to know where the enemy was.

It was a bold but flawed plan, and its coordination was frankly sloppy, even under the stressed circumstances. Mannerheim had ordered Öhqvist to take no risks – the army, which he had husbanded so tenaciously, could simply not afford them – and to pull back, calling off the attack, as soon as he met any major or unforeseen difficulties, which, it must be said, Öhqvist soon did. In his memoirs after the event, Mannerheim himself was relatively charitable concerning the scheme: 'It soon became apparent that the plan of attack had not been worked out in sufficient detail and that not enough allowance had been made for the friction which so easily occurs – particularly under winter conditions – when an offensive on a large scale is undertaken.'[9] And it was, by any measure, a large-scale plan. It would also prove to be the blooding of the reserve 6th Division in battle, with not altogether encouraging results.

On the morning of the 23rd, stung by the gleeful (or scornful) comments in the Western press concerning the performance of the Red Army, the major press organs of the Soviet State – *Pravda*, *Isvestia* and *Kransnaya Zvezda* (*Red Star*) – ran this very cross editorial: 'The foreign press, especially the French and the British, regard the rate of advance by Soviet troops as too slow, attempting to explain by this the 'low fighting capacity' of the Red Army ... such vilification of the Red Army can be explained either by overt and crude slander or by the ignorance of its authors in military affairs.'[10]

THE FINNISH 6TH DIVISION, attempting to start their sweep around Muronkallio, immediately ran into the enemy less than a mile in front of the line, as Russian fire from both artillery and machine guns, and accurately coordinated by observers in captive balloons, raked them thoroughly. Infantry regiment JR17 fared particularly badly and was clearly shaken by the experience. General Heinrichs, in his account of the war (he was not directly involved in this aspect of the counter-offensive), ruefully described the 6th Division as 'showing signs of disintegration' by the day's end.

Other units of the Finnish attack force fared almost as badly. In the centre of the attack, 5th Division quickly encountered both infantry and armour – they had outrun their anti-tank units and were forced to stop. 1st Division went the farthest, almost to Lake Perkjärvi, but were again stopped by heavy resistance and large numbers of tanks in laager formation, adopting the by now almost instinctive defensive formation of the Red Army. Lack of Finnish artillery (it had failed to arrive) prevented any more ambitious attempts, particularly disappointing given that the Finnish advance had revealed some useful targets of opportunity. Öhqvist, sensibly using the discretion mandated by Mannerheim, called off the attack at 2.40 p.m.; he had little choice.

Finnish losses were grievous – the II Corps took 1,300 casualties, killed, wounded and 'missing in action' with a further 200 cases of frostbite – more than 1 per cent of the Army of the Isthmus.[11] Morale was also hit badly, not helped by a degree of mutual finger-pointing among the commanders, which further lowered confidence in them on the part of those they commanded.

MILITARILY, THE COUNTER-OFFENSIVE might have been a failure against its expectations, but it had a certain success on the political level – certainly the Russians were startled at its boldness and in fact were not to mount another serious attack on the Viipuri gateway for many weeks.[12] The importance of it in forcing Stalin to suspend offensive ground operations on the Karelian Isthmus should not be underestimated, if only on the grounds that the Russians were startled to have been attacked at all. It may also have triggered something else.

The core infrastructure of the Finnish forces had been disorganized somewhat by the counter-offensive and offered a severe blow to Finnish morale at a time – just before Christmas – when it needed most support. One who spotted this was the commander-in-chief of the *Lotta* organization, Fanni Luukkonen. This formidable lady, having heard that the army transportation commissariat had been pessimistic at the prospect of being able to deliver Christmas packages to the front in time, commandeered a scarce aircraft and flew straight to General Headquarters at Mikkeli where she instructed Mannerheim as to his proper responsibilities. Rather unsurprisingly, he agreed with her, picked up a telephone and gave the order.[13] The transportation was arranged forthwith and gifts of knitted clothing, delicacies, coffee and, this being Finland, brandy, tobacco and aquavit, were distributed to the front. For the men at the front, this represented a miracle of organization – for the population as a whole, it represented a matter of pride. Happily, the Russian offensive was now slowing.

CHAPTER NINE

Manoeuvres: The Gate of the Year

It's jolly to look at the map
And finish the foe in a day
It's not easy to get at the chap
These neutrals are so in the way...

Baku, or the Map game – *A. P. Herbert, 1940*

WHILE ENERGETIC *LOTTAS* were distributing Christmas gifts to the hard-pressed soldiers at the front, the evolution of Allied policy was following its confused and erratic path in London and Paris. The King's Christmas message, broadcast at 3 p.m. on 25 December, rather summed it up:

> A new year is at hand. We cannot tell what it will bring. If it brings peace, how thankful we shall be. If it brings us continued struggle, we shall remain undaunted. In the meantime I feel that we may all find a message of encouragement in the lines which, in my closing words, I would like to say to you: 'I said to the man who stood at the gate of the year, "Give me a light that I may tread safely into the unknown". And he replied, "Go out into the darkness and put your hand into the Hand of God. That shall be to you better than a light, and safer than a known way."'[1]

The hesitancy with which the King spoke these words in his message to the nation reflected rather more than his naturally shy disposition and chronic stammer. The whole country was confused – it was at war with Germany and thus faced with the prospect of engaging with the most formidable war machine ever mobilized, but nothing significant had happened. The only actual fighting that seemed to be going on was up near the Arctic Circle and the King himself, it was reported, had exchanged his study wall map of the proposed Western front for one of eastern Scandinavia.[2] The 'little Princesses', it was further reported, had responded to their father's initiative (and what was now becoming a national obsession) by knitting mittens for Finnish soldiers.

The balls of wool were being produced all over Europe. The Catholic ladies of Paris, putting their traditional disdain for heretical Lutherans[3] on one side (Bolshevism was, they reasoned, infinitely worse), contributed to the greatest clicking of needles heard since the Revolution, and the churches filled up, not only for the Feast of St Nicholas, but in extended prayers for the handsome Marshal Mannerheim and his splendid army.

In fact, the Finnish front soon went rather quiet. The news broke at New Year of the destruction of the hapless 163rd Division at Suomussalmi, followed by the further victory on the Raate road, after which, militarily, the situation seemed to switch to a relatively dull – and to foreign observers at least – anti-climactic war of position.

The reason was Stalin. Almost as King George was speaking, he had made it clear to Meretskov at a Kremlin conference that, in the light of the clear deterioration on the Karelian Isthmus (after three attempts to break through), as well as the looming disaster in the north: 'The authority of the Red Army is the guarantee of the USSR's national security. If we struggle for a long time against such a weak opponent, this will stimulate the anti-Soviet forces of the imperialists.'[4] Judging by the public outcry and clear policy developments in Britain and France, he was right.

His solution, very pragmatically, was to scrap the entire extant plan, and dust off Shaposhnikov's original effort, which had called for a concentrated and focused attack on the Isthmus alone. In doing this, Stalin not only confirmed the worst fear of the Finnish General Staff that this would be the logical blueprint for any invasion of Finland, he also condemned those remaining Red Army units still engaged in combat away from the Isthmus to a quite dreadful ordeal. He had no choice, however – they could not be successfully withdrawn: the Eighth Army was maimed and in disarray, the Ninth was in the process of virtual destruction and the Seventh was stalled and frozen in front of the Finnish defences, and clearly of dubious reliability. Only the Fourteenth Army, in possession of Petsamo (virtually unopposed), had fulfilled its primary war objective, however much it was struggling with its secondary one.

The Baltic fleet, too, was clearly ineffective and its Air Force, although it had wrought a high level of destruction, was taking heavy losses against a bemusingly fierce Finnish Air Force. Further, the role of the Air Arm, however tactically successful, was serving to bring down such international contumely upon the Russians that its utility was becoming questionable. So the northern elements of the Red Army were forced to stay on station, either because they were surrounded, or because they were in the process of annihilation already, amid the coldest weather of the war so far, as temperatures started to plunge yet again.

On 28 December, as the order for a 'temporary defensive posture'[5] went out, a special session of the Main Military Soviet was convened, at which a volunteer was called for to carry out the Shaposhnikov/Vasilevski plan, for which a new command was to be created – the North-Western Front. There was really only one candidate, another Stalin crony, but this time a competent one – the present Commander of the Kiev Special Military District, Semyon Konstantinovich Timoshenko.

Timoshenko, then 45, had been a junior cavalry commander in the First Cavalry Army during the civil war (after service as a youth in the ranks of the Tsar's army as a machine-gunner[6]) and had also served in Poland in 1920. In fact he had just returned from there once more, after the annexation operation of September. Cannily, he had disassociated himself from the doctrine of 'war of manouevre' as laid down by Tukhachevski (dismissively describing it as 'degenerate'[7], which was certainly an unusual view for a man who had actually fought on a horse) preferring the 'wall of fire' approach that, when all was said and done, had served General

Brusilov well enough during the Great War. In fact, Tukhachevski's death in June 1937 had served Timoshenko rather well on more than one level, but there is no evidence whatever that he connived at it. He was not a 'political general'.

In keeping with the clear political importance of the task before him, Timoshenko's preparations were, to say the least, thorough. He demanded, and received, a free hand, an almost unheard of privilege for a Red Army commander, possibly a reflection of the genuine concerns Stalin himself had over Western (and German) intentions. The most obvious manifestation of the total authority that Timoshenko received, though, was not a matter of resources, it was the abolition of the system of dual command that had hamstrung the Seventh Army so badly since the start of the invasion and already cost more lives than anyone, least of all L. Z. Mekhlis, the commander responsible, would admit. Possibly it was this single career-threatening development that drove Mekhlis to such lengths when dealing with the 700 pathetic remnants of the 44th Division – the Finnish campaign was now a soldier's, not a commissar's war.

Some radical reorganization on the Isthmus had already taken place, in fact. The Seventh Army had been reorganized into two separate commands, its right wing now being known as the Thirteenth Army. This was now under the command of Grendal' and would be reinforced with the full resources of the entire Red Army, as opposed to merely those units attached to the Leningrad Military District, the very existence of which was now suspended; at a stroke it became the North-Western Front.

IN LADOGA-KARELIA, General Hägglund was ready by the turn of the year for the final phase of his operation against the beleaguered 168th and 18th Divisions, both still penned in around Kitelä and Lemetti respectively, the latter with the 34th Tank Brigade in attendance. This was no small task, and so he had few reserves with which to bolster the defences at Kollaa, where Teittinen's soldiers were still, against every rational expectation, holding their ground; four battalions were still surviving against two divisions and their attendant armour, outnumbered almost ten to one and under unceasing pressure. Heavy falls of snow had helped them somewhat, at least in hampering the Red Army's advance (while improving their own mobility on skis) but so poorly equipped were the defenders at Kollaa that the plunging temperatures that January brought with it handicapped them almost as much as the invaders.

As Mannerheim reviewed the situation he had every reason to be relieved, at least temporarily; from a dangerous and chaotic first few days, the war had stabilized somewhat and, thanks to the efforts of Siilasvuo, Talvela, Pajari and so many others, Finland had not collapsed under the strain of this enormous attack. Most importantly, the supply situation had been eased by the capture of so much booty from the Red Army, particularly arms and ammunition, a windfall that would pay further dividends through January. Not only that, but there were small amounts of *matériel* arriving from and through Sweden, so some of his resource concerns as expressed in his memoirs at the outbreak of war were eased.[8] But he was acutely aware that a fundamental shortage – that of soldiers – simply would not go away. He was faced with another of the commander's nightmares: a brave and willing army, but no means by which it could be rested through a reserve system – his reserves, such as they were, were either committed already, or about to be. He was, whichever way he calculated it, at least three divisions short. But January would bring a relative respite.

Nor was Mannerheim the only one boosted, however temporarily, by the unexpected failure of the Red Army. All over Europe there was scribbling. In Paris, Senator Bardoux, an independent Radical tasked by Daladier to test the climate of opinion, had happily confided to his diary on 23 December, the very day that the Finnish counter-offensive on the Isthmus was launched:[9]

The Russian disaster in Finland is a capital event. Henceforth, far from trying to split Germany and Russia, we must, on the contrary, weld them together more tightly, for a weak ally is a ball and chain and opens a

breach in the common front. We must enter into it resolutely. By
intervening to aid Finland, we shall create, together with the neutrals
and Italy, the definitive bloc. It is possible to offer the Crimea to Hitler, to
utilise the Ukrainians, the Transcaucasians and the Persians. We can
roll up everything, all the way to the Caucasus.[10]

Napoleonic! This may make risible reading now, but these are
the thoughts of a serious politician, representing a sizeable slab
of public opinion, who also had the ear of his government. And
this sentiment was being expressed a month before the true scale
of German intentions became clear.

Somewhat energized by the Russian collapse at Suomussalmi-
Raate (which was widely and gleefully reported in the West on
9 January) General Maurice Gamelin was moved to write to
Daladier magnifying the potential scope of the operation in Scandinavia already mentioned in December – to his pleasure, he found
he was singing to the choir. Even further east than Finland, from
his base in Syria, the sprightly (and *very* conservative) General
Maxime Weygand wrote to tell Gamelin that an operation against
the oil-wells at Baku would surely prosper, and reminding him
that he had the aeroplanes to do it: 'I regard it as essential to break
the back of the Soviet Union in Finland ... and elsewhere.'[11] Some,
rather further to the left than General Weygand, were more
detached. Arthur Koestler recalled that the French delight at
Finnish victories recalled nothing so much as 'a voyeur who gets
his thrills and satisfaction out of watching other people's virile
exploits, which he is unable to imitate'.[12]

But unhappily for Koestler, he was paying for his political
opinions, by languishing in frightful sordor at a French internment camp specially reserved for Communists. We may imagine
that conditions in this camp (at Vernet) did not improve materially
as the broad swathe of French public opinion moved rapidly to
the right and, emotionally at least, to the north.

Clearly, Senator Bardoux and those who shared his pleasure at
the plight of the Russians were far ahead of the vanguard of opinion
in terms of Scandinavia as, although the Supreme War Council

had listened to Daladier's exposition on the subject of the Swedish iron ore, and by now had had it reconfirmed by Churchill (who had not, of course, been present on 19 December), it was at this point that the two outlooks, French and British, started to diverge wildly, but this fact was not immediately clear. General Ironside had reported rather scornfully to his own diary on 18 December, the night before the Supreme War Council meeting: 'Winston Churchill is pushing for us to occupy Narvik in Norway and prevent all the iron ore going to Germany All his ideas are big, if nothing else. He talks of occupying the islands and controlling the coast.'[13]

No talk of Finland yet from Churchill – his plan was still small and practical, if bold, but essentially the same one as suggested by the First Lord the very day before the Finnish war erupted and a purely naval undertaking. But in the wake of Daladier's enthusiasm, which was clearly infectious, others were soon minded to be more adventurous, including Ironside himself.

NOWHERE (outside Finland, at least) was the performance of the Red Army studied with such interest as in Berlin. As the first phase of the battle of Suomussalmi came to an end, a German General Staff report, dated 31 December and clearly sourced from information gained in Helsinki and elsewhere, evaluated the Red Army in these staccato, but plainly less than terrified terms:

In quantity a giant military instrument. Commitment of the 'mass' – organisation, equipment and means of leadership unsatisfactory. Principles of leadership good – leadership itself, however, too young and inexperienced. Communications systems bad; transportation bad – troops not very uniform – no personalities. Simple soldier good-natured, quite satisfied with very little – Fighting qualities of the troops in a heavy fight, dubious. The Russian 'mass' is no match for an army with modern equipment and superior leadership.[14]

There was probably never a military intelligence assessment more unfortunately timed, for, as we have seen, Stalin himself had come to very much the same conclusion nearly a week before.

Mannerheim's own assessment of the Red Army also drew on his own experience as a Tsarist commander: 'The Russian infantryman showed himself brave, tough and frugal, but lacking in initiative ... he was a mass fighter who was incapable of independent action when out of contact with his officers or comrades.'

GIVEN THE CLEAR POLITICAL agenda that was now being openly discussed in Western Europe, there was little time for Timoshenko to lose – he was given twenty-one days to study the Shaposhnikov plan, introduce the necessary reforms within his army, and bring the offensive operations to a state of readiness. Instructions confirming his appointment, and the military reshuffle that went with it, were put out on 7 January, as the miserable 700 remnants of the 44th Division, with their doomed Commander Vinogradov unwisely going ahead, were trudging back towards the border.

Which made Wuolijoki's approach to Kollontay rather well timed. On New Year's Day, Hella Wuolijoki wrote to Väinö Tanner, offering her services as an unofficial envoy to Stockholm, where the Soviet minister plenipotentiary was an old friend of hers. Perhaps she could help? Tanner knew Wuolijoki rather better than he would have liked – as a Social Democrat of the *very* far-left type (which Tanner was definitely not) she had been a thorn in his side for some considerable time. She was also definitely an 'agent of influence'[15] of the Comintern, with connections to those organizations that have already been mentioned. Tanner was pessimistic as to how useful this might be, but given the lack of success he was having with any other potential intermediary (Blücher, toeing the Berlin line – in public at least – turned him down on 4 January) he rather speculatively authorized her to fly to Stockholm on 10 January; she made contact two days later. The news that the British ambassador to Moscow, Sir William Seeds, was returning to London 'on leave' cannot have filled him with confidence concerning the other obvious source of mediation.[16]

Alexandra Kollontay was a diplomatist in virtual exile. As an ex-Menshevik (like Tanner) she had been fortunate indeed to survive the purges, as there is plenty of evidence that she kept her own counsel, at least on matters of foreign policy. Such a famous revolutionary had she been (and, in her younger days, such a beautiful one[17]) that there is some thought that she was 'untouchable' – it is even possible, although unlikely, that a residual sentimentality on the part of Stalin kept her alive. She had been in post, off and on, since 1923. She was also part-Finnish, and had even been born there; Wuolijoki (*née* Murrik) was Estonian. Tanner held no particular hopes for the mission, but other doors seemed to be closing.

In fact, Molotov had already stated to von der Schulenberg, when the subject came up in a discussion on 10 January, that the door to negotiation might well be ajar, if not open. Again, the Finnish victories of a few days before in the northern forests would certainly have played a role in framing his reply to Schulenberg's enquiry concerning an opening up of diplomacy. Rather than a flat refusal such as he had given the League of Nations a month before citing Kuusinen, Molotov now became Delphic: 'It was late, very late' to resume conversations.[18] But with that hint, Kuusinen's 'government' was consigned back into the desk drawer from whence it had come.

It is worth quoting from the W. P. and Zelda Coates book regarding the Kuusinen government, if only to experience the flavour of Moscow's later propaganda:

> As a matter of fact the relations of the Soviet Government with the Terijoki Government illustrated strikingly the Soviet respect for the independence of Finland. No doubt when the Terijoki Government was formed it was thought or hoped that it might receive sufficiently wide popular support among the Finnish people to overthrow the bourgeois Government of that time and the military and Fascist cliques which to a large extent were the real rulers of Finland. This did not eventuate – whether because the Schutz Corps (protective guards) and Fascists were too strong or because the masses of the Finnish people were not yet prepared for a wholehearted Socialist Government is immaterial to the argument – but the fact was that the Terijoki Government did not gain power over the whole of Finland.

Any Imperialist Power faced with this position and having Finland at her mercy as the Soviets then had would have undoubtedly have simply ridden roughshod over the bourgeois Central Finnish Government and forced upon the country the government which she had recognised a few months previously...

The Soviet Government acted otherwise, it declared that the form of Government in Finland was the affair of the Finns themselves and after consultation between the Soviet and Terijoki Governments the latter agreed to dissolve itself.[19]

STAFFORD CRIPPS had not been in England when the *Tribune* made its unfortunate endorsement (over his byline) of Soviet policy in Finland, and was thus uninformed as to government deliberations over the matter. Nor did he necessarily know that the editorial board of *Tribune* had performed a hasty (but very pragmatic) volte-face on the subject. Not being privy to the Supreme War Council conversations, he was somewhat startled when he embarked on a tour of China, to be asked by the Soviet ambassador in Chungking what his view was of the possibility of Britain and Germany now turning on Russia. He recorded in his diary:

I thought this a rather odd question ... I told him that many friends of Russia thought that she should have waited to get the readjustments that she wanted without copying the Nazi methods of aggression, and that I should like to know what he thought was the answer that should be given to those who accused the Russians of imperialism ... I told him that the Russians often seemed to overlook the difficulties of their friends in other countries who were of some value to them and that they ought to make a statement for that purpose.[20]

This hardly counts as a full-blooded disapproval of Soviet action, despite the change of heart at *Tribune*; rather it is a qualified admonition from an 'embarrassed' friend.[21]

FIRST CONTACTS BETWEEN Yartsev, Erkko and Kollontay took place on 21 January, the day after Churchill gave a controversial speech that seemed to imply that the British were preparing to come to Finland's aid (of which more in the next chapter). For a week the Russians stalled, a matter that bothered the Finns little – Mannerheim's counsel, when consulted by Ryti, was that 'in war, one never really knows how it is going to turn out in the end, but at this moment the situation was good and gave no grounds for a spirit of panic.'[22]

Mannerheim's view, however, was predicated upon the arrival of 30,000 trained soldiers and attendant hardware (see p.222). He also suggested a small modification to the proposals which the Finns had made before war broke out, although pointed out that the cession of any territory in the region of Hanko was out of the question. He had calculated that if Finland acquired everything for which she had asked (a total of 400 aircraft, for example) then the situation would remain stable.

By 29 January, Molotov's attitude (possibly even influenced by Cripps's rather uninformed comments in Chungking) seemed to have changed somewhat; Kollontay met with the new Swedish Foreign Minister, Christian Günther, and read him the following telegram: 'The U.S.S.R. has no objection in principle to concluding an agreement with the Ryti-Tanner government. As regards the initiation of negotiations, it will be necessary to know beforehand what concessions the Ryti-Tanner government will be prepared to make.' Given that Molotov already had an 'agreement' with the Kuusinen administration, this was on the face of it a huge climb-down. But, the note went on:

> It is also indispensable to note that the requirement of the U.S.S.R. are not limited to those which were presented in Moscow at the time of the negotiations with Messrs. Tanner and Paasikivi, because since those negotiations, blood has been shed on both sides, and that blood, which has been shed contrary to our hopes and through no fault of ours, calls for augmented guarantees to the security of the frontiers of the U.S.S.R. … It must also be noted that the promises the government of the U.S.S.R. made to the Kuusinen government are not applicable to the Ryti-Tanner government, nor can the government of the U.S.S.R. consent to make such promises to the Ryti-Tanner government.[23]

Kollontay's intention, Günther related, was to involve Sweden in the negotiations, not merely as host, but as principal, an initiative that Sweden had rejected immediately, which the Finns initially found comforting – the prospect of undue pressure being brought to bear on Sweden, resulting in Finland being bounced into an ill-advised agreement, was unpleasant, to say the least. Immediately a difficulty arose, which would dog these conversations (of which very few notes were kept) for weeks. The initial role of Wuolijoki was as a go-between, to 'break the ice' between Helsinki and Moscow; her self-appointed function now, it seemed, was to 'spin' the Russian proposals from Stockholm somewhat, and Tanner later recalled dryly: 'Later events showed that it was necessary to deal cautiously with reports from both ladies.'

Ryti, Tanner and Paasikivi drafted a guarded response, which reflected willingness to step up guarantees to the USSR regarding territory, even to demilitarize the Gulf of Finland by international treaty, but declining the lease of Hanko that, they noted naively, had not been mentioned in Kollontay's initial message to Günther.

But at least contact had been made, albeit at arm's length, and the removal of Kuusinen as an obstacle was a minor triumph at least – indeed, it was a vindication of Mannerheim's core defence policy, of fighting on the way to the conference table. It would become clear that what Kollontay said was not necessarily what Molotov or Stalin actually meant, but that realization was some way off when Ryti took the reply to Stockholm on the last day of January. The next day the relative lull on the Isthmus, which had given some measure of comfort, even relief, to the Finns, abruptly ended.

CHAPTER TEN

A Hare-brained Scheme...

Cheer up; the worst is yet to come.

Philander Chase Johnson, 1920

BEFORE WE RETURN TO THE battlefield it is important to show what effects the Finnish war was having on the other European nations, particularly Britain. On New Year's Eve 1939, the chiefs of staff produced for the British War Cabinet, as requested, their considered assessment of the project to seize the Swedish ore fields. General Ironside, as the man to 'take the lead' in this matter, had started, however, to have some reservations, and by no means all of them concerned the plan; of equal weight was the competence and abilities of his Cabinet superior, Leslie Hore-Belisha, about whom, his diary tells us, he had been exercised for some time.

So had others. Hore-Belisha's apparent inability to master the carefully prepared briefs with which he was copiously supplied (not least by a diligent Ironside), coupled with the persistent friction between himself and Lord Gort[1] and other senior generals, had made him extremely unpopular; the Cabinet meeting of 2 January, which met to discuss the General Staff paper, probably did for him, although Cadogan's diary suggests that his career was already doomed.[2]

Hore-Belisha had followed faithfully the Churchill line on Norway since it had first been produced. Unhappily for him, he had also thought it wise to show enthusiasm for this 'larger plan', possibly assuming (perhaps because he never read his briefs properly) that the two were really one. An enthusiasm for the big picture, however, was not enough, and at the 2 January War Cabinet meeting, despite a warning from Ironside, he was unwise enough to support Churchill's cherished naval efforts in Norway, but also then stated (prophetically, as it turned out) that he would 'far rather we sent British troops to Finland'.[3] Essentially, Hore-Belisha had already grasped the core issue, and not entirely because he agreed with Daladier. But in terms of a collective Cabinet policy, he was jumping the gun.

Of course, Hore-Belisha had a point – there was a League of Nations resolution to support such action, but Ironside was clearly livid: 'He is incapable of realising the simplest problem. He does not read the papers sent to him and has them read to him a few minutes before he enters the Cabinet ... I cannot get him to consider the bigger questions. He did not read my paper on the strategy for the war and had no idea what I had said.'[4]

There was rather more than professional pique in this, for clearly Hore-Belisha had failed to realize that the only possible access point to the Finnish mainland was not, in the light of Swedish and Norwegian nervousness, through either country but via Petsamo, which was, of course, (as Ironside heavily pointed out) precisely why Petsamo was already in Red Army hands. Any approach through the Baltic was obviously out of the question, as it was teeming with both Russian (and German) warships and, particularly, submarines. Significantly, the French would also shortly embrace a plan for Petsamo.

Clearly, such a rash and ill-thought-out opinion from a minister for war, going in the face of the opinion of both Chamberlain and Churchill concerning the unwisdom of war with Russia, was less than useful at a time like this. Further, Hore-Belisha's previous unswerving support for Churchill's plan also irritated Halifax, whose stated concern for the niceties of Scandinavian neutrality made his own position on Churchill's plan rather more than equivocal, let alone justifying an expedition to Finland, and Halifax had the ear of the King. So did Lord Gort, via the Duke of Gloucester, a close friend of the Earl of Munster, Gort's military assistant.

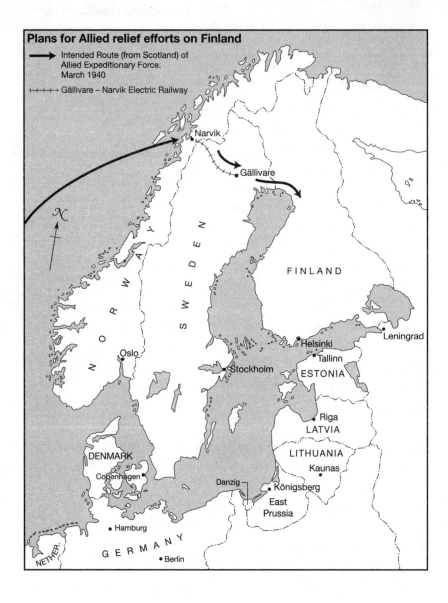

Plans for Allied relief efforts on Finland

➤ Intended Route (from Scotland) of Allied Expeditionary Force. March 1940

⊢+++++ Gällivare – Narvik Electric Railway

Narvik

Gällivare

N O R W A Y

S W E D E N

FINLAND

Leningrad

Helsinki

Tallinn

Oslo

Stockholm

ESTONIA

Riga

LATVIA

DENMARK

LITHUANIA

Kaunas

Copenhagen

Danzig

Königsberg

East Prussia

Hamburg

NETHER.

G E R M A N Y

Berlin

On 4 January Chamberlain effectively requested a shocked Hore-Belisha's resignation. According to Henry 'Chips' Channon (as well-connected a gadfly as any): 'The Crown decided to intervene dramatically, and sent for the PM ... The PM, startled by the complaint, gave in, and that turned the scales.'[5]

An unusual (and rare) intervention, to say the least, but most commentators at the time who knew of the burgeoning crisis between the chiefs of staff and the War Minister, were sanguine about 'Horeb's'[6] departure, reasoning that it was better to lose a war minister than the entire General Staff.[7] Needless to say, the press did not agree, so for a few days Finland was removed from the front pages of the tabloids, just as a *very* unofficial peace feeler from Moscow was being considered in Helsinki.

Meanwhile, Chamberlain had finally come round to Churchill's plan of a limited naval intervention off the Norwegian coast in order to strangle the ore traffic, reasoning that if Norwegian protests proved too vehement (and calculating that a German invasion of southern Norway was affordable) the task force involved could easily withdraw. This was tentative, to say the least, but at least it was a *policy*. A British presence off the Norwegian coast was also justifiable, given that German U-boats had already sunk two British (and one Greek) merchant vessels *within* Norwegian territorial waters, this itself a clear violation of that questionable neutrality.[8]

It fell to Halifax to deliver a note to the Norwegian (and, as a diplomatic courtesy, Swedish) ministers in London, citing the sinkings and proposing to send Royal Naval vessels into Norwegian territorial waters 'from time to time'. Iron ore was not mentioned, an omission which must have caused the 'Holy Fox's' strict Anglo-Catholic conscience at least a mild inguinal twinge.

MOSCOW, MEANWHILE, had not been inactive in greater Scandinavia either. On 5 January Alexandra Kollontay had delivered a very stiff note to the Swedish Foreign Minister, no longer, to Finland's distress, Rickard Sandler, who had (on 2 December) gone the way of Leslie Hore-Belisha, and for not unassociated reasons –

his enthusiasm for a clearly pro-Finnish policy. His successor, Christian Günther, was informed that the Soviet Union viewed the violent Swedish press campaign developing against the USSR as being hostile in the extreme, and that rumours of 10,000 Swedish volunteers arriving in Finland were inconsistent with stated Swedish neutrality – this might lead to 'undesirable complications in the relations between Sweden and the USSR.'[9] Simultaneously, Kollontay's opposite number in Oslo, Plotnikov, delivered to Halvdan Koht, the Norwegian foreign minister, a very similar message.

Given that news of Halifax's note arrived in both capitals the very next day, the Swedish and Norwegian governments were now under extreme pressure, which did not stop there. On 9 January in Berlin, Weizsäcker met a presumably nervous Norwegian Foreign Ministry official:

> I tried to explain to M. Johannsen [Commercial Counsellor, Norwegian Foreign Ministry], as I have done with other visitors, our urgent desire that Norway not become a theatre of war. Norway's attitude would begin to *assume importance for us* whenever, succumbing to British or French influence, Norway began to grant our enemies facilities and concessions which are incompatible with our interests.[10]

The Norwegians were swiftly conciliatory to both Plotnikov and his German counterpart, Carl Bräuer, but extremely hostile to Halifax's note. Given the pressure being applied, this is not surprising. The Swedes, perhaps somewhat stiffened by the news of the fate of the 44th Division of the Red Army on the Raate road, were a little more assertive than that to Kollontay, Günther stating to her that the volunteer numbers were exaggerated (and a private matter anyway, about which nothing could properly be done) and that the people of Sweden had a 'warm sympathy for Finland, which finds its expression in the press.' Not a response calculated to inspire even remote comprehension in a minister plenipotentiary from the Soviet Union, whatever her own private instincts may have been.

Molotov's public response, that: 'The reply given by the Norwegian government and particularly by the Swedish government cannot be regarded as wholly satisfactory', can only have served to heighten nervousness in both Scandinavian capitals, which is perhaps why Günther was positively grovelling to the German minister in Stockholm, Prince Viktor zu Weid, who reported their rather one-sided conversation to Weizsäcker on 10 January:

> Sweden was prepared energetically, and if necessary, by force of arms, to repel any attempts by the western powers to establish bases in Sweden or to transport British and French troops through Swedish territory. This also held for British and French military supplies of all kinds. Transit permits would be granted, however, for war material that was the property of the Finnish Government.[11]

As for Lord Halifax's note, it had merely been a courtesy copy, for which no reply was expected, but he got one anyway, or rather the British chargé in Helsinki did, from Boheman, the General Secretary at the Swedish Foreign Ministry, who asserted crossly that if the Royal Navy moved, then so in all probability would the *Kriegsmarine*: 'I should have thought that the British Government had the fate of a sufficient number of smaller states on their conscience as it is.'

This was not a promising situation in which Churchill's modest little plan could prosper; an opportunity that was seized by Lord Halifax, whose fretfulness concerning Scandinavian neutrality had proved to be so accurate. A see-saw series of angry Cabinet debates resulted in Chamberlain changing his mind again, and 'the smaller plan' was finally, after weeks of vacillation, consigned to the dustbin. It was a low moment for Churchill; he was moved to write shortly afterwards, in response to an anxious, even deferential note from an apologetic Halifax, which stated how much the Foreign Secretary regretted being unable to support him: 'My disquiet was due mainly to the awful difficulties which our machinery of war-conduct presents to positive action. I see such immense walls of prevention, all built and building, that I wonder whether any plan will have a chance of climbing over them ... Victory will never be found by taking the line of least resistance.'[12]

SUCH OBSTACLES to decision-making were clearly still a thing of the future in the Third Reich; the intense diplomatic traffic, assuring Berlin of both the neutrality and slightly cringing good offices of both Sweden and Norway, however comforting and believable, did little to convince Adolf Hitler of their ability to withstand Allied pressure, particularly in the case of Norway. Accordingly, Hitler had now instructed OKW (Armed Forces High Command) to investigate the possibility of an invasion of Norway under the code-name *Studie Nord*. At this stage, the Führer was doing little more than hedging his bets; 'Case Yellow' – the climactic battle with France, already discussed in *Mein Kampf* – was still uppermost in his mind.[13]

As these chaotic discussions continued all over Europe, a bizarre and unsettling incident on the German–Belgian frontier provided a temporary distraction from Allied concerns about Scandinavia and served to concentrate distracted minds. A German light aircraft (clearly lost in fog and 70 miles off course) had crashed inside the Belgian border on 10 January; aboard were two Luftwaffe officers – a courier, Major Reinberger, and the pilot, Major Hoenmanns – who were both captured. In Reinberger's possession (he was supposed to have taken a train to Cologne, but reasoned that an aircraft would be quicker[14]) was a full set of operational plans for 'Case Yellow', which had been expected by the nervous western powers since the fall of Poland.[15]

Despite the appalling weather – little better than in southern Finland – it was generally assumed that the capture of the plans, which Reinberger claimed to his superiors that he had burned, heralded a full-scale attack. A full alert was ordered (the Belgians said nothing about the capture of the papers for *three days*) and the Allies prepared to move into Belgium to meet the Wehrmacht. Of course, nothing happened. Initially (and briefly), this incident was presumed to be a hoax, but the German diplomatic telegram traffic confirms that it was far from that. The Allies would later discover that 'Case Yellow' had been postponed over a dozen times since 1 November, one reason being the distracting outbreak of war in Finland, the other – more significant – being the dropping temperature. On 20 January, in fact, 'Case Yellow' was postponed yet again, this time until May 1940.[16]

Now that Churchill's plan was abandoned completely – although he would continue to press its merits for a long time afterwards – the War Cabinet, assuming a false alarm in Belgium (there were no confirming troop movements), turned its attention back to the matter of iron ore. Naturally, neither the Norwegians nor the Swedes had been informed about the change of tack, but that detail did not trouble Halifax unduly as he relaunched his mild diplomatic offensive on 18 January.

Two days after the unfortunate Reinberger's aeroplane came down, Brigadier Ling[17] returned from Helsinki, where he had been sent in late December, bearing the news that Marshal Mannerheim would need 30,000 trained soldiers in the field by May, but who also expected a serious Soviet attack within weeks. He had a particular need, Ling reported, for long-range artillery, but also aircraft – could any eight-gun fighters be spared? It was decided that a squadron of twelve Hawker Hurricanes could indeed be spared – a generous gesture on the face of it, given the possible imminent pressure on the Western Front, but not entirely. Their dispatch, from RAF St Athan, was formally approved on 20 January. These aircraft were not a gift, however, they were sold – under protest from the Air Staff – at an eye-watering £9,000 apiece.[18] In a rather touchy private response to a very public criticism,[19] Chamberlain later wrote:

> They began by asking for fighter planes, and we sent the surplus we could lay hands on. They asked for A.A. guns, and again we stripped our own imperfectly-armed home defences to help them. They asked for small arms ammunition, and we gave them priority over our own army. They asked for later types of planes, and we sent them 12 Hurricanes, against the will and advice of our Air Staff...[20]

But this is only tangentially true; Chamberlain was remembering with advantage. The Finns bought, and were to buy, almost everything. And, further, like the deliberations on intervention itself, which was now at the forefront of British foreign policy, there was absolutely no sense of urgency involved in supply, a matter that had already vexed Gripenberg hugely. This was not *aid*, it was, in effect, business. Some of the sting of this might have been drawn by the fact that the King visited the Finnish pilots, who had arrived for familarization and training, for lunch on 9 February.

The Hurricane squadron, uncomfortably decorated with their *hakaristi* markings,[21] were prepared and sent in convoy in late February. They would arrive in theatre in the very last few days of the war.[22]

HALIFAX'S INITIATIVE, to put the Swedes and Norwegians under courteous pressure on the pretext that Churchill's smaller plan was still under consideration, did not bear fruit. On the contrary, the Norwegian reaction was quite uncompromising. First a note, delivered the next day: 'The circumstance, that Great Britain is fighting for its life, cannot give it a right to jeopardise the existence of Norway.'

This was reinforced by a truly wild statement from a rattled Halvdan Koht to the Storting (Norwegian Parliament), also on 19 January, that as 'we have no proof left of who is responsible' when a ship is torpedoed, then blame for the sinking of British shipping in Norwegian waters must remain an open question. The implication behind this, that the Royal Navy was as likely to be responsible for the sinkings as the Germans (or even, more remotely, they were merely a *misfortune*) was not only craven (towards Berlin) but deeply insulting, given that Norway, if anything, appeared at present to be neutral on the side of Germany, a perception rather reinforced by these provocative Norwegian remarks. Winston Churchill had had enough.

The same day that Koht made this unwise reference, Neville Chamberlain personally approved, in the War Cabinet, an initiative to conduct a Scandinavian expeditionary mission. The chiefs of staff of both France and Britain had convinced each other that such a plan could prosper. With the hapless Hore-Belisha safely consigned to the back benches, Churchill himself could now grandstand the issue. On the evening of 20 January, he made a broadcast in the orotund, gurgling lisp that would become so familiar to his audiences later, in which (although it was never included in the printed record of his collected wartime speeches, for reasons which may become clear), he 'had a go' at the neutrals. After a properly exaggerated résumé of the war at sea and a positive paeon to those neutrals prepared to fight if necessary (particularly Holland), he then came to Finland:

> Only Finland – superb, nay, sublime – in the jaws of peril – Finland shows what free men can do. The service rendered by Finland to mankind is magnificent. They have exposed, for all the world to see, the military incapacity of the Red Army and of the Red Airforce. Many illusions about Soviet Russia have been dispelled in these few fierce weeks of fighting in the Arctic Circle [*sic*]. Everyone can see how Communism rots the soul of a Nation; how it makes it abject and hungry in peace, and proves it base and abominable in war…

> …We cannot tell what the fate of Finland may be, but no more mournful spectacle could be presented to what is left of civilised mankind than that this splendid Northern race should be at last worn down and reduced to a servitude worse than death by the dull brutish force of overwhelming numbers. If the light of freedom which still burns so brightly in the frozen North should be finally quenched, it might well herald a return to the Dark Ages, when every vestige of human progress during two thousand years would be engulfed.

He then invoked the League of Nations covenant (never mind that this institution was now clearly in a state of coma) urging the neutrals to stand together, before lambasting them thus:

> Each one hopes that if he feeds the crocodile enough, the crocodile will eat him last … All of them hope that the storm will pass before their turn comes to be devoured. But I fear – I fear greatly – the storm will not pass. It will rage and roar, ever more loudly, ever more widely. It will spread to the South; it will spread to the North.
>
> There is no chance of a speedy end except through united action; and if at any time Britain and France, wearying of the struggle, were to make a shameful peace, nothing would remain for the smaller States of

Europe, with their shipping and their possessions, but to be divided between the opposite, though similar, barbarisms of Nazidom and Bolshevism.[23]

This may have been ripping stuff, but if Churchill had been hoping to put some backbone into the undeclared neutrals to join the Allied cause, then he was to be sadly mistaken, although Paris, for reasons of its own, rather liked it; the linkage between the League of Nations, 'Nazidom and Bolshevism' would have suited Senator Bardoux and his circle admirably.

One who heard this broadcast with some optimism was the Finnish minister in London, George Gripenberg. In common with his colleagues in the chancelleries of Europe and Washington, Gripenberg's hyper-activities had taken on some of the characteristics of a one-person business. Of all the senior Finnish ministers and Foreign Service officers, Gripenberg was perhaps the closest to Marshal Mannerheim – indeed, as already noted, they were related by marriage – and, given that the best prospect of immediate material assistance, for reasons of recent commercial history, seemed to lie in London, he was more than usually energetic. He requested an immediate meeting with Churchill; he was granted one, but vexingly only on the evening of the 22nd, 48 vital hours later.

If Gripenberg had thought that Churchill's broadcast presaged any public endorsement by a Cabinet minister of a public hardening of official policy, he was to be sorely disappointed. Churchill was 'friendly but reserved' and Gripenberg quickly realized that whatever the First Lord's agenda was, it did not necessarily include anything meaningful in terms of direct assistance. He was not to know that Churchill was in serious trouble over the speech, nor was he to know (or, if he did, he was too polite to say so in his memoirs) that for Churchill, Finland was merely a stalking-horse; the prime objective of the larger plan was still – *and would remain* – to exert a stranglehold on Swedish ore exports to the Reich.

The reception of Churchill's speech, which he had not cleared with Lord Halifax, was, to say the least, cool. In response to Halifax's polite, but rather querulous memorandum, which requested:

> Would you think it unreasonable of me to ask in future, if you are going to speak with particular reference to Foreign policy, you might let me see in advance what you had it in mind to say? ... I have no doubt that you would feel the same if the roles were reversed, and I was making general speeches about Naval policy, etc.[24]

Churchill replied, charmingly: 'This is undoubtedly a disagreeable bouquet. I certainly thought I was expressing yr view and Neville's...'

It was a fair point, but Halifax was also very careful *not* to point out that the response from other Allies was, by and large, hugely favourable, but of course Churchill would find that out for himself quite soon.[25] Given the enthusiastic French response to Churchillian oratory, it was now rather difficult for Chamberlain to exclude Churchill from the next Supreme War Council meeting, to be held in Paris on 5 February. Winston Churchill, at 65 years of age, was finally going to take tea with the grown-ups.

TO THE BELEAGUERED FINNS, Churchill's injunctions to the neutral countries – he did not at any point in the speech advocate *intervention* in Finland – was probably something less than helpful, as it did not serve to ease the cause of Scandinavian cooperation, upon which much depended. With both Germany and the USSR putting ferocious diplomatic pressure upon Stockholm and Oslo, this latest contribution only induced paralysis in both places. While he had intended to stiffen the wider Scandinavian resolve in resistance to totalitarian pressure, he had also signally failed to see that this was inordinately hard for them to do – their hesitation over the League of Nations issue had already suggested that. Finland's plight, despite its nervousness concerning the intentions of others, was already stretching them somewhat. Perhaps the response to this speech as recorded by Josef Goebbels (after he had taken soundings) puts this into some perspective: 'Churchill's speech is still going the rounds and arousing the neutrals' outrage. We ignore it. [We] have no intention of helping out these tiny dwarf-states. They deserve to disappear.'[26] Goebbels had little reason to know of the German General Staff study concerning Norway. In fact, Hitler was not ignoring Churchill's speech of 20 January – he had already anticipated it.

The same day that Goebbels confided to his diary, the German minister in Oslo, Curt Bräuer, reported – clearly rather tickled – to Baron Weizsäcker, what the effect of Churchill's speech had been on its principal target:

> It was incomprehensible [said Koht] that one of the ranking members of the Cabinet should have delivered such an address which would drive the neutral countries into opposition to British policy even if they were in sympathy with England. The speech was provocative and silly... He had known Churchill for thirty years and considered him a 'demagogue and a windbag' (sic!).
>
> ...He, Koht, had at the time been very much astonished that Churchill had been taken into the Cabinet at just so difficult a period and had been given a position of such importance in the British government which called for the greatest tact and the deepest wisdom. This could be explained on the grounds of the lack of realism of Chamberlain, who 'means well, but is a bungler [ein schlechter Musikant].[27]

Clearly, on this issue, everyone agreed that this time Churchill's oratorical effort had been something of an exploding cigar and that German policy (concerning Sweden and Norway, at least[28]) was working *very well indeed*.

There was real exasperation in the higher reaches of the British government, at least from those who were less outwardly fastidious than Lord Halifax concerning the finer feelings of the Swedes and Norwegians. Hugh Gaitskell, then a rising star in the Ministry of Economic Warfare (and later to be briefly leader of the Labour Party) bewailed the dilemma to his friend Hugh Dalton: 'What can we do about these neutrals? The Foreign Office won't let us bully them and the Treasury won't let us bribe them.'[29]

IF THERE WAS INDECISION in the civil service, however, Ironside was gently pushing his own priorities, and for this the quiescent state on the Western Front allowed him to suggest that certain elements of the British Army should learn to ski – accordingly, the slopes of Chamonix acquired a strangely pre-war, even festive atmosphere, as British soldiers encountered winter sports for the first time.

CHAPTER ELEVEN

The Red Army Reforms Itself

Impetuosity and audacity often achieve what ordinary means fail to achieve.

Niccolo Machiavelli, Discorsi, *1531*

THIS FIRST PHASE OF the Russo-Finnish War had revealed some staggering (and depressing) deficiencies in the Red Army, which only reflected the greater dysfunction of the State as a whole. This deterioration – from the most feared instrument on Earth, which Tukhachevski and his circle had made it, to the brave but insubordinate rabble which the Finns had held off so skilfully – had taken less than three years. Timoshenko, however, now had a mere three weeks to reverse this trend.

The rebellion of the Baltic fleet at Kronstadt in 1921[1] cannot have been far from the minds of Russians as they surveyed this dismal situation. There was already ample evidence of individual unit insubordination in the Red Army; the prospect of this occurring on a larger scale was too dreadful to contemplate. Full circle, in fact. Now, as Timoshenko and his staff (he was given *carte blanche* in selecting them) surveyed the condition of the Red Army, it was instantly clear to him that what he really needed was an army that could fight like the Finns. The Red Army, by its purpose, indoctrination and, critically, the individual motivation of its soldiers,[2] was not by any measure an expeditionary force.[3] Clearly, neither was the Finnish Army. Both were essentially defensive – the vital difference between them lay in what they were fighting for and the will of the defenders. Ignorant of the occasional chaos in Finnish command and control, Timoshenko was faced with the prospect of an interim overhaul of the entire structure of what had been the Leningrad Military District – it would be hurried, but comprehensive; the Finns had to be beaten. Accordingly, the entire Soviet *apparat* was now put to work.

Despite the suspension of dual command, the political elements of doctrinal reform were not ignored, merely repositioned, and in some cases suspended. In microcosm, the motivational problems of certain Red Army soldiers had to be addressed in a manner which rather prefigured the situation in the summer of 1941 – a straightforward, atavistic appeal to Russian nationalism. From the bottom up, in the case of the soldiers themselves, and from the middle outwards in the case of the officer cadres, the process commenced immediately.

The problem of troops' morale was addressed by a straightforward mobilization of the Russian home front. Appeals went out for gifts for the Red Army soldiers – for supportive, patriotic letters to be written to them at the front (according to templates laid down) with a relaxation of military censorship – not, judging by some of the letters recovered, that this had previously worked well.

There must have been concern in Moscow, too, at the state of civilian morale, particularly in Leningrad, as the Finland Station presented a scene of horror as the troop trains kept coming, piled with wounded. In a memorandum to Berlin from Schulenberg written on 10 January, (the same telegram in which he describes his encounter with Molotov), the German minister points out the general climate among the civil population:

> I should like to add that according to all our observations the food situation, which is worse than it has been for a long time,[4] letters with unfavourable news from the Finnish front and the lack or inadequacy of support given to the families of the soldiers are creating unmistakable dissatisfaction among the population.

It would have been lost on no one that bread riots had proved a decisive trigger before – in 1917 and 1921.[5]

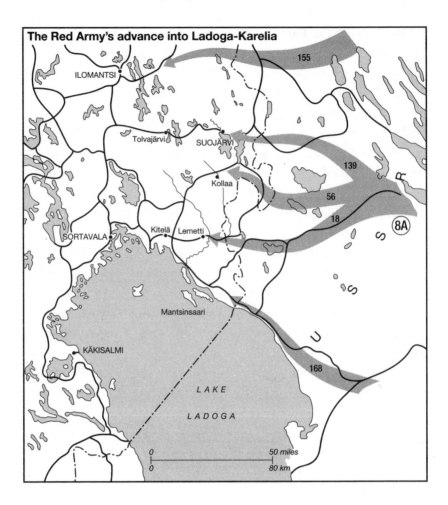

The Red Army's advance into Ladoga-Karelia

ILOMANTSI

155

Tolvajärvi   SUOJÄRVI

139

Kollaa

56

18

SORTAVALA   Kitelä Lemetti

8A

Mantsinsaari

KÄKISALMI

168

LAKE

LADOGA

0   50 miles
0   80 km

In terms of the Party's relationship with the Red Army, dual command might have been suspended, but *politruki* were not. Their job now became once more driven by objectives of political education, as the 'journalists'[6] of the army (and State) journals now started to produce embellished folk tales about Russian military heroes from the past – particularly Suvurov and Kutuzov,[7] punctuated by very pointed articles concerning military discipline, which, all agreed, was lax at best. The climate of nostalgia was thus heightened; the *politruki* ensuring that the articles were read by as many as possible, or if they were illiterate in Russian (as very many were) read to them out loud.[8]

There was coercion, too; the breaking of a 'soldier's oath' would now involve the punishment extending out to the culprit's relations – in this sense, the unspoken code of the purge that the whole family of a victim could be 'suppressed' for the crime of one member was now extended down into the ordinary ranks of the Red Army.

Given that the political-military model for the Red Army was essentially *industrial* – the Red Army as a great khaki factory – some allowance was now made for the essential difference between an industrial worker and a soldier, or a factory manager and an officer – in effect upgrading the status of the soldier as opposed to the worker who was not risking his life. This would develop further after the war.

There was even a sense of light-heartedness about this – one manifestation being uniquely Soviet, the second being particularly Russian – the difference is clear. The strip cartoon *Vasia Tërkin*, the 'perfect Soviet revolutionary soldier', clean, cheerful, resourceful and creative – first appeared in the pages of *Na Strazhe Rodiny* at the end of December 1939 as a potential role model offered up for the discontented soldiery and others.[9] A far more *Russian* alternative, *Pasha the Liar*, was to appear (briefly) later. Pasha is dirty, undisciplined, gossiping, lazy and cynical. His fictional letters to the press mocked everything about the Red Army, from food to transportation, including weaponry, discipline and even traffic jams – he cannot ski, or even shoot straight, and doesn't care overmuch.[10] We may imagine which character the soldiers preferred.

At the purely military level there was, Timoshenko and his staff determined, much to be done. The successive failures on the Mannerheim Line were worse than embarrassing, as Stalin had already pointed out, as they might well lead to an underestimation of the Red Army and invite attack, a matter that was now being discussed openly in the Western press and, critically, not being strenuously denied. 'The main argument against any genuine wholehearted assistance to Finland', reported the *Daily Sketch*, 'is that it would distract our attention from our main business in the war, which is the defeat of Germany. The argument seems to me unsound. Our task in this war is to defeat Hitlerism, but it is still Hitlerism if the aggressor is called Stalin.'[11] And, a week later, this was expanded to: 'There would be more to be said for sending military reinforcements to Finland than to France, *where they may never be needed*. [emphasis mine].'

The press it seemed (largely fictional reports 'from the front' notwithstanding) was starting to build a momentum all its own. Some papers, particularly Beaverbrook's *Express*, held back (we may see the hand of Churchill in this) but generally, the more left-wing, the greater the pressure to act, with the *Daily Mirror* and the usually pacific *News Chronicle*[12] in the vanguard. By the end of January, however, even Beaverbrook allowed Captain Basil Liddell Hart (ex-military adviser to Leslie Hore-Belisha and therefore at something of a loose end for that very reason[13]) to at least sit on the fence in the *Sunday Express*, with an astonishingly obvious, rent-a-quote 'balanced view'. Fleet Street had caught a very heavy dose of Finland fever, it seemed, and, ever nervous about being wrong-footed by events, started to climb aboard the trundling bandwagon. This cannot have gone unnoticed, for in truth, people were discussing little else; the music of Jean Sibelius preceded most BBC news broadcasts on the wireless;[14] Finland had assumed a simple importance (although for radically different political reasons) that Spain had had so recently.[15]

IT WAS NOT LONG before George Gripenberg became very busy indeed. As early as 12 December, the Finnish Aid Bureau was established, initially at the Finnish Legation in Smith Square, later (after the legation was bombed) at a large private house loaned for the purpose and, as soon as the matter became public, an astonishing volume of gifts and money started to pour in that, coupled with the huge demands placed upon him for military orders (in a system that was still glacially slow), kept him extremely busy – and worried, as his instructions from Helsinki were less than exact. The British director of the Bureau with responsibility for volunteer efforts was Colonel Harold Gibson, MC, with whom Gripenberg dealt very well – importantly, Gibson, who had presented himself to Gripenberg on 4 January, was a member of the War Cabinet secretariat and had the ear of Halifax, who approved the plan to raise a volunteer force on the 8th. Other members of the Bureau included Leopold Amery, Lord Nuffield, Lord Dawson (the King's physician), Lord Balfour and several other *prominenti*. It was thus a powerful and well-connected cadre; it is perhaps surprising, then, that it was not more effective.

In France, Edouard Daladier was impatient, to say the least. On 8 January he had ordered General Audet to prepare a *Force Spéciale*, specifically to conduct ground operations in Finland; from Sidi bel Abbes[16] to Syria, the call for volunteers went out.[17] At this stage the British Cabinet was still rather circumspect, but Daladier's action forced the approval of the raising of volunteer forces the next day. Within a week of that, Gripenberg had opened for business, on the understanding that there was to be a strictly bilateral note to this – British officials could not be involved (the first responses from Sweden and Norway have already been noted) and the Finnish government would contract with volunteers on a private basis. Beaverbrook, whatever his personal thoughts may have been, contributed £100,000 towards the cost of this.[18]

The news that volunteers were being raised soon filtered out, as it was intended to. One of the few Members of Parliament to actively support the Soviet Union was the redoubtable Communist Willie Gallacher, who tabled a *very* hostile question on 6 February to: 'Ask the Secretary of State for War whether he will inquire and inform the House who is responsible for offering inducements to conscripts ... to leave the Army for service with the forces of Baron Mannerheim; and whether an office for directing such activities has been opened in London?' He avoided describing these men as mercenaries, but the meaning is clear. This was followed by a rather loaded supplementary: 'Is it not in the knowledge of the Hon. Member... that there has been a private army under Baron Mannerheim in Finland since 1918, and is it not in the knowledge of the War Office that such a private army has existed since 1918?'[19]

Which was an odd (if properly right-on and odiously politically correct) way of describing the Civil Guard, at that very moment fighting for its life against Gallacher's employers of last resort. Another nominally Labour member, Denis Nowell Pritt (who would go the way of Stafford Cripps shortly), developed the legality of the recruitment enterprise as a theme ten days later, citing the Foreign Enlistment Act (1870).[20] This was countered by the government with the League of Nations resolution. Naturally, Pritt (a lawyer) made no reference to the persuasive precedent established by the volunteers for the International Brigades in Spain during the Civil War.[21]

The peculiar relationship between the volunteers and the Finnish government *was* of course legally questionable, but it was a merely useful stalking-horse, for by the time Gallacher asked his question, the Supreme War Council had already met and Gallacher and others would not know the official outcome of its deliberations for some time. They would naturally assume the worst, obediently following the Moscow line.

The disclosure that there were volunteers signing up to actually fight in Finland was something of a boon to the press, and quite soon exaggerated estimates of the numbers involved were bandied about – between 'several hundred' (*The Times*) and 'more than 8,000' (*The Evening Standard* – then a Beaverbrook paper). But none of this excited as much attention as the news that the commander of this valiant band would be none other than Major

Kermit Roosevelt, MC, second son of Theodore, and a man who was driven by very much the same instincts as his father. As a soldier (he had served in Mesopotamia in the Great War and won the Military Cross) and big-game hunter, he was also a naturalized British citizen and presumably just the sort of fellow of whom Marshal Mannerheim might approve.

Unhappily, Kermit Roosevelt was also a deeply troubled man – he drank very heavily, took drugs and, although he took the task in hand seriously (he informed *The Daily Telegraph* that he regarded the issue of Finland as a 'crusade') there is some thought that it was his surname, rather than anything else, which the Bureau (and the War Cabinet – if not the Foreign Office) needed most – he was, after all, Franklin Roosevelt's cousin.[22] Gripenberg himself recalled:

> ...but the British Foreign Office, with which I discussed even this matter, would not at first give its approval; America was neutral, and although Major Roosevelt was a British subject, it was feared that his selection might not meet with approval in Washington because he bore the President's name – one of the many reasons that had prompted us to select him.[23]

Given Washington's attitude to Finland, it may be surmised that 'approval in Washington' was not high on the list of priorities for the Finns, who were becoming more and more scandalized at the lawyer's view being exercised by Cordell Hull, not to mention the relative inaction of the President himself.

As for the volunteers themselves, no skiing in Chamonix for them – unless, of course, they could afford it.

THE STATE OF public opinion in the *entente* now made the Red Army's task rather urgent. But, in terms of 'chewing' its way through Finnish defences, Timoshenko already had a template, expressed in the mid 1930s to Mikhael Solov'ev, then a military correspondent, and by early 1940 working under Mekhlis. Here we have a chillingly brutal picture of what Timoshenko had in mind:

But while it cannot be gainsaid that in a war of manoeuvre we shall be the weaker party, the position is different with regard to frontal attack. In frontal attack no enemy or combination of enemies can hope to compare with us. By making a succession of direct attacks we shall compel him to lose blood, in other word to lose something he has less of than we have. Of course we shall have enormous losses too, but in war one has to count not one's own losses but those of the enemy.[24] Even if we lose more men than the enemy, we must view it dispassionately.

I know of no army in Europe that could hold up our mass advance. And despite everything, that advance will deny the enemy any possibility of manoeuvre on a strategic scale and will force him into a frontal war, advantageous to us and disadvantageous to him.

…we concentrate our army into an enormous fist. The very fact that such a fist exists will prevent the enemy from dispersing his forces in a war of manoeuvre, he will not be given any opportunity to loosen the close 'interlinking' of his army; on the contrary, he will be forced to concentrate, to go over to the defence on as restricted an area as possible. In other words, we get conditions of a frontal war, we force the enemy to accept our view of the character of the war.

Having forced the enemy into this position, our object being his wholesale destruction, we strike a pulverizing blow, not through a combination of sectional manoeuvres, not in the hope that the sum of those manoeuvres will develop into a general success, but by frontal action, doing all we can to smash the enemy's front. Of course we strike simultaneously at his flanks. For us, that frontal battle together with pressure on the flanks will constitute a single engagement; for the enemy it constitutes three different tasks.[25]

Such a doctrine, the backbone of Russian Army policy since Tsarist times, had been developed in step with new technology, particularly tanks and aircraft, but at its heart was a dependence on artillery. It was a policy that could have been bespoke for an assault on fixed fortifications, whatever the cost; hardly, then, the equivalent of factory work, however arduous. Five years after Timoshenko spoke to Solov'ev, his view, as expressed to another in January 1940, was that: 'To chew through the fortified region in winter in a severe frost is more than difficult. Success in a given day is measured in ... metres. History has not yet known such a war and not one army, except our own, is capable of conducting an offensive in such conditions.'[26]

As Timoshenko said this, clearly hedging his bets somewhat after his analysis of the Red Army's previous performance, temperatures were about to plunge once more as the Winter War now entered its coldest phase.

MANNERHEIM HAD already told a concerned Brigadier Ling that he expected a major offensive within weeks, but the scale of the one envisaged by Timoshenko's interpretation of the Shaposhnikov plan would wind even the pessimistic Marshal; the previous suicidal, piecemeal attacks of the Red Army were now to be initially at least a thing of the past. What the Finns were now facing had simply not been faced before and, although the various judgements on Russian ability had already been made, the Red Army that would now attack was radically different from the one that the Finns hoped they had already fought to a standstill; the difference was to be immediately obvious.

For the exhausted Finnish soldiers of General Öhqvist's II Corps on the far side of the line behind Summa, there was a suspicion that perhaps something was about to happen after the relative quiet of the last three weeks of January, but confidence was still remarkably high none the less. They had shown that in defence they could tolerate almost anything that the Red Army had shown itself capable of throwing at them. There were rumours of significant amounts of Western aid on the way, and their numbers were now leavened by some very welcome volunteers, tangible and friendly evidence of the international support that those who could read foreign papers already understood. Politically, the Finnish Cabinet were no longer wobbling, and the press seemed confident that Mannerheim's policy, of fighting until help arrived, was working. All they had to do, many reasoned, was to hold out. Physically the Finns were, in relation to their enemy, comfortable, though extremely tired and inevitably stressed. They were well enough fed and relatively warm, however, and during the quiet phase (which had characterized the time taken by Timoshenko to prepare his plan) much captured *matériel* – mainly small arms – had been redistributed along the line. Supplies of anti-tank ordnance had been marginally increased, both captured and Swedish-sourced,[27] and morale was buoyant as a result[28]. Above all, the Finns had learned that the soldiers of the Red Army were not ten feet tall; they could be halted, driven back and humiliated.

An ominous novelty for the defenders in the line was the appearance of more observation balloons, tethered above the small village of Boboshino[29] – a rather nineteenth-century touch in what was to become a very twentieth-century encounter, except of course for those other, later moments which were to prove themselves quite medieval. More contemporary (if unfamiliar) were the weird autogyros[30] that had suddenly appeared, extending the observational capacity of the Red Army up to the line itself, indeed across it. Slow, small but manoeuvrable, the autogyro proved to be an extremely difficult target.

There was to be pressure along the entire Isthmus front that early February, not merely at Summa. Activity at the other end of the line, at Taipale, would also produce vast stresses, the Soviet hope still being that the Finns would be forced to disengage in Ladoga-Karelia, where they were still holding down five stranded Red Army divisions, and come south to bolster the line on the Isthmus. This would allow a resumption of the Soviet attempt to move round the north of Lake Ladoga to turn the Finnish line, as well as offer up those remaining Finnish forces by then within range into the meat grinder that Timoshenko had prepared for them. It was not to be; General Hägglund, in close contact with Mannerheim's new headquarters at Otava, stayed firmly put and so, therefore, did the beleaguered Russians.

The putative rescue of these encircled Russian divisions north of the Ladoga was a purely secondary objective for Timoshenko; they had already failed. The primary task, of punching through the defences in front of Summa and racing for Viipuri to deliver the ancient capital of Karelia into Soviet hands, remained paramount. Beyond that, Timoshenko had no particular remit, or even interest. The Eighth and Ninth Armies were no concern of his. After the military objective, strictly narrow and limited, had been achieved the political agenda would intercede. Surely, in military history, no commander has had at his disposal such huge resources with which to secure so modest an objective, as well as so much discretion to deploy them. As the artillery of the Seventh and Thirteenth Armies lined up, wheel to wheel, across the Isthmus and no less than twelve fresh infantry divisions were rotated into the lines, the architects of the previous failure watched the new front commander's efforts with presumably mixed feelings.

Mannerheim was not so optimistic and neither could he afford to be; he had briefly allowed himself to be carried along on the wave of euphoria that had resulted in the ill-advised and disappointing counter-offensive of 23 December. Now, as usual in full possession of the military and logistical realities, he was far more circumspect. Outnumbered as the Finnish forces were, even one more adventure of that kind could prove disastrous, and he was also acutely aware that supplies of artillery shells were now critically low.[31] His fears were confirmed when an aerial reconnaissance, carried out under conditions of almost suicidal bravery, revealed that the concentration of Russian artillery in front of Summa alone was easily in excess of 400 pieces of heavy (200–280 mm) ordnance, which the Russians had not even bothered to camouflage, together with a host of smaller (75 mm and 45 mm[32]) pieces. To Mannerheim, holding ground was Holy Writ, particularly this ground; once Viipuri fell, the war would be over – there was nothing between the Karelian capital and Helsinki.

CHAPTER TWELVE

Endgame: Red Storm

It is with artillery that war is made.

Napoleon

COMMANDER TIMOSHENKO had had only three weeks to reorganize the whole thrust of Red Army military doctrine, with but a single purpose: the delivery of Stalin's original political ambition, so confidently set out in September 1939, of destroying – utterly – the Finns' ability to fight. The obstacle of the Mannerheim Line, however, still remained; while it was perfectly clear to the new Soviet commander that the resources required to break through it were considerable, it was also clear that the political and personal prices paid for failure in this war were terminally high, as the late Commanders Vinogradov, Gusev and so many others had recently learned.

As a veteran of the First Cavalry Army during the Russian civil war, Timoshenko enjoyed the same privileges as Voroshilov, Budenny, Chuikov, Meretskov, Zhukov and, after his brush with the purge, Rokossowski. Despite this, he was careful not to antagonize the party *apparat* unnecessarily; he hoped (and was largely to succeed in this) that the emphasis on rigorous training would serve to eclipse the malign influence of the commissar cadres, rather by putting them into the shade by comparison and demonstrating that the army could function perfectly well without them. He was aware that his proposals would not necessarily find favour with the Voroshilov–Mekhlis axis, that direct link between

Kremlin power and political control of the army, and which had proved so incompetent.

In formulating his new policy Timoshenko turned his back on the haphazard, piecemeal disaster of Meretskov's original plan, and produced a doctrine that owed something to the alternative drawn up by Shaposhnikov in 1939, which had already been rejected once by Stalin. Further risking his political reputation, Timoshenko reintroduced elements of the strategy of the Tsarist General Brusilov and used by him (with some success) in the First World War.[1] It was thus a hybrid policy that was even, vaguely, reminiscent of Tukhachevski's 'deep battle' theories, which would not further endear him to the Politburo should it fail. But he was a conservative general and, perhaps unusually for a cavalryman, viewed war of manoeuvre, irrelevant as it was in this context, as a 'degenerate' concept. Timoshenko was, in early February 1940, taking a huge personal risk. That this could reward him with Voroshilov's job was something he may have hoped, but was not something of which he could be certain; the culture of mediocrity as represented by Voroshilov's very existence made all aware that the purge was not yet a thing of the past.[2]

In essence, Timoshenko stressed the role of coordinated combined arms, with the somewhat counter-revolutionary rider that the direction of battle would now be exclusively the responsibility of the front commander; Moscow, of course, had little alternative but to agree. With one stroke, he thus maimed the career of the sinister Mekhlis, sidelined Zhdanov away from the military process and – most helpfully for his troops – consigned the hated *politruki* to a purely 'supporting' role. In removing the possibility of the political officers thus taking credit for the work of other men, he of course piled responsibility upon the shoulders of those very men, who frankly were not used to it. This presented potential tensions that would be tested, almost to destruction, very soon. Unfamiliarity with unified command was one thing; unease with such new responsibility was quite another, but meanwhile, there was a job to be done.

Timoshenko demanded, and received, huge resources. Significantly, there was no intention to relieve the beleaguered Red Army divisions who were still clustered in *mottis* to the north (but see page 253–4). Rather, the offensive would concentrate purely on the Isthmus and, particularly, on the Viipuri Gateway in front of the village of Summa, which straddled the main road to Viipuri. Here was the strongest line of defence; here was the widest strip of land unencumbered by lakes;[3] here, to borrow from the vocabulary of the Wehrmacht, was the *schwerpunkt*. And part of the task before Timoshenko and his division commanders was to disguise this clear and obvious objective from the enemy – for the moment.

THE FIRST BARRAGE crashed into the line at Summa at 12.45 p.m. on 1 February. For the Finns, ensconced as they were in relatively deep earthworks, the ordeal was still uniquely dreadful. There was, of course, more than one motive for the ferocity of this attack; on the one hand the apparent defeat of the Red Army's efforts thus far had served to ridicule it in the eyes of foreign observers,[4] but on the other, the embarrassing climb-down over the legitimacy of the 'Ryti–Tanner–Mannerheim gang' had, at least within ruling Finnish circles (within which the Soviet *démarche* was kept close) heaped even more contumely upon the head of the hated Kuusinen. Important, then, that Moscow was seen in Helsinki and Stockholm (not to mention London and Paris) to be negotiating from a position of infinite strength as opposed to having been fought, via a standstill, to the conference table. On top of this, the natural focus of Soviet attention on the Finnish war had also served to create bottlenecks in the contracted supply of raw materials to Germany. The schedules of delivery were punishing at the best of times, but any lapse in the schedule, so vital as it was to German war ambitions, served to set alarm bells ringing in Berlin.

Unhappily, the urgent *matériel* needs of the Finns, exacerbated by the renewed intensity of the Soviet attack, thus coincided with what was perceived to be the most dangerous phase of the war so far. It was reasoned that if the Red Army could go to war in weather like this, then why not the Wehrmacht? So, the impor-

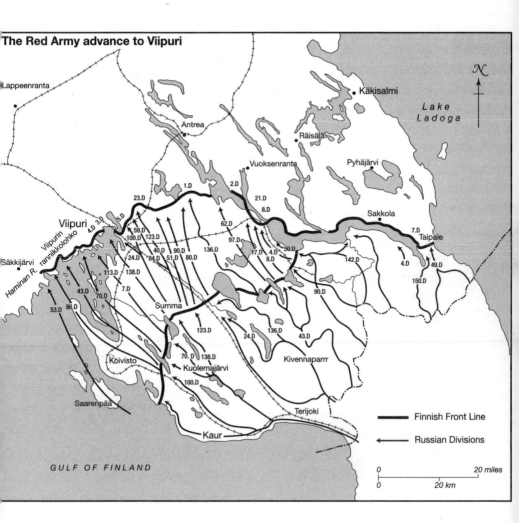

The Red Army advance to Viipuri

Lappeenranta

Antrea

Käkisalmi

Lake Ladoga

Räisälä

Vuoksenranta

Pyhäjärvi

1.D   2.D

23.D   21.D   8.D

Viipuri   5.D   62.D   Sakkola   7.D   Taipale

4.D 3.0   59.D   97.D

100.D 123.D   50.D

Säkkijärvi   40.D 90.D   136.D   17.D 4.D   142.D   4.D   49.D

24.D 84.D 51.D 80.D   8.D   150.D

113.D 138.D   90.D

43.D 7.D

53.D 86.D 70.D   Summa   123.D   24.D 136.D   43.D

70.D 138.D   Kivennaparrr

Koivisto   Kuolemajärvi

100.D

Saarenpää   Terijoki

Finnish Front Line

Kaur

← Russian Divisions

GULF OF FINLAND

0   20 miles
0   20 km

tunate Finnish ministers who prowled the corridors of the chancelleries of Europe, not to mention the energetic Hjalmar Procopé in Washington, were met with tea and sympathy, but little else. Any progress in procurement in mainland Europe (and there had been some) up to 10 January was swiftly stalled by the revelation of the scope and, more critically, the potential timing of the German plans in the West.

THE SUPREME WAR COUNCIL met on 5 February to ratify the decision to intervene in Finland. Churchill, in his maiden attendance and still on probation since his speech of 20 January, is not recorded as having made any contribution whatsoever, Daladier rather setting the pace of the conversations. Perhaps the most critical conclusion reached, however, was that the whole operation would now be under British command – now that Daladier had his way politically, he was quite happy to allow the British General Staff to run the military risk of the project. Ironside reported to his diary: 'Everybody purring with pleasure. I wondered if we should all be in the same state if we had a little adversity to touch us up. All is plain sailing. The French are handing the operation over to us and are sitting back pretty.'[5]

Still, nobody told the Finns of the plan. A disbelieving George Gripenberg, attending a reception on 8 February, was startled to be told of the proposed operation by several newspapermen who asserted that, 'within a week, a French, British and a Polish Division were to land in Finland.'[6] This after he had spent a fruitless afternoon at the Foreign Office on the very matter, attempting to find out the decision of the Supreme War Council as rumours to this effect were circulating rapidly; he had been fobbed off by a junior official. In fact, his journalistic sources reported, Daladier had leaked the news two days before. Clearly, a certain instability was becoming obvious. Also, a chilling realism. Ironside had further confided: 'One is almost frightened at the boldness of the plan, knowing what slender means one has at the moment to carry it out. We must see that we are politically strong and that we remain quite cynical about everything except stopping the iron ore.'[7]

Naturally, the rumours of intervention had their effects on an otherwise depressed French stock market. For years, the bond certificates of French-financed Tsarist Russian corporations had been pushed about by bored stockjobbers in a desultory manner, mainly for their curiosity value. Now, as the dreams of men like Senator Bardoux started to affect a wider audience, the price of these certificates, long in default and effectively wampum since the Russian Revolution, actually started to rise – a sure sign that someone in Paris was taking this very seriously indeed. So was Väinö Tanner who, as the Supreme War Council met, was on his way to Stockholm.

AS THE FIRST WEEK of February came to an end, it became apparent to the Finns that the Red Army's initial artillery assault on the Isthmus was rather limp – not a rehearsal for something quite vast. Red Army casualties were, despite the artillery preparation, still on the scale that had forced them to suspend offensive operations in December. It was not clear to the Finns that the Soviet attack was being intensively monitored, as Timoshenko drew up the final details of the assault that was to come. The offensive (or what appeared to be an offensive) was better coordinated than before, but little more than that at present.

During the intervals between bombardments in the first days of February, the Seventh and Thirteenth Red Armies conducted what were referred to by the Russians as 'demonstration' operations to attack at five points along the Finnish defence line. In effect, these were experiments in the exercise of independent, delegated command at regimental strength, under live-fire conditions: vivisection. By and large they were successful, but at some cost. Horrified, the Finnish defenders watched as T-28 and T-26 tanks operated in close support with swarms of infantry, the lighter T-26 machines, equipped as 'chemical tanks', spewing forth flaming liquid naphtha at defender and attacker alike, the Russian machines grinding the living and dead bodies of friend and foe beneath them. Russian infantry followed in echelon behind the triple-turreted T-28 tanks; for the first time it was observed that the disparate arms of the Red Army were operating in something like close cooperation as the huge machines ground their way toward the Finnish blockhouses.[8]

The defenders were not to know that the storm groups were in direct contact with their respective artillery support units and, for the first time, were able to call down and, critically, correct previously inaccurate fire by means of the field telephone cables that now trailed back to the guns. It would make a crucial difference in the February offensive, this improved communication, particularly as the Red Army soldiers came to make their final assault. Rather than rely on divisional or regimental artillery, however, the assault groups were ordered to destroy the Finnish strong points by using high explosive charges, which they would themselves deliver. The explosives were carried in armoured sledges that the tanks towed behind them, and the infantry would place these charges against the strong points.[9] To the Finns this appeared to be mere gimmickry.

Naturally, the Russian commanders in the field had only the haziest idea of the strength of the individual Finnish fortifications, or even of the exact location of many of them, so well camouflaged were they. Rumours had even spread that the concrete bunkers were protected by sprung steel plates (like the side skirts of a tank), a bizarre variation on which was that they were further coated with rubber sheets, causing grenades and other projectiles to bounce off. Such had been the slaughter involved so far, there were soldiers in the attacking divisions who would have been happy to believe anything.

A different matter was the new KV1[10], a 47-ton behemoth, which now saw its first large-scale service in this phase of the war, after occasional previous forays in December. It was to all intents and purposes invulnerable to anything but a lucky direct hit from a medium or heavy shell, a matter that was reduced to only an academic probability as the Army of the Isthmus started to run out of field artillery rounds; Mannerheim's initial back-of-the-envelope calculation concerning ordnance supplies was proving to be depressingly accurate. The delays in trans-shipping weapons from Norway and Sweden were starting to prove vital – a cargo arriving in Norway could, due to the lack of suitable transport, take up to a month to reach the Karelian front. Telegrams flew out of Helsinki in an urgent appeal for more war *matériel*; in London, Ironside saw General Enckell who, shuttling between London and Paris, passed on a request for artillery from Mannerheim: 'These demands are heartbreaking to refuse', the ex-gunner recorded sadly.

IN WASHINGTON, poor Hjalmar Procopé was in something of an emotional state. Having ascertained that there were 200 17-pounder field guns sitting in a war surplus warehouse, he was now attempting to buy them.[11] They were of British design and manufacture and had seen service with the American Expeditionary Force in 1918. As such, they were comparatively 'state of the art' as compared to the current Finnish artillery park, which as we have seen was, in parts at least, of museum quality. In essaying this undertaking, the entrepreneurial (and tearfully frustrated) minister came up against Secretary of State Cordell Hull at his most pious:

> I then made it clear to the Minister and his two associates the entire improbability of this government selling arms, ammunition or implements of war to the Government of Finland. I said I did not want them to be misled for a moment. They sought to bring up the technical law in the matter. I replied that wherever fighting was taking place and whatever it might be called in technical law, the one matter of concern in this country is that this Government does not engage in acts or utterances that might materially endanger its peace and safety by causing it to be drawn into war. In these circumstances, I stated that, in my opinion, it need not be expected that this Government would sell arms, ammunition and implements of war to the Government of Finland.[12]

This rather relieved General George Marshall, who had been forced to admit at least the existence of the guns (along with some 8-inch howitzers of similar vintage) until, that is, he received a memorandum from the White House, 'suggesting to the General that the next move in supplying the Finns was up to him.'[13] Marshall did not assume this questionable responsibility – the responsibility for Finland was now passing around faster than a hockey puck. Which was a pity for Finland – Ironside, already critically short of artillery of his own, knew full well of the existence of these weapons (as well as anything else which might be available – worldwide) and would indeed request them on Finland's behalf: 'It is difficult to follow such a mentality, but there it is, clear enough…'[14]

Procopé did not give up, but was in danger of losing what little composure he understandably had left: '…if this government refused to sell arms to his government at this juncture, the decision would be tantamount to signing a death warrant for his country' reads a memo penned by an embarrassed White House aide. What Procopé (and many others) failed to realize was that the American agenda would not, and could not, include an acceptance of the European status quo as being anything other than fragmentary and rotten to the core. The fact that Finland – indeed the whole of Scandinavia – represented perhaps a shining exception to this dismal norm no doubt caused Roosevelt to 'wobble' over the matter of the Winter War, but not sufficiently to allow him to run the risk of veering away from the Holy Writ of his stated policy.

Americans, as a rule, disapproved strongly of the chaos of European politics, which had permitted the emergence of the dictators who now threatened world stability. A series of public opinion polls had revealed by 1937 that the majority of Americans believed that participation in the Great War had been an error[15] – twenty years after the USA had joined the war, here was the result – Hitler, Mussolini and Stalin (whose predecessor had actually been put in to place by the *Germans*), with the confused French and the indolent British (with their morally questionable empire) unable to dominate events. The price to be paid by those whose motives were perhaps more honourable, more *American* – particularly the Finns – was regrettably high, but, as Ironside had remarked, 'there it was, clear enough'.[16]

In one sense, then, American policy regarding the political crisis that had led to a state of war between Germany and the Allies was not so dissimilar to the Soviet one – to let them fight it out, resulting in a 'radical reduction in the weight of Europe'[17] but the near-death experience suffered by the Finns certainly served to weaken some of this resolve, as the internationalist cause within America found a *cause célèbre*, and with it, a very loud voice. Even the state of Minnesota would struggle to absorb 3.8 million new residents, however welcome they would be.

One American who would grasp the significance of the events in Finland was the talented and prolific Robert E. Sherwood, ironically at this moment also employed as a speechwriter for Roosevelt. After hearing the Christmas broadcast made by CBS's Bill White 'from the Finnish Front',[18] Sherwood was moved to write *And There Shall Be No Night*, which quickly received its first airing on Broadway in 1940. One of its themes is the transformation, from pacifist to activist, of a Finnish family. The play won Sherwood yet another Pulitzer Prize for his already crowded mantelpiece.[19]

THE MORNING OF SUNDAY, 11 February, saw a thick, milky fog descend upon the Karelian Isthmus, making the scheduled Soviet aerial attack impossible. Not so artillery; accordingly, the barrage that had been scheduled for 10.30 a.m. was unleashed an hour early. It was to be the first movement of a truly shocking symphony; an artillery barrage the like of which had not been seen since the Great War and would not be seen again until 1944.[20] Not only was it audible in both Leningrad and Viipuri, but across the frozen Gulf of Finland as far as Estonia.

It lasted until noon, whereupon the yellow signal flares drifted up into the clearing sky and Gorolenko's L Rifle Corps moved forward. There were two rifle divisions in the van; Ermakov's 100th and Alabushev's 123rd.[21] These two units were to attack either side of Lake Summajärvi.

The Russians had been issued vodka[22] with their breakfast – they would need it. Tension was high as the divisions moved forward. Alexander Tvardovski recalled a junior officer being berated on a field telephone for being slow off the mark – 'Attack, f..k your mother!' – by a more senior commander, safe in the command post.[23] Or so he thought, until Finnish artillery rounds started to land nearby; the Russians were simply staggered that the 'sons of bitches' could even return fire, let alone this accurately.

The 100th Division was so badly mauled by the dense Finnish cross-fire that it was forced to withdraw back to its start point and regroup by the evening. The 123rd fared better, and by the end of the 11th, had advanced east of Summajärvi, 1,200 yards into the main defence line towards Lähde, and had set about blowing up Finnish fortifications. There were two bunkers in particular that commanded the road through Lähde up to Kämärä station, which were the primary targets. Aliabushev's men had rehearsed the procedures necessary – to the rear, full-scale mock-ups had been constructed in January to familarize the attacking troops with the structure and bulk of the obstacles.

The first structure to fall was the 'Poppius' bunker, whose crew evacuated it to continue the fight in the open. It had been comprehensively wrecked already, and the Russian tactic, of simply parking an armoured vehicle in front of the firing embrasure, meant that it was effectively useless, armed as it was only with machine guns. It was captured at 1.30 p.m.

The second strong point, the 'Million' bunker, also extensively damaged, took rather longer.[24] Finnish resistance was so fierce that the fighting lasted through the night, but the result was by now a foregone conclusion as the Russian tanks dragged up sleds laden with thousands of pounds of explosive. At 5 a.m. on the morning of the 12th, the Million bunker was destroyed in a truly massive explosion, which killed every defender within it. Consistently, the 123rd Division seemed to set a higher standard than any other Red Army unit in the area and was awarded (as a unit) the Order of Lenin three days later by a relieved Kremlin – the first of a tide of awards and decorations.[25]

Finnish units kept counter-attacking with savage, spoiling jabs, each of which were expensive for them, but vitally serving to keep the Red Army forces off balance. However, as soon as the line was breached even once (and the loss of the two key bunkers was seriously important), it became uncomfortably clear that its integrity, its ability to support itself, was also lost. Without the murderous cross-fires behind prepared defences, which the design of the modest line allowed, the Finnish Army was now faced with the prospect of fighting itself to exhaustion in open battle or, more prudently, falling back to its modest prepared defences.

The Finnish instinct – to counter-attack in the face of this setback – was still strong, however. The Kannas Army simply no longer had the resources to launch a major offensive along the lines of the 23 December operation, but none the less, it tried to plug the gap in the line that the 123rd Division had made. It was a grotesquely uneven fight against tanks supported by infantry, and by nightfall, after sustaining terrible losses – some entire Finnish companies were wiped out completely – the gap remained, and it seemed that the war, and Finland, would now come swiftly to an end.

Inexplicably, possibly because of exhaustion, the Russians failed to press home their advantage. Had the Seventh Army (or even L Corps alone) poured through the gap and spread out in the rear of the Mannerheim Line, then subsequent events (indeed, the Second World War) would have been radically different, and yet Meretskov did not order a general advance for some days. It is of course equally possible that the simple speed of the initial success on 11 February took the Red Army command (and the Kremlin) by as much surprise as it had the Finns.

AS THE RED ARMY was making its first serious breakthrough, events in Norway were further raising the tension. It had been generally suspected for some time that the principal supply ship of the *Admiral Graf Spee* (which had been scuttled by its captain off Montevideo in December) was carrying several hundred British merchant seamen, survivors from the activities of the German pocket battleship in the South Atlantic. The vessel, the *Altmark*, had been spotted inside Norwegian territorial waters by the Fleet Air Arm on 16 February.

This was a ticklish situation; to board the *Altmark*, even to release prisoners, was a technical breach of both international law and Norwegian neutrality, which, as we have seen, was under enough pressure already. A carefully worded dispatch was sent out by Churchill to Captain Philip Vian, commanding the destroyer HMS *Cossack* and a small flotilla, who had sped to the reported location. A stand-off ensued between the *Cossack* and two (outmatched) Norwegian torpedo boats, who claimed that the *Altmark* was unarmed, a matter which, they claimed, they had ascertained by a previous search of the German vessel. After the *Altmark* attempted to ram the *Cossack*, she ran aground and Vian's sailors boarded her; four German sailors were killed in the ensuing fight but in the hold Vian discovered 299 British prisoners.

The *Altmark* was armed, the prisoners were there, and the Norwegians had not searched the ship.[26] To British public morale, the *Altmark* incident provided a boost not seen since the action against the *Graf Spee* and went some way to offset the gloom at the news that the Mannerheim Line had been broken, a matter to which the British Cabinet, perhaps calmed by the public approval that action (and enemy deaths) in Scandinavia had received, now turned itself.

GIVEN THE LOW TEMPERATURES the Gulf of Finland, like the Ladoga, was frozen enough to allow even the heaviest of vehicles to cross it. This was the third element of Timoshenko's attack, a flanking movement over the ice in an attempt to turn the Finnish defences from the opposite end from that which had been the task of the Eighth Army, which was still mired and dying in *mottis* north of the Ladoga.

Initially, the venture on to the ice was conducted by marines of the Baltic fleet in battalion strength, later reinforced by armour.[27] They were vulnerable to the ever-vigilant Finnish coastal batteries, but were sensibly dressed in winter coveralls and almost invisible on the ice. Not so their armoured support, when it arrived.[28] The

Finnish guns simply blasted holes in the ice, with the same predictable results that had proved to be the dreadful end of so many of
the 163rd Division fleeing over the frozen lake from Suomussalmi.

For the next month, pressure on the coast of Finland from the
frozen Gulf would intensify as the Red Army, still taking horrendous losses on land, started to attempt a leapfrog to leave the
Mannerheim Line and its fall-back positions isolated and irrelevant. Quite shortly, the focus shifted radically – from a frontal
assault through stiff resistance, despite the breach in the line, to
a full-blown race for Viipuri before the ice in the gulf melted. As
the intense cold that had characterized this strange winter, and
which had compromised everyone's planning, showed no signs of
abating, the coincidental benefits that had helped the Finnish
Army and had hindered the Baltic fleet, now started to act against
the Finns. In effect, the solid ice in the Gulf of Finland presented
a broader front than any Soviet commander could have wished
for, and about which any Finnish commander – Mannerhiem
included – could only have had nightmares. Coastal defences
suddenly found themselves functionally inland. It seems that this
aspect of Timoshenko's attack was, although important (indeed,
would constitute a large proportion of the Red Army's final effort),
a matter of opportunistic expediency.

The Finnish Air Force, acquitting itself with a brio and skill
(not to mention persistence) easily the equal of the Royal Air Force
only months later, was offered some startling targets of opportunity as February ground on.[29] Leavened by some welcome reinforcements (but still outnumbered by at least eight to one) it was
merciless in its strafing of the soldiers on the ice. Russian casualties were quite appalling, as they were effectively defenceless
against air attack. Further, as their mass increased, the Finnish
shore batteries, short of ammunition as they were, simply fired
to break up the ice around them. Little accuracy was needed.

IF THE SITUATION to the south was becoming critical, north of the
Ladoga General Hägglund's forces were slowly grinding the
Russian's 18th Division down. Unlike the 54th further North,

which would hold out (partly due to aerial resupply) until the end of the war, these men were in dire straights, and had been since their initial encirclement in January. They had commenced killing and eating their transport horses early on as their rations had run out, but again, as at the Raate road, Finnish interdiction of field kitchens and open fires prevented the cooking of them on a large scale. In essence, the 18th Division was in a state of every man (and woman – there were many) for himself. The effect of these conditions on a soldier's digestion is not hard to calculate.

A diary found at the east Lemetti *motti*, and apparently written by a soldier in the 34th Tank Brigade (attached to the 18th Division) reveals some of the aspects of merely existing under these horrible conditions. These recovered extracts trace the period between 1 and 8 February: 'Feb 2nd – 7 a.m. It's particularly cold this morning, nearly –35°C. I was unable to sleep due to the cold. Our Artillery has been firing through the night. After I woke, I went for a shit, but at that moment the Finns opened fire, one bullet hitting the ground between my legs. I hadn't had a shit since January 25th.' The unfortunate soldier did not manage to do so until 6 February, when: 'My stomach is completely empty. Some soldiers around me are frying some horse meat. Some have gone out to gather horse bones.' And the next day:

'The driver … is boiling intestines and offal and eating the soup. It sickens me, but I'm nearly willing to try it, and perhaps I'll be forced to it as I'm steadily running out of food, no matter how well I regulate my personal stock … I'm feeling dizzy in the mornings.'[30]

In an environment where a human requires a *minimum* of 4,000 calories per day merely to get, even inactively, through it, these soldiers (the record ends on 8 February) were receiving perhaps a tenth of that – not a situation that could have been expected to persist without their total collapse. There is also evidence that a serious influenza bug was further debilitating their ability to fight.

By the time it was clear that the Mannerheim Line was breached (and would stay breached) Hägglund had stepped up the pressure at Mannerheim's order; the situation on the Isthmus required more men than the Finnish Army now disposed of. Mannerheim was fully aware that help might be on the way, but it was also clear to him that the Allied assistance that had been discussed was not going to arrive immediately, despite the optimism of Gripenberg's journalistic sources.

IN PARIS, the Finnish minister Harri Holma was suddenly a very popular man, but for reasons that rather eluded him. In constant receipt of extravagant undertakings as to the level of Allied support that his country was about to receive (this despite the fact that the French had put the responsibility for the management of the support operation in the hands of the British), Holma's understanding therefore differed radically from that of Gripenberg in London. Gripenberg's main points of contact were either uncooperative clerks in the Foreign Office or Alexander Cadogan, who dealt with him as plainly as he could according to his remit, which, as a result of British War Cabinet indecision, shape-shifted rapidly. Gripenberg's encounters with Halifax were, despite the Finnish minister's respect for the man (clear from his memoirs), less than revealing. Holma, on the other hand, was dealing with Daladier, who, as this crisis unfolded, started to exhibit a self-regard – an almost chemical need to set the pace – that was quite inconsistent with the Supreme War Council agenda agreed on 5 February. It was this paradox – the French extravagant, the British regretfully realistic – which would come, quite logically, to govern Finnish attitudes over the coming weeks. It would also, for exactly opposed reasons, govern British ones.

One diplomatist who had not, in Finnish eyes, covered himself in glory was the British ambassador in Helsinki, Thomas Snow. He had, according to Tanner, 'lost his nerve when the first bombs fell' and was recalled on 15 February. His replacement, Gordon Vereker, who was a relative of Lord Gort, presented his credentials (in a bunker during an air raid, which rather impressed the Finns) on 24 February, accompanied by Brigadier Ling who had brought with him news of firm Allied proposals, which were already uncomfortably at variance with what Holma had been told in Paris only ten days before.

Allied response speed was rather outside the pace of the unfolding deterioration in Finland – the first breakthrough at Summa was made only a week after the last Supreme War Council meeting and the diaries of those involved reflect, particularly at the political level, a creeping paralysis, not the least reason for which was the natural concern that if Finland fell, then the tenuous justification for what the Council was proposing to do – the League of Nations resolution – would fall with it in the manner that the Allied guarantees to a dismembered Poland had. Certainly the Swedes thought so, as a depressed Väinö Tanner started to come under pressure from that quarter to treat with the Russians.

His Cabinet colleagues were rather split on this issue. Defence Minister Niukkanen, still adhering to a bullish view (entirely at odds with the military realities), insisted that more aid from Sweden would buy enough time for the Finnish Army to survive until the spring thaw, which would have the effect of shortening the front dramatically. His view carried some weight, as it turned out. Mannerheim urged a settlement; his concern, that Finland should still have an effective army, was paramount.

Accordingly, this first break in the Mannerheim Line finally goaded the Allied planners into action – if they were to justify a military presence on the greater Scandinavian peninsula as the Finns started to crack under the pressure of Timoshenko's assault, then they would need to move swiftly. It was certainly not lost on Ironside that two months had passed since the original initiative at the December Supreme War Council, and as the initial probing attacks of the first week of February had marked a step up in Soviet activity, he had noted: 'Reports are not so good from the Mannerheim Line ... I am wondering what will happen if it bursts before the date upon which we can act. The Cabinet will try to rush me, and I shall have to resist.'[31]

THE RESPONSE OF the Finnish General Staff to the crises at Summa and Lähde was, within the overall context of its dismay, relatively measured, even calm. Naturally, there were contingency plans ready – to fall back on the western half of the Isthmus to an intermediate defence line – the V-line – as retaking Summa was hardly a realistic possibility; even as the Red Army was slow in exploiting its advantage, Russian superiority of numbers was now higher than it had yet been. Accordingly, Mannerheim ordered Östermann to withdraw the II Corps at his discretion, an option he exercised immediately on 16 February. Three days later Östermann submitted his resignation; he was distracted by the news that his wife, injured in an air raid, was far from well and cited his own ill-health as his reason. Mannerheim consented with little comment, replacing him with Heinrichs (Öhqvist was – and would remain – out of favour). To take over Heinrichs's III Corps, the Marshal appointed General Talvela.

The situation on the Isthmus was now critical, with only a handful of committed reserves, most of whom were designated to reinforce the hard-pressed troops in Ladoga-Karelia, still holding out against a reinforced Russian attack that had been stepped up as Summa fell. There were isolated small units available, but nothing in more than reduced battalion strength apart from the 13th Division, at present on its way under Hägglund's orders to relieve Kollaa. Reluctantly, the II Corps withdrew under the cover of the shore batteries at Björkö.

The withdrawal was completed by 21 February, whereupon the Björkö garrison was ordered to use up what little ammunition it had left and then destroy its tired guns. The Finnish soldiers were forced to trek past the extreme left of the Red Army, across the frozen Gulf, 25 miles back to the new defence line, which was already under pressure. A blizzard on 23 February afforded them some cover.

At the V-line, it seems the Red Army reverted to its suicidal tactics of December – massed infantry, uncoordinated with armour. Again, it proved expensive – it may well be that the intensity (and disorganization) of this attack was designed as a decoy against the planned Russian move over the ice to attack Viipuri from the frozen sea. With the Björkö batteries now abandoned, there was some more room for the Russians to manoeuvre, but this phase of the plan relied upon the single fundamental of the strength of the ice. Errors in estimating this might result in the biggest military disaster since the Pharoah's attempted crossing of the Red Sea. The risk was deemed justifiable and, in the event, it was.

IN STOCKHOLM, little progress was made. Negotiations, such as they were, were taking place under conditions of total secrecy. Given that Tanner was a well-known face in the Swedish capital, he could initially only meet with Kollontay in Wuolijoki's suite in the Grand Hotel, late at night. He could not even take the elevator – he had to use the staff stairway, a necessary indignity that he bore stoically. His subsequent meetings were arranged with the reluctant (but necessary) offices of the Swedish Foreign Ministry. The Soviet terms that had emerged by the time Summa fell were harsh, to say the least – Hanko Cape, most of Karelia, including all the Isthmus, Viipuri and Sortavala, together with all the offshore islands over which the October–November haggling had taken place. In short, Peter the Great's border, sweeping aside the Treaty of Tartu in its entirety. The Swedes were starting to urge the Finns to accept these terms, punctuating this with a public announcement that Sweden would send none of its army to Finland.[32]

For Swedish and Soviet policy regarding Finland were now effectively one. Despite the assurances received by both Count Rosen and Sven Hedin, Hansson's government remained far more concerned about German intervention on the Scandinavian peninsula than they were about Russian expansionism. The fact that the Finns had fought the Red Army to a bloody standstill naturally made the latter contingency less likely, but Allied plans were now an open secret, which put Norwegian and Swedish relations with Finland – at the government level at least – under a huge strain. At the popular level, it was rather different. The private fund-raising initiatives, tolerated – even encouraged – by the Swedish government, were of a genuinely massive order. It seems that the departed Foreign Minister Sandler still had his supporters, particularly on the right.

Thus, the political tensions by the middle of February were vast; the Allies separated by motive – the French seeking a new front, the British intent on the iron ore with greater Scandinavia fully aware of that – against a Germany anxious for a settlement for economic reasons, and the Soviet Union still pursuing territorial rectification even though the Red Army had failed to take the whole country. All these forces now rotated around the fulcrum of Finland.

The initiative to inform Britain of the Russian proposals was launched on the evening of 22 February, when Maisky approached one of the few people in government still to speak to him, Richard Butler. Butler had in fact invited the approach when lunching with Maisky on the 16th. The proposals, which unknown to the British Cabinet had already been put to Tanner in Stockholm, were discussed the next day in Cabinet. Cadogan noted: 'About 7.15 H [Halifax] back from Cabinet. They had reacted strongly against Maisky's suggestions of last night to R.A.B. about peace terms for Finland. I am v. glad R.A.B. disgusted – I am sure he saw here another chance of appeasement.'[33] Perhaps he did, but Halifax passed the proposals on to Gripenberg, only commenting that the Cabinet felt them to be too harsh to merit further comment, and the government would not act as an intermediary between Helsinki and Moscow on that basis. Gripenberg, uninformed as to Tanner's detailed progress in Stockholm, interpreted the approach not as a serious peace feeler, rather an attempt to make the secret talks guardedly public in order to forestall the Allied intervention that Moscow feared so much; he was almost certainly correct. The prospect of peace would wreck Allied designs – every reason, then, to decline the role of peace broker. Put crudely, the longer this war went on, the more chance of successful mischief in greater Scandinavia.

Gordon Vereker's first task as British Ambassador, after presenting his credentials, was to state Allied intentions. He explained to Tanner that between 20,000 and 22,000 men could be available to depart from Britain on 15 March provided the Finnish government made a formal request for their dispatch by 5 March, which was ten days away (1940 was a leap year) when he provided the details on 24 February. He stressed that the soldiers would be heavily armed: 'In firepower, they correspond', said Vereker, 'to ordinary forces of at least double the number.'[34] Brigadier Ling, who was present, managed to keep a straight face – he knew exactly the composition of the force, but four days before, when closely questioned by Mannerheim as to its various qualities, had hedged somewhat concerning how many would actually arrive.

The force was, in fact, rather smaller in number than Vereker had suggested. Ironside and General Audet had between them managed to identify a modest force of 15,500, coded Force Avonmouth, drawn from the Brigade of Guards, the Foreign Legion, the Polish Brigade and the Chasseurs Alpins;[35] all excellent soldiers, certainly, but also unsupported by advanced kit – everything would have to be delivered to Finland, via the ore fields at Gällivare by the single electric railway. It had already been noted, by Ironside at least, that the Swedes by the simple expedient of switching off the electrical power could effectively strand this mixed infantry division exactly where they chose. Of course, sabotaging the power supply would also mean that the iron ore could not move either – but was this worth the fortunes of an entire division? The answer, given the importance of the ore, was probably in the affirmative.

But others on the Allied Staff were not so sure. In France, General Alan Brooke, soon to be Ironside's successor (and a commander of exceptional ability) entertained persistent and early doubts:[36]

> The proposed plans fill me with gloom. They are based on the assumption that the Germans will not attack on this front during the spring. Personally I hold diametrically opposed views. Any forward move of the Germans on this front must necessarily bring operations in subsidiary theatres to a standstill, but unfortunately by then we shall have seriously reduced our strength on this front and will be less well able to meet any attack.'[37]

Shortly afterwards, Brooke wrote to General Sir John Dill from France: 'There is only one front that matters in this war during 1940, and that is this front. It is the only front during the present year on which the war can be won or lost, and it is quite shattering to see its security endangered.'[38]

THE QUESTION OF whether the Norwegians and Swedes would grant the force right of passage – within the terms of the League of Nations resolution – was obviously uppermost in the minds of all concerned. Further, should passage be demanded, would the Norwegians and Swedes resist? Given the experience of the *Altmark*, perhaps the Norwegians would not. The Swedes, in need of further confirmation that Germany would 'permit' either escalation of their role or look away while Allied troops crossed through to Finland, would not be encouraged by Hitler's response to Sven Hedin on 4 March, when he stated firmly that any Allied presence on the Scandinavian peninsula would trigger a response by the Reich, although material extra-Swedish aid to Finland would not. The Führer also took the opportunity to restate his personal gripe against the Finns, and expound on what he considered to be British policy: 'The British care nothing about Finland *per se*, and when the Finns had played their part in the British plans, the British, smiling coldly [*kaltlächelnd*] would drop them. One thing was sure: If England got a foothold anywhere in Scandinavia, then Germany for her part would intervene at once, since she could not permit such a threat to her flank', ran the official German record.[39] Actually, three days before, Hitler had stepped up the theoretical *Studie Nord* to a full-blown operation – *Fall Weserübung*.[40] The architect of the final plan for this was General Nikolaus von Falkenhorst, who had served with von der Golz in 1918. Von Falkenhorst had no particular knowledge of Norway, and so on 21 February, Hitler and Keitel invited him to acquire some. Accordingly, he went shopping for a second-hand Baedeker guide at lunchtime and 'retired with it to my hotel room'. By 5.00 p.m. his *pro forma* plan was ready; by such methods are significant plans occasionally made.

Falkenhorst's outline was, for such a compressed effort, quite brilliant. Stressing the importance of combined operations, case *Weserübung* was to be the first encounter on the ground between the Reich and the Western Allies and the outcome would have a profound effect. Grand Admiral Raeder would come to regret his enthusiastic sponsorship for the initiative, however; it would cost the German Navy dear.

But by that time, what had been clear to Marshal Mannerheim for some time was also evident to anyone else who could read a map; Finland was not going to manage to hold out much longer. With the Red Army in possession of the eastern islands and the original defence line, it had also stepped up the offensive over the ice in the Gulf of Viipuri, now threatening the city from the south-west. Repeatedly, the Finnish troops beat it back whenever it forced a beachhead, but now no less than four fresh divisions, with full armoured support as well as air cover, were making tiny incremental gains behind the new defence line. Viipuri itself was already under artillery attack from railway-borne cannon parked on the Leningrad–Viipuri track. Ancient and inaccurate though these weapons were, they were also huge. Finnish radio traffic was monitored in order to discover the effect of the bombardment on the population. It was dire.

Such was the pressure now that Mannerheim decided to attempt to bolster the coastal defence with a new commander – he reluctantly sent for Wallenius, whose Lapland command, nearest the Swedish border, had been bolstered somewhat by the arrival of Swedish and Norwegian volunteers.[41] When Wallenius arrived at the Isthmus he was stunned at the state of affairs. Compared to the wilderness from which he had come, with the Red Army held in check with relative ease in rolling, open country, the crowded, panicked maelstrom he found on the coastal region, with Russian troops pouring across the ice and the most desperate fighting of the war so far, his nerve collapsed completely – he retreated to his command post and became very drunk indeed. After he disappeared on a three-day bender, Mannerheim dismissed him, effectively cashiering him as well. His reputation and nerve ruined, Wallenius left the Finnish Army, never to return. Mannerheim replaced him with his own deputy, General Oesch.

On 26 February, the ever-vigilant von Blücher's latest report arrived in Berlin. It was already somewhat dated (dispatched four days previously)[42] and with his usual perception, he summed up the condition of the Finns quite accurately. He mentions in it the presence of Ling and the French General Ganeval, and further points out that Allied intervention (probably at Narvik) seemed more likely now given the *Altmark* incident – Norwegian neutrality, as the Führer had already concluded, had been tested and found rather wanting. He concluded:

> 'In view of the uncertain basis of these speculations, I shall at present refrain from going into German military countermeasures. There is no doubt in my mind, however, that the neatest [*eleganteste*] solution would be to compose the Finnish-Russian conflict before the Western guardian angels have time to arrive and take the Swedish ore, instead of Finland, under their wings.'[43]

This time, there was no rebuff from either Ribbentrop or Weizsäcker. Indeed, the Foreign Minister now scrawled a marginal note: 'For F. [Führer]. Von Blücher had finally found his audience, and probably repaired his career[44] – and Ribbentrop had reached the upper limits of his own.

By contrast, Kurt Bräuer, perhaps energized by the assurances of Koht (however unsatisfactory Schreiber's conversation with Admiral Diesen had been) seemed relaxed as to Allied intentions in Norway.[45] Of the two opinions the Führer, not unnaturally, favoured von Blücher's. The big decision, with a spring thaw (however late) now critically important, was whether to press ahead with *Fall Gelb*, or to trigger *Weserübung*. He decided on 3 March (according to General Jodl's diary) to take care of Norway first 'with a few days' interval' between them. France was important, but the major objective, the destruction of the Soviet Union, was far more so. For that, copious amounts of strategic metal were going to be needed, much of which, under the trade agreements already extant, Germany was receiving from the Soviet Union.

Originally, *Studie Nord* had included the occupation of Sweden; when Göring discovered this he was appalled. He entertained (personally, highly flexible) notions of honour, and he had previously given his personal assurance to von Rosen that Sweden would remain inviolate. It seems that his conversation with Rosen had not had the authority of the Führer behind it, as Göring had pretended it had. The representations he now made to Hitler included an offer to resign if Sweden were attacked or occupied[46]. The Führer's reply was pragmatic: would the Swedes permit transit of German troops? Göring saw no problem, he assured him.[47] Relieved (despite the fact that Hitler refused to support Göring's original warranties to Rosen), he wrote to his stepson Thomas von Kantzow, at present in service with the Finns: 'You will just have to go on taking my word for it that it will never happen.'[48]

OTHER NEGOTIATIONS in Stockholm were going nowhere – in a rerun of the autumn talks, Tanner was handicapped by both secrecy and the Cabinet's indecision as it attempted to respond to the positive news from Ladoga-Karelia and Lapland rather than the unfolding disaster around Viipuri. It became clear that the back door diplomacy that Tanner and Kollontay were essaying (they got on fairly well, in fact) was fruitless. So impatient was the Kremlin that the message went out that unless Finland accepted the revised Soviet terms, then the dreaded Kuusinen government would reappear.[49] Kollontay attempted to be calming – perhaps Stalin would make a grand gesture? The Finnish response to this was to request more time (the decision to request the Allied troops had been due on 5 March) from London and Paris as to their needs for assistance, which, although it triggered alarm, was extended by Daladier, with British acquiescence, to 12 March.

The battle for the Gulf of Viipuri was now reaching its hysterical and bloody climax. Waves of Russian infantry were slaughtered as they poured pell-mell across the ice, which, it was reasoned, might start to melt at any time. Tanks, trucks, horses, motorized sleds – even appropriated private cars – raced, skidding across the frozen and bloody surface, to be met by a desperate, withering fire from the few remaining Finnish coastal batteries, which were fast running out of ammunition. Finally, on the evening of 5 March, an entire division (the 173rd Motor Rifle) managed to establish a beach-head, and Viipuri was now effectively cut off from Helsinki.

The suggestion came, on 6 March, that a Finnish delegation be sent to Moscow and Risto Ryti accepted with alacrity, arriving the next day, accompanied by Paasikivi, Walden and Väinö Voionmaa, a Cabinet secretary and official of the Diet. Because of Soviet refusals to entertain a truce, or even a brief ceasefire while talks were going on, the pressure upon the group was vast.[50] Importantly, the dilatory Finnish Cabinet, even the previously optimistic Niukkanen, could now see that the situation was rapidly becoming hopeless. They resolved to buy as much time as possible, and the only weapon at their disposal now, apart from the exhausted Finnish Army, was the possibility of Allied intervention.

Now that matters were coming to a head, with the Finnish delegation safely (he assumed) in Moscow, Adolf Hitler chose the moment (8 March) to reply to Mussolini's protesting note of three months before. After a wide-ranging review of the state of affairs, he came to the point which had annoyed Mussolini so much:

Finland! Germany, as I have already stressed, Duce, is fighting for her existence ... I believe that a modicum of reason and objectivity in examining and deciding these problems would have given the Finns better counsel than that of resorting to arms. Russia, I am convinced, never intended to take up this fight, for otherwise she would have chosen a different season of the year; and in that event there is no doubt in my mind that Finnish resistance would have been broken very quickly. The criticisms which have been made of the Russian soldiers[51] in consequence of the operations to date are not borne out, Duce, by the facts ... The scorn heaped upon the Russian troops, however, has in my opinion made it very hard for Stalin to accept, not to speak of to offer, a compromise. But in this instance England has no other aim than to secure a legal basis under the terms of the League of Nations by which other nations could be gradually drawn into the war. We are watching this manoeuvre, Duce, with calm attention.

He ended by drawing attention to the anti-German sentiment expressed by Finland, but: 'This does not imply, Duce, that the German people feel any hatred for the Finnish people; it merely signifies that we have no cause to champion Finland's interests.'[52] Or not yet, at least.

After a visit from Ribbentrop, who delivered the letter, Mussolini seemed satisfied with Hitler's explanation and agreed to a summit in the near future. Ribbentrop had used a strange form of words when discussing the Finnish situation referring, dismissively, to Tanner as a 'Menshevik', which he certainly had been in his youth.

THE FINNISH CABINET was handed a report from Heinrichs and fully endorsed by Mannerheim, who was by now both exhausted and quite ill. He had flu and a high temperature, and was sitting out these unseemly political deliberations at General Headquarters, wrapped in a blanket and shivering. Heinrichs had submitted this:

> As Commander of the Isthmus Army I consider it my duty to report that the present state of the Army is such that continued military operations can lead to nothing but further debilitation and fresh losses of territory. In support of my view I set forth the loss of personnel which has occurred and which is still going on. The battle strength of battalions is reported now generally to be below 250 men [53] with the aggregate daily casualties rising into the thousands. As a consequence of physical and spiritual exhaustion, the battle fitness of those who remain is not what it was when the war started. Considerable losses of officers further reduce the utility of these diminished units…
>
> …Lt. General Oesch, the Commander of the Coast Corps, has emphasised to me the scanty numbers and the moral exhaustion of his forces, and does not seem to believe he can succeed with them. Lt. General Öhqvist, Commander of II Army Corps, has expressed the opinion that if no surprises take place, his present front may last a week,

but no longer, by reason of the expenditure of personnel, particularly officers. Major General Talvela Commander of III Army Corps, expresses his view by saying that everything is hanging by a thread.

Tanner, commenting, stated flatly: 'This is the Commander-in-Chief's view. Our situation is such that we are faced by a forced peace. We must make haste before the collapse occurs. After that our views would not be asked.' It was sensible advice.

THE DIFFICULTY NOW arose of whether to ask for Allied intervention in support of the hard-pressed army. The Marshal, consistent to a fault and determined to preserve his beloved army, had known all along that the Allied force could not arrive at the Finnish front until mid April at the earliest; he further knew that the Finnish Army, having fought itself almost into a coma, could not hold out that long. His decision was critical – if he counselled that Allied assistance should be summoned, there is little doubt that the Cabinet would have supported him, but the very possibility of an Allied force of any weight being dispatched would surely spur the Red Army on to greater efforts. It was now a distinct possibility that Viipuri would fall, and shortly after, Helsinki. He now had until 12 March to call for help.

He did not; publicly, Mannerheim would blame Norwegian and Swedish obduracy as the reason for Finland remaining unassisted, even though it was clear that the Allies would arrive anyway and demand passage – the more important consideration in Mannerheim's view was that the greater war should be kept out of Scandinavia. In this, of course, the Finnish policy was to prove a failure – Hitler had already taken steps to ensure that.

Ryti was in an unenviable position in Moscow. Not only had the proposal for a ceasefire been rejected out of hand, but Stalin himself was absent from the conference table. Instead, he and his colleagues were faced by a stern trio: Molotov, Zhdanov and Shaposhnikov's protégé, General Vasilevski, these latter two having been completely uninvolved up until now. Certainly a 'grand gesture', as offered by Kollontay seemed off the agenda, given that Stalin had failed to turn up. Even worse for Ryti, there were now more demands. While the Soviets offered to vacate Petsamo (its capture had been purely for prophylactic purposes) they now demanded the construction of a railway to the Finnish border with Sweden. 'Madame Kollontay must have forgotten to mention that,' stated Molotov dismissively.

All cables to Helsinki had, perforce, to travel via the Swedish Embassy, and so it was not long before the Swedish Cabinet had access to them. Günther, while telling Tanner that Swedish policy could not change, rounded privately on the embarrassed Kollontay, accusing her angrily of bad faith – her government had behaved 'intolerably'.[54]

As the Finns had been leisurely in their sense of urgency the previous autumn, so now Moscow, knowing the war was effectively won, were painstaking and plodding – to a distressed Ryti, who knew that as every hour went by, dozens, possibly hundreds more young (and not so young) Finnish soldiers were dying. The experience of attempting to negotiate against 'the logic of war' was quite agonizing – the transmission/reply cycle of cables to Helsinki was a full twelve hours.

On 10 March, General Heinrichs reported that a further collapse was likely – savage fighting was taking place in the suburbs of Viipuri, and Soviet strength was increasing as the X and XXVIII Rifle Corps poured across the beach-head created by the 173rd Motor Rifle Division. On the same day, Vereker reminded the Finns by note that they must make their request for Allied intervention by 12 March; but this time, he could not guarantee its arrival, given Swedish and Norwegian intransigence.[55] This was extraordinary (and we may see Halifax behind it); the Russians were fighting in the suburbs of Viipuri and Mannerheim, assessing the value of Allied assistance very accurately indeed, was according to this, expected to keep his army fighting on the off chance that Sweden and Norway would suddenly change their minds.

Despite the clear urgency on the Karelian Isthmus, the British Cabinet was still considering the tricky matter of Norwegian refusal to allow passage to the Allied forces, which were at that moment boarding their transport ships in the Clyde. On the 11th, Ironside recorded:

Finland again this morning ... Corbin[56] came to see Halifax and said that Daladier would resign if we did not do more over Finland. That we made much of the difficulties in telegraphing to them. That people were beginning to doubt whether we were in earnest. As a matter of actual fact [the French] have been promising far more than they can ever carry out, and doing it very deliberately in order to force the Finns to ask for help. The French, who are not responsible for the military execution of the plan, put forward the most extravagant ideas. They are absolutely unscrupulous in everything.

The Cabinet decided this morning to go on with the Narvik plan at all costs and to arrive off the port and make a demand for passage through to Finland ... I can see our great big Scots guards shouldering the sleepy Norwegians out of the way at 5.a.m. in the morning. It seems inconceivable that the Norwegians should put up any resistance if they are in any way surprised. Of course, we ran up against the Foreign Office, who wanted to protect themselves by giving notice to everyone, including the Americans, in order to 'put ourselves right with the world.' They live such a leisurely life ... We are not good poker players.'[57]

On the same day, the Finnish Cabinet bowed to the inevitable once Ryti had reported that 'not a single comma' was up for negotiation in Moscow at a meeting that had taken place the day before. They agreed to Moscow's terms: 'Let the hand wither that is forced to sign such a paper' cursed President Kallio, the ageing Karelian farmer whose personal heritage was now history.[58]

The treaty was signed on the evening of 12 March, with hostilities to cease at 11 a.m. the next day, which activity rather left Allied policy irrelevant. This, however, did not stop the Allies attempting to formulate it. On the very night that Ryti and his colleagues signed the Moscow treaty, Ironside, who had only the previous day so relished the prospect of action in Norway, now reported gloomily to his diary:

We had a dreadful Cabinet. Everybody had a different idea about how much force we would have to use at Narvik … A more unmilitary show I have never seen. The Prime Minister began peering at a chart of Narvik and when he had finished he asked me what scale it was on. He asked me what effect an 8-inch shell would have on a transport and finished up by saying he was prepared to risk a 4-inch shell but not an 8-inch shell. He then asked what the weight of the shells were. Chatfield, an Admiral of the Fleet, first said that we should not risk firing at the Norwegians, and then said that we should not be bluffed by a mere Lieutenant in charge of a shore battery. The Cabinet presented the picture of a bewildered flock of sheep faced by a problem they have consistently refused to consider … I came away disgusted with them all.'[59]

ALL, HOWEVER, with exquisite irony, was finally ready. The Allied force, code-named Avonmouth, had been sitting patiently in the Clyde aboard the *Aurora*, awaiting both Finland's call to arms and the arrival of the French, under General Audet. The former never arrived, of course, but the latter did.

The nominated commanders of Force Avonmouth, General Macksey and Admiral Evans, spent a depressing evening surveying the wreckage of their drafted orders to commanders on the ground once the civil service had 'edited' them. General Kennedy, on the planning staff, recalled:

The meeting began with Evans giving an enthusiastic exposé of the whole plan, with all its details. The Prime Minister looked tired and lugubrious enough when he began; but as Evans warmed to his subject, Mr. Chamberlain looked more and more horrified. Halifax listened in grave silence. The draft instructions to platoon commanders were passed; they were hedged about with a great many provisos, and were based 'on the same principles as those which apply to military action in aid of the civil power': this phrase has an evil connotation in the Army, since it is popularly interpreted as 'whatever you do, you'll be wrong.'

We then went on to the instructions for the Force Commander. By the time these had come through the mangle they were extremely detailed, and gave the commander little discretion…[60]

After Ironside's insistence that the 'Government would be in the hands of the General' a frisson of unease passed through the collected Cabinet. Halifax commented, most unhelpfully: 'Well, if we can't get in except at the cost of a lot of Norwegian lives, I am not for it – ore or no ore.' 'The meeting came to an end', recalled Kennedy. 'The Prime Minister shook hands with us as we filed out of the room, saying, "Good-bye, and good luck to you – if you go"'. As an exercise in military-political cooperation in time of war, this was less than encouraging for future efforts.

THE WAR, MEANWHILE, went on in Finland. Instructions regarding the ceasefire, scheduled for 11. a.m. Finnish time on 13 March, were couriered to the respective front lines, but there was widespread disbelief, as the Red Army appeared to redouble its efforts at the last minute. Salvo after fresh salvo suddenly crashed out, as the Russian artillery attempted to use up all its available ammunition. It was a spiteful, frustrated gesture, designed to inflict as much damage as possible up until the very moment of peace. Then, at the appointed hour, a colossal, echoing silence.

CHAPTER THIRTEEN

Outcomes

If an unjust and rapacious conqueror subdues a nation, and forces
her to accept hard, ignominious and unsupportable conditions, necessity
obliges her to submit, but this apparent tranquility is not a peace;
it is an oppression which she endures only so long as she wants the
means of shaking it off, and against which men of spirit rise on the first
favourable opportunity.

Emmerich de Vattel, The Law of Nations, 1758[1]

COMPARED WITH THE carpet-bagging of eastern Poland (not to
mention the crude intimidation of the hapless states of the
southern Baltic littoral) the Winter War had been, for the Soviet
Union, a dismal and embarrassing failure. The Leningrad Military
District had set itself modest objectives and signally failed to
achieve them; Shostakovich's trite little piece had failed to find
an audience, and certainly not one in Helsinki.[2]

Despite this, the events of the 105-day conflict had a profound
and depressing effect in Finland. Essentially, Finnish policy had
failed, and at all levels; it had survived initially by grit and later
as a result of Moscow's failure. Internationally, useful support had
been *de minimis*; whatever modest credits had been available in
Washington had, perforce, been devalued by the commercial
slippage of barter with Britain; whatever commercial acuity had
been displayed by the deft swapping of American loans for British
weaponry via the food market, it was unavoidably clear that
whatever had arrived (the Hurricanes being the best example) had

arrived late. Thanks to Germany, by either blockade or sheer military presence, most other armament markets were closed. In truth, Finland had captured and redeployed more Soviet weaponry against its original manufacturer than it had received from its friends, save that which can be described as having arrived from 'surprising sources'.

But most of what Finland had received, had been bought; cash on the nail. Gripenberg lost no opportunity in demonstrating this. The occasion was a meeting he attended on 14 March, the day after the news of the armistice broke. Present were Halifax and Chatfield; the subject was the return of British war *matériel* and equipment at present en route, a matter that he had discussed hotly the previous day with Cadogan, who had professed astonishment when Gripenberg acquainted him with the economic reality of what had taken place.

The encounter between Gripenberg and his interlocutors must have been a memorable one, for it is not one upon which either of the British participants chose to elaborate in their papers. Gripenberg's restrained recollection is worth reading:

> Cadogan told me he had been instructed by Halifax to ask for this meeting. The British Government wished me to put a stop on all the war material now en route to Finland. The Government itself would halt the export of those weapons that had not yet left England. 'Don't do that, Sir Alexander!' I broke in, no doubt somewhat anxiously. 'You haven't the right to do it. The material is our property...' And I told him of my arrangements with the War Office and the Export Credit [Guarantee] Department.
>
> Cadogan said he was not acquainted with these agreements. 'I thought that you had got the goods on loan from the War Ministry...'
>
> The amiable Cadogan, for whom I had always felt a genuine affection, asked me to 'do what I could [to ascertain the exact details] without going to too much trouble.'

The next day, still somewhat reeling from the news of the peace settlement, Gripenberg met with Halifax. With the Foreign Secretary was the estimable Lord Chatfield, chairman of the

Defence Coordination Committee. Halifax, informed of Gripenberg's ire, passed the buck to Chatfield:

'Chatfield, perhaps you should explain to his Excellency why we wanted this talk.' The defence Minister then proceeded to explain that since the war in Finland was now over, the Finnish Army would no longer need the weapons it had received from England. The British Government therefore desired that these should be returned as soon as possible, and he mentioned the items of most concern to the Defence Ministry.

'If I were to forward such a request to my Government', I replied, 'it would give them and my countrymen a real shock. It would not be understood. It would be said – and I wanted now to be very frank – that England never really wanted to help us.'

'I find it impossible to understand,' broke in Lord Chatfield, with some irritation, [and demonstrating neatly why he has not gone down in history as a particularly *clever* man] 'why they should say anything like that.'

Gripenberg explained that Finland was now in more danger than she had been in November of the previous year – three cities lost, a ruined army, no defence line and a million Red Army soldiers on the border – a matter which, remarkably, does not seem to have even occurred to Halifax either:

'Naturally, we do not want to do anything which would be interpreted in Finland as a stab in the back, or that would appear like we were abandoning our friends. I think that at least for the time being you need not inform your government about this conversation.'

I replied that I would be happy to comply with his request...

'...All right' he said, 'you have promised not to report this conversation to your government.'...At the door, he put out his hand: 'Remember what you promised me,' he said with a smile...[3]

EDOUARD DALADIER did not survive the Finnish crisis for long. He had already indicated his willingness to resign due to the clear differences of opinion between London and Paris; he had also announced to the Chamber of Deputies, by way of hedging himself against disaster, that the matter was in the hands of the British, even citing Scandinavian neutrality as a possible obstacle. He would survive the vote of confidence in the French Senate on 14-15 March, but there were seventy abstentions – a tactic which was filed and noted in London. Daladier faced another vote in the Chamber of Deputies on 20 March – the result was rather stark: For the Government: 239. Against: 1. Abstentions: 300. Outwardly dejected, Edouard Daladier returned to the Elysée Palace, muttering plaintively: 'Leon Blum does not like me.'⁴ He resigned that evening. He would be back in office, however – inappropriately enough as minister of defence.

Despite all the evidence to the contrary, the collapse of Finnish resistance came as a massive shock to the general public and to many a politician. Daladier, who had threatened his resignation in the light of British slowness to come to Finland's aid only days before, was the first to go; Neville Chamberlain was nearly the second. The House of Commons opened its Finland debate on 19 March. Ranked against Chamberlain were many of the Members of Parliament, crucially on his own side, who would bring him down a few long weeks later, and they were a disparate group, but one united by the same sense of outrage and humiliation that had led General Ironside to comment: 'We need more drive at the top.'

Perhaps the trickiest issue for Chamberlain to circumvent was the official secrecy of the whole Scandinavian operation – while the press, fuelled by casual leaks from all levels of the French government, had been discussing intervention in Finland as if it was a foregone conclusion, barely a word had been uttered in either the House of Commons or the Lords, where both Halifax and Chatfield sat. Some of the remarks are worth quoting.

Two MPs in particular, from the Conservative benches, made telling contributions: Richard Law, son of a former prime minister (Andrew Bonar Law), and Harold Macmillan, who was a future one. Law, after polite and fulsome praise for Chamberlain, went in for the kill with this derisive and cutting conclusion:

> ...In the last few years I and every other Hon. Member have witnessed one or other prominent member of the Government – the Prime Minister

or the Chancellor of the Exchequer or the Lord Privy Seal – come down to the House and stand at that Box in the midst of the wreckage of some policy or other, in the midst of some defeat or other, and explain that there was nothing that could possibly have been done. That has happened time after time. It happened in the case of Austria. It happened in the case of Czechoslovakia, it happened in the case of Poland, and now it has happened in the case of Finland. Each time it happens it makes the next time easier and the next time more likely.[5]

Macmillan, who spoke with more authority than many, as he had been in Finland during the war (as a political counterbalance to Walter Citrine's TUC sponsored visit), then undertook a brutal and forensic analysis of Chamberlain's previous statements concerning assistance rendered, which left no one in any doubt that the Prime Minister had been less than accurate in his reporting of the situation. Macmillan used the opportunity to grandstand the issue, in rather the same way that Churchill had in January. He had, during his visit, kept a diary, certain passages of which he had circulated privately, to Chamberlain's intense irritation.

To read the full text of Macmillan's attack is to read an audition for the role of 'glamour boy' but, as an ex-Grenadier guards officer, with a fine service record in the previous war, he, like so many who had come to utterly despise the received wisdom concerning dictators, felt that this fiasco was perhaps worth exploiting. His remarks are at the same time both sinuous and challenging. First, a little scene-setting from his travels in Finland:

When I went into the ticket office to find out if there was any chance of getting a train … I found that a woman had taken the place of the railway man, who had gone to the war … I tried through an interpreter to discuss with her how it was she took everything so calmly, and she gave the rather pathetic reply 'the women of Finland will fight on, because they believe that you are coming to help them.'[6]

Macmillan then proceeded to skate on very thin ice; amid several interruptions that cautioned him on the issue of national security, he pointed out that whatever the Prime Minister's recollection of events, the Finns saw it rather differently. Further, he emphasized, had the Prime Minister not chosen to make a public statement concerning the level of assistance given to the Finns, he would have been quite happy to keep the matter in secret session. This was, by any measure, a serious attack; it called into question the basic concern – that this government was both economical with the truth and, far worse, incompetent. One or the other is occasionally permissable – but to be both at the same time is indefensible when the country is in a state of war.

Other criticisms, from a still-smarting Leslie Hore-Belisha and a slightly ponderous Colonel Josiah Wedgwood (who referred, quite accurately, to the whole venture as 'harebrained'[7]) also took their toll on the dignified, struggling but essentially still-vain Chamberlain. The darts were thrown with no pity; significantly, most of them originated from the government, rather than the opposition side – perhaps not surprising, given that Clement Attlee himself was engaged in a serious cull of those who had expressed themselves as being on the wrong side of agnostic so far as the Soviet Union was concerned. Pritt would be the first to go.

All in all, it was a bruising experience for the Prime Minister, but given that the discussion of Finland took place as part of a much more wide-ranging session on the progress of the war, there was no vote per se as there would be later on the subject of Norway. But a fatal indecision had been revealed at the highest reaches of government and, spirited though Chamberlain's defence of his policy was, it was clear that confidence in him was waning, and doing so rather quickly. It was not known at this time, of course, that the Prime Minister was grievously ill – he would die, from cancer, in November.

FOR GERMANY, the end of the Winter War represented as much of a success as it was a disaster for the Allies. Both the Red Army and the League of Nations had been pleasingly humiliated and the decision-making process of the Allied Supreme War Council had been revealed as utterly chaotic and flawed at both a military and political level. Further, the general domestic popularity of

Germany's policy of neutrality on the Russian side had been very low throughout the conflict and relations with Italy had also suffered badly. This was now relieved.

For the German people, the plight of Finland, coming as it did immediately in the wake of the non-aggression pact with Moscow, was the cause of genuine distress, and for a population politically weaned on concentrated, virulent anti-Bolshevism, the Nazi Party's apparent volte-face was as hard to understand for them as it had been for Benito Mussolini.

The German Foreign Ministry, not having ignored the remarks of von Blücher entirely, arranged with the Economics Ministry for preliminary conversations concerning a resumption of Fenno-German trade, the core of which concerned the German acquisition of strategic metals, particularly the output of the Petsamo mines, which, they had noted with relief, had been returned to the Finns with little comment by the Soviets. Blücher had noted as early as 2 March that the Soviets clearly 'put no value on Petsamo'. This would change, but within two weeks of the peace of Moscow, the now rather ticklish issue of Fenno-German relations was top of the agenda. Counsellor Kreutzwald from the Helsinki legation, fully briefed by von Blücher, opened the inaugural meeting on 28 March with the unwelcome information that sentiment towards Germany was 'outspokenly unfriendly' and that the Finns were, despite the fiasco of the Allied intervention policy, still oriented towards the Western powers. That would change too, and soon, but all would be surprised by the pace of it. For the moment, though, the attention of German diplomacy was concentrated on building – and rebuilding – bridges.

Despite the fact that Russia had achieved war aims that were as limited as they had been embarrassing, the loss of the Karelian Isthmus had implications for Germany almost as serious as they were for Finland, in that the path to the interior of the entire Scandinavian peninsula now lay open to the Red Army. Russia had not merely acquired effective control of both sides of the Baltic littoral for purposes of the defence of Leningrad, but it had also acquired the key to the vast resources of the Scandinavian interior as a whole, which despite the clear fact that they were replicated inside the Soviet Union itself, offered the uncomfortable possibility of Russian interdiction of raw material supplies. This would threaten the drive to the west for which, now that the horrendous winter was over, the German plans were being dusted off. But the Winter War had created a new imperative for which *Fall Gelb*, it was decided on 2 April, would have to wait.

The Allies had also shown their hand in this particular and as a concerned Wipert von Blücher had pointed out so early in the conflict, the safety of the Swedish iron ore supplies, not to mention the cupro-nickel deposits in Finland itself, were now within the grasp of the Allies and the Russians respectively. Scandinavian neutrality, which translated as craven weakness in Berlin, could clearly not be depended upon as, with the exception of the Finns, they were clearly not prepared to fight for it.

Weserübung was conceived in a small bubble of need-to know participants. It was of itself a relatively small plan compared to the grandeur of what was to come and basically involved the delivery to Norway, by sea and air, of a compact but diversified occupation force to seize the key ports along the coast. A separate force was hastily put together to invade Denmark. A planned spin-off of the undertaking would be to shatter any of that residual sense of Scandinavian collective neutrality, which had been tested to destruction over the issue of Finland. This may not have been intentional, as Hitler had been, until the *Altmark* incident, quite relaxed about Norwegian neutrality, or so he said, but given that plans would shortly be laid that directly affected Finland (whose discussions with Sweden for a military alliance were public knowledge), the secondary effect would be important.

The rapid evolution of events between the launch of *Weserübung* and the successful completion of *Fall Gelb* on 20 June stunned the world. The sheer bravado of the German efforts, whatever their impact in theatre, had further important consequences outside their immediate area. One of the most significant was the simple economy of the moves. German casualties, against contingency planning, had been slight at best. Within six weeks, Germany had wrapped an arm around the north-west Scandinavian peninsula and gained a measure of control over the routes to north Russia and at the same time crushed what was considered to be the strongest army in Europe, for the loss of less than a tenth of what the Red Army had lost in Finland. The ignominy of Dunkirk also served to reorient opinion among the political class in Helsinki. Even the staunch anglophile Risto Ryti started to reserve his opinion.

Nearby, the Soviet Union acted swiftly. By the time that part of Europe which had not already succumbed to Hitler turned its gaze back eastwards, Lithuania, Estonia and Latvia had effectively disappeared into Stalin's pocket, all pretence at 'mutual assistance' quite abandoned; they were fully occupied, with twenty divisions. Rapidly, commissars had appeared like early mushrooms and radical left-wing groups and publications followed them. This seizure of the southern Baltic states while Europe's attention was elsewhere, followed the by now established pattern; a German victory simply had to be followed by a Soviet one. While all knew that Finland had been a tougher nut to crack (there was, unsurprisingly, no measurable resistance at all elsewhere in the Baltic states to this new Soviet initiative) it was also true that Finland was now utterly exposed, effectively unarmed and, when all was said and done, still collectively mourning the loss of both territory and soldiers. Strategically, Finland would keep, and the Soviet Union would come to regret that judgement.

Once the southern Baltic coast was secured – according to sound Tsarist principles – the Kremlin swiftly consolidated its cheap gains, and very large forces indeed were installed, far greater than any perceived threat locally would justify. Simultaneously, the Romanian provinces of Bessarabia and northern Bukovina were annexed in a like fashion. These events, particularly those which affected Romania, were not greeted with unalloyed pleasure in Germany; Articles III and IV of the 1939 pact mandated that any action 'affecting the common interests' of both signatories should be transparent, and Romania was, both sides agreed, a vital (oil and agricultural commodities) German interest.

The thorough reorganization of Scandinavia and western Europe represented by *Weserübung* and *Fall Gelb*, combined with the reactive Soviet expansion, left both Finland and Sweden rather nonplussed. There they sat, sandwiched between a rampant Germany and an uncoiling Russia. Yet they could not act; Soviet pressure on Finland, predictably nitpicking in the context of the peace of Moscow, had vetoed any Finnish military alliance, and Germany, superficially now a smiling neighbour of Sweden, still ostensibly kept to the letter of the 1939 pact. As a result, both Sweden and Finland were now effectively hostages to fortune.

In Finland, the plight of Norway in the wake of its occupation actually aroused some genuine sympathy, despite that country's apparent behaviour in the Winter War. But not for long, as the pressure from Moscow, in direct proportion to German success elsewhere, started to bite, and at every level. Round two of 'Finlandization' had begun. The instinctive reaction of a traumatized Finnish government had been to seek alliance with Sweden. Given that Rickard Sandler had already paid for his support for Finland with his career, this naturally threw up some potential difficulties in Stockholm, but they were as nothing compared to the objections thrown up by Molotov on the basis of Article 3 of the 12 March Moscow treaty (see Appendix).

In the Baltic, tensions rose rapidly in the summer of 1940. On 14 June, an unarmed Finnair liner was shot down by fighters of the Baltic fleet. Simultaneously, the Comintern front organization, the Finnish-Soviet Friendship Society, started serious political agitation. Ten days later, Molotov commenced pressure for a Fenno-Soviet corporation to be started in order to expolit the nickel deposits at Petsamo, never mind that it was already a British concession. Within a week of that, a separate démarche went out for a Soviet consulate on the Åland archipelago. On 8 July, demands were made for unlimited Soviet access to the Finnish railway net in order to facilitate military traffic between the Hanko Cape and the new border.

And so the unremitting pressure went on. None of this went unnoticed in Germany; on 3 July, at a conference at Berchtesgaden, Hitler announced that operations would take place against the Soviet Union in the spring of 1941. Two weeks later, an initiative went out to Toiro Kivimäki, the Finnish minister in Berlin, to effect an introduction between Marshal Mannerheim and another crony of Göring's, Josef Veltjens, who had been the original conduit of early weapons supply prior to Soviet objections. Veltjens had served with Göring during the Kaiser's war – he was trusted, discreet and bore with him a huge list of available ordnance, much of which had been captured in France and the low countries. For reasons which need no explanation, much of it was pristine. Within a week, Veltjens met Mannerheim and the stage was set – what had been, in November 1939, an unlikely possibility of Fenno-German cooperation in an attack on Russia was, thanks to Soviet conduct by the end of August 1940, now almost a certainty.

The Russo-Finnish Treaty of Moscow, 12 March 1939

THE GOVERNMENT OF the Republic of Finland on the one hand and The Presidium of the Supreme Soviet of the Union of Soviet Socialist Republics on the other hand, desiring to put an end to the hostilities which have arisen between the two countries and to create lasting peaceful relations between them, and being convinced that the creation of precise conditions for reciprocal security, including the security of the cities of Leningrad and Murmansk and of the Murmansk railway, corresponds to the interest of both contracting parties, have to this end found it necessary to conclude a peace treaty and have appointed as their representatives for this purpose:

[For] THE GOVERNMENT OF THE REPUBLIC OF FINLAND:

Risto Ryti, Prime Minister of the Republic of Finland,

Juho Kusti Paasikivi, Minister,

General Rudolf Walden, and

Professor Väinö Voionmaa.

[For] THE PRESIDIUM OF THE SUPREME SOVIET OF THE U.S.S.R.:

Vyachaslev Mikhailovich Molotov, Chairman of the Council of Peoples' Commissars of the Union of Soviet Socialist Republics and Peoples' Commissar for Foreign Affairs,

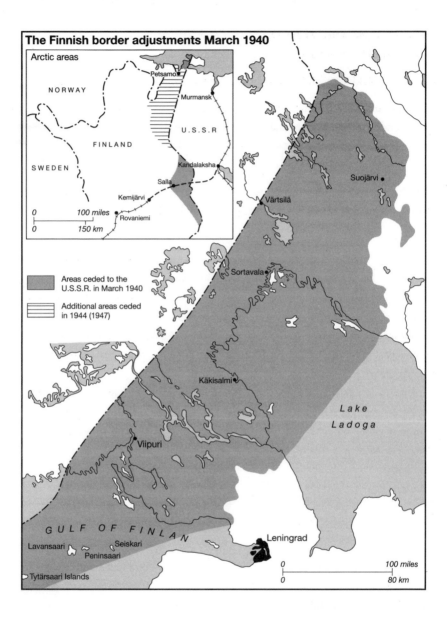

The Finnish border adjustments March 1940

Arctic areas

NORWAY

FINLAND

SWEDEN

Petsamo

Murmansk

U.S.S.R

Kandalaksha

Salla

Kemijärvi

Rovaniemi

0   100 miles

0   150 km

Areas ceded to the
U.S.S.R. in March 1940

Additional areas ceded
in 1944 (1947)

Suojärvi

Värtsilä

Sortavala

Käkisalmi

Lake
Ladoga

Viipuri

GULF OF FINLAN

Leningrad

Lavansaari   Seiskari

Peninsaari

Tytärsaari Islands

0   100 miles

0   80 km

Andrei Aleksandrovich Zhdanov, Member of the Presidium of the Supreme Soviet of the Union of Soviet Socialaist Republics,

Aleksander Mikhailovich Vasilevski, Brigade Commander.

The above-mentioned representatives, after exchange of credentials, which were found to be in due form and good order, have agreed upon the following:

ARTICLE 1

Hostilities between Finland and the U.S.S.R. shall cease immediately in accordance with procedure laid down in the protocol appended to this treaty.

ARTICLE 2

The national frontier between the Republic of Finland and the U.S.S.R. shall run along a new line in such fashion that there shall be included in the territory of the U.S.S.R. the entire Karelian Isthmus with the city of Viipuri and Viipuri bay with its islands, the western shore of Lake Ladoga with the cities of Kexholm and Sortavala and the town of Suojärvi, a number of islands in the Gulf of Finland, the area east of Markajärvi, and part of the Rybachi and Sredni peninsulas, all in accordance with the map appended to this treaty.

A more detailed determination and establishment of the frontier line shall be carried out by a mixed commission made up of representatives of the contracting powers, which commission shall be named within ten days from the date of the signing of this treaty.

ARTICLE 3

Both contracting parties undertake each to refrain from any attack upon the other and to make no alliance and to participate in no coalition directed against either of the contracting parties.

ARTICLE 4

The Republic of Finland agrees to lease to the Soviet Union for thirty years, against an annual rental of 8 million Finnish Marks to be paid by the Soviet Union, Hanko Cape and the waters surrounding it in a radius of five miles to the south and east and three miles to the north and west, and also the several islands falling within that area, in accordance with the map appended to this treaty, for the establishment of a naval base capable of defending the mouth of the Gulf of Finland against attack; in addition to which, for the purposes of protecting the naval base, the Soviet Union is granted the right of maintaining there at its own expense the necessary number of armed land and air forces.

Within ten days [that] the date this treaty enters into effect, the Government of Finland shall withdraw all its military forces from Hanko Cape, which together with its adjoining islands shall be transferred to the jurisdiction of the U.S.S.R. in accordance with this article of the treaty.

ARTICLE 5

The U.S.S.R. undertakes to withdraw its troops from the Petsamo area which the Soviet State voluntarily ceded to Finland under the peace treaty of 1920.

Finland undertakes, as provided by the peace treaty of 1920, to refrain from maintaining in the waters running along its coast of the Arctic Ocean warships and other armed ships, excluding armed ships of less than one hundred tons displacement, which Finland shall be entitled to maintain without restriction, and also at most fifteen warships or other armed ships, the displacement of none of which shall exceed four hundred tons.

Finland undertakes, as was provided in the same treaty of 1920, not to maintain in the said waters any submarine or armed aircraft.

Finland similarly undertakes, as was provided in the same treaty, not to establish on that coast military ports, naval bases or naval repair shops of greater capacity than is necessary for the above-mentioned ships and their armament.

ARTICLE 6

As provided in the treaty of 1920, the Soviet Union and its citizens are granted the right of free transit across the Petsamo area to Norway and back, in addition to which the Soviet Union is granted the right to establish a Consulate in the Petsamo area.

Merchandise shipped through the Petsamo area from the Soviet Union to Norway, and likewise merchandise shipped through the same area from Norway to the Soviet Union, is exempted from inspection and control, with the exception of such control as is necessary for the regulation of transit traffic; neither customs duties nor transit or other charges shall be assessed.

The above-mentioned control of transit merchandise shall be permitted only in the form usual in such cases in accordance with established practice in international communications.

Citizens of the Soviet Union who travel through the Petsamo area to Norway and from Norway back to the Soviet Union shall be entitled to free transit passage on the basis of passports issued by the appropriate officials of the Soviet Union.

Observing general directives in effect, unarmed Soviet aircraft shall be entitled to maintain air service between the Soviet Union and Norway via the Petsamo area.

ARTICLE 7

The Government of Finland grants to the Soviet Union the right of transit for goods between the Soviet Union and Sweden and, with a view to developing this traffic along the shortest possible railway route, the Soviet Union and Finland consider it necessary to build, each upon its own territory and insofar as possible in the year 1940, a railway which shall connect Kandalaksha with Kemijärvi.

ARTICLE 8

Upon the coming into force of this treaty economic relations between the contracting parties shall be restored, and with this end in view the contracting parties shall enter into negotiations for the conclusion of a trade agreement.

ARTICLE 9

This treaty of peace shall enter into effect immediately upon being signed, and shall be subject to subsequent ratification.

The exchange of instruments of ratification shall take place within ten days in the city of Moscow.

This treaty has been prepared in two original instruments, in the Finnish and Swedish languages and in Russian, at Moscow this twelfth day of March, 1940.

[For the Government of the Republic of Finland]:
RISTO RYTI
J.K.PAASIKIVI
R.WALDEN
VÄINÖ VOIONMAA

[For the Union of Soviet Socialist Republics]:
V.MOLOTOV
A.ZHDANOV
A.VASILEVSKI

PROTOCOL APPENDED TO THE TREATY OF PEACE CONCLUDED BETWEEN FINLAND AND THE UNION OF SOVIET SOCIALIST REPUBLICS ON MARCH 12TH, 1940.

The contracting parties confirm the following arrangement for cessation of hostilities and the withrawal of troops beyond the national boundary established by the peace treaty:

1 Both sides shall cease hostilities on March 13, 1940, at 12:00 noon Leningrad time.

2 As from the hour fixed for the cessation of hostilities there shall be established a neutral zone, one kilometre in depth, between the positions of advanced units, whereupon within the course of the first day forces of that party to the treaty which under the new national boundary find themselves in territory pertaining to the other party to the treaty shall withdraw to one kilometre's distance.

3 Withdrawal of troops beyond the new national boundary and advance of the troops of the other party to this national boundary shall commence on March 15 from 10:00 a.m. along the whole frontier from the Gulf of Finland to Lieksa, and on March 16 from 10 a.m. at points north of Lieksa. Withdrawal shall be effected through daily marches of not less than seven kilometres, the advance of troops of the other party taking place in such fashion that there shall be maintained between the rear guard of the withdrawing troops and the advance units of the other party to the treaty an interval of not less than seven kilometres.

4 The following time limits are established for withdrawal, on various sectors of the national boundary, in accordance with Paragraph 3:

a) In the sector comprising the upper course of the Tuntsajoki River, Kuolajärvi, Takala, and the eastern shore of Lake Joukamojärvi the movement of troops of both parties to the treaty shall be completed on March 20, 1940, at 8:00 p.m.

b) In the Latva sector south of Kuhmoniemi, troop movements shall be completed on March 22, 1940 at 8:00 p.m.

c) In the Lonkavaara, Värtsilä, and Matkaselkä station sector, troop movements of both parties shall be completed on March 22, 1940 at 8:00 p.m.

d) In the Koitsanlahti sector at Matkaselkä station, troop movements shall be completed on March 25, 1940, at 8:00 p.m.

e) In the Enso station sector at Koitsanlahti, troop movements shall be completed on March 25, 1940 at 8:00 p.m.

f) In the Paationsaari sector at Enso station, troop movements shall be completed on March 19, 1940 at 8:00 p.m.

5 Evacuation of troops of the Red Army from the Petsamo area shall be completed by April 10, 1940.

6 The command of each party undertakes, while troops are withdrawing to the other side of the national boundary, to put into effect in the cities at localities to be ceded to the other party necessary measures for their preservation undamaged, and to put into effect measures necessary to the end that cities, localities, and establishments of defensive and economic importance (bridges, dams, airfields, barracks, storehouses, railway communications, industrial plants, telegraphs, electric power plants) shall be preserved from damage and destruction.

7 All questions which may arise upon the cession by one contracting party to the other of the areas, localities, cities, or other objectives referred to in Paragraph 6 of this protocol shall be settled on the spot by representatives of both parties to the treaty, for which purpose the command shall appoint special delegates for each main route of movement of both armies.

8 The exchange of prisoners of war shall be carried out in the briefest possible time after the cessation of hostilities on the basis of a special agreement.

March 12, 1940.

[For the Government of the Republic of Finland]:
RISTO RYTI
J.K.PAASIKIVI
R.WALDEN
VÄINÖ VOIONMAA

[For the Union of Soviet Socialist Republics]:
V.MOLOTOV
A.ZHDANOV
A.VASILEVSKI

Notes to the Text

PROLOGUE
Naboth's Vineyard

1 Mannerheim had two Marshal's batons; one had been presented to him as an unofficial gesture of recognition by his own military circle in 1928, another, formally, by the government in 1933. He carried, on this occasion, the earlier one, claiming that 'it was lighter'.

2 He had, perhaps unwisely, written an open letter, published in Finland on 2 November 1919, advocating immediate intervention to capture Petrograd (St Petersburg); an impulsive act, to be sure, and one which kept him out of public life until 1931.

3 V. I. Lenin, *Letters from Afar* (International Publishers, NY, 1932).

4 He would be made Knight Grand Cross of the Order of the British Empire the next year.

5 He had even bagged a python, which seems a little unsporting, or at best opportunistic. They are brave animals, but not *swift*.

6 General Erik Heinrichs.

7 Mannerheim, *The Memoirs of Marshal Mannerheim*.

8 See in particular the two-volume biography of Mannerheim by J. E. O. Screen.

9 Where Mannerheim's estranged Russian wife Anastasie had lived in resentful exile until her death in 1936. Born Anastasie Arapova, she was the daughter of one of Nicholas II's closest personal advisers, Generale à la suite Arapov. The marriage had been arranged, partly to ease the penury in which the dispossessed Finn (his father had been declared bankrupt in 1880) found himself, and partly to bind him to the Russian establishment. Arapova was no beauty, but she was rich – Mannerheim had briefly acquired an estate on the Courland peninsula as a result. They had in fact dealt well enough together after a reconciliation following their divorce.

10 He was not; he despised all totalitarian regimes, referring to both Stalin and Hitler as 'tyrants'.

11 Lenin, as a frequent visitor to Finland (and seldom by choice) was, as an icon, extraordinarily popular as the man who was seen (and promoted as, by the far left) the granter of Finland's freedom; in fact he had tried to crush Finland when his agenda was questioned.

12 About 11 per cent of the population spoke Swedish as a mother tongue, including Anaheim and the other national treasure, Jean Sibelius. Of all the languages Mannerheim spoke – Russian, Swedish, English, German, French and Finnish – he spoke the latter least intelligibly, about as well as Winston Churchill spoke French.

13 His hobby. He was the chief sponsor, it seems, of Dmitri Shostakovich.

14 People's Commissariat for Internal Affairs. Until 1933, this organ was known as the GPU, and was often referred to as such until 1940.

15 John Erickson, *The Soviet High Command*.

16 Cited by Martin Amis, *Koba the Dread* (Jonathan Cape, 2002).

17 Except Russia, which, largely dependent upon commodity exports, was hit very hard indeed by the collapse in global demand.

CHAPTER ONE

Naboth's Vineyard

1 Tartu is in Estonia. It is also known as Dorpat.

2 Thrashed – soundly – at Poltava in the Ukraine in 1709.

3 The autonomous Grand Duchy (last incumbent Nicholas II), had owned 40 per cent of the usable agricultural land.

4 Exact historical exchange rates are hard to find; the markka had plunged during the depression from c. 100 to the pound to c. 300, but was in strong recovery by 1939.

5 Geoffrey Hosking, *A History of the Soviet Union*, p. 213.

6 Robert Conquest, *The Great Terror*, p. 532.

7 The Scandinavian model of co-operative commerce had been the brainchild of the Swede, Martin Sundell and the Finn, Hannes Gebhardt, and was based upon their observations of the buying power of the mill workers of Rochdale, England in the mid nineteenth century.

8 Ryti's role in the economic evolution of Finland has been compared to that of Alexander Hamilton, with some justification.

9 In Finland the depression started rather early with the collapse in construction materials prices, particularly lumber, in 1928, a signal which wiser heads had chosen to ignore.

10 See H. B. Elliston, *Finland Fights*, p. 112.

11 *Ibid.*, p. 115.

12 A separate convention from the Treaty of Tartu, although obviously associated with it. Moscow (indeed, Stalin) had signed the Treaty of Tartu – having granted Finnish independence and then lost the attempt to scupper it, they had no choice – but the Ålands were another matter and the Soviet Union did not sign the 1921 convention, which was sponsored by the League of Nations.

13 Jakobson, *The Diplomacy of the Winter War*, p. 35

14 C. V. Wedgwood, *The Thirty Years War* (Jonathan Cape, 1944) p. 275.

15 The infantry were more often Scottish.

16 Yartsev was a work name; his real name was Rybkin.

17 Jakobson, *The Diplomacy of The Winter War*, p. 8.

18 Jakobson, *ibid.*, p. 26.

19 To be precise, Finnish exports to the USSR comprised 0.6 per cent of total trade and imports 1.9 per cent of the same, by markka volume. Given the huge mutual border, observers have noted that in economic terms this amounted to virtual blockade.

20 Wuolijoki was totally deranged, in the view of some, but certainly a Comintern agent as well as queen bee of the limousine left. An Estonian by birth, she also wrote under the pseudonym of Juhani Tervapää. She worked with Bertholt Brecht, while he lived with her in 1940 at her grand country house, the Villa Marlebäck, in the village of Iitti, north-west of Helsinki. She had been married, briefly, to the Social Democrat M. P. V. Wuolijoki, who was a close associate of Kuusinen, and whom Tanner had known as well as he wished.

21 One of Kuusinen and V. Wuolijoki's first cooperations had been the translation of 'the Internationale' into Karelian, for repetitive broadcast into Finland from the Soviet Union.

22 Both Tanner and Ryti studied trade and commerce with an all-consuming passion; Tanner in order to strengthen the co-operative movement (and stamp hard on any *poujadiste* tendencies which might emerge elsewhere – he had little time for shopkeepers) and Ryti as a theoretical, even philosophical matter. Both men clearly missed the point concerning Soviet advances on this – trade, like everything else, was but a single piece of a very complex ideological jigsaw.

23 A good example was Corps Commander Vitovt Putna, Soviet miltary attaché in London, recalled in September 1936 and executed in the same week as Tukhachevski.

24 Or more probably Otto Kuusinen, who was a prolific, if talentless, ghost writer.

25 A more twenty-first-century job title would be Minister of Diversity *within the Soviet Union.*

26 He was General Secretary by 1923 (his name appears on the famed Zinoviev letter – he may even have written it).

27 I think he meant *majority*; see D.N. Pritt, *Must the War Spread?* for a fuller text.

28 It has been estimated that up to 30,000 'Reds' died in captivity in the spring of 1918.

29 See Conquest, *op. cit.*, p. 432.

30 Variously known as the Civil Guard, the Civic Guard, the White Guards and, by the far left, the *Schutzcorps*, to create linkage, inaccurately, with the *Schutzstaffel* – SS – in Germany. It was, of course, nothing of the sort.

31 Named, apparently at Mannerheim's suggestion, after the wife of a soldier in Runeberg's epic poem.

32 Mannerheim held Czechoslovakia in no particular regard, for reasons that went back to the Russian civil war – the Czech Legion had handed over the White Admiral Kolchak to the Bolsheviks – for *money* – with predictable effects upon his life expectancy.

33 Mannerheim, *Memoirs*, p. 296.

34 In contrast to General Gamelin's publicly stated confidence.

35 Mannerheim, *op. cit*, p. 298.

36 In fact, he merely had to choose between being a League delegate or a minister – he was being paid for both jobs, which raised some auditors' eyebrows, and he chose the League – the salary was higher!

37 His table manners while in Geneva had given some cause for offence; he had been overheard describing Adolf Hitler as a 'madman' and Mussolini as a 'syphilitic demagogue'. He was possibly drunk.

38 Mannerheim, *op. cit.*, p. 300

39 The same day, Adolf Hitler – in the context of demanding a free hand in the East, particularly Poland – stated openly his intentions to Dr Carl Burckhardt (The League of Nations' High Commissioner in Danzig): 'All I intend is to take Russia to task [*gerichtet* – this, with different emphasis, can imply an almost *Biblical* connotation]; the West is too stupid and blind to understand this. I have become swayed [persuaded?] to an understanding [*verständigen*] with the Russians, to attack the West, and then after their defeat, with my assembled strength, to turn on the Soviet Union. I need the Ukraine, so that no one need starve, as in the last war.' C. J. Burckhardt, *Meine Danziger Mission*, p. 348. This very free translation is mine.

Interesting that Hitler chose, outside his immediate circle, to confide in Burckhardt, a Jewish official of an organization of which Germany was no longer a member (but of which the USSR, in August, still was.) But see also Kershaw, *Hitler*, vol. II, pp. 201–3. See also *Mein Kampf* – rather a lot of it, in fact.

40 General Josef Doumenc was a staff officer to Gamelin.

41 Admiral Sir Reginald Aylmer Plunkett Ernle-Erle-Drax, admiral commanding the Nore.

42 Erkko to H. B. Elliston, December 1940.

CHAPTER TWO
Bear-baiting: The Emerging Crisis

1 *Ironside Diaries*, p. 106. Or, in Churchill's case, pretended to be. On 26 July, he and Ironside had 'made a night of it' at Chartwell when, interestingly, Churchill had tabled a naval plan for the Baltic, later to be christened Operation Catherine.

2 *Ibid.*

3 And failed sisal planter, as his critics gleefully pointed out. See Graham Stewart, *Burying Caesar*.

4 There were isolated partisan actions, but not on an organized basis.

5 In fact, there were persistent (and often quite severe) border tensions between the two sides across the new boundary until June 1941.

6 Although Russian timing was largely driven by the completion of Zhukov's battle at Nomonhan, it is quite possible that the Soviet Union had full knowledge of Gamelin's initiative; on 27 September a clerk in the Communications Department of the British Foreign Office was arrested as a Soviet spy. He was jailed for ten years, after which a comprehensive (and clearly necessary) 'tightening up' of security procedures took place. See *Cadogan Diary* (ed. D. Dilks), p. 208.

7 R. Sontag & J. Beddie, *Nazi-Soviet Relations*, p. 100; a draft apparently in Stalin's own fair hand.

8 By one account 800,000, against an army of 200,000.

9 Edward Smigly-Rydz, Marshal of Poland 1935–9, Inspector General of the Polish Army and C-in-C.

10 He was, he hoped, referring to the fact that Poland had acted as a bulwark for much of central Europe.

11 Despite the fact that, its strident atheism notwithstanding, Bolshevism was *technically* a Christian heresy. An indication of the moral flexibility at work from the outset is seen in the statement by Lunacharsky, the first Soviet commissar for education, who stated: 'Christ, if He were ever to come back to earth, would immediately join the Communist party.' See Oscar Levy, *The Idiocy of Idealism*, (William Hodge and Co., 1940).

12 *Time and Tide*, 8 August 1938.

13 J. F. C. Fuller, *The Conduct of War*. Fuller did his own reputation no particular good in the 1930s by being an adherent of Mosley, but his argument is none the less elegant.

14 Victor Gollancz, who finally wrested control of the Left Book Club back in the spring of 1940 (for reasons not unassociated with events in this book), described its branches as 'bastard CP [Communist Party] locals'. Not, as a fellow-traveller, that he would have been particularly concerned, save, of course, at Soviet conduct.

15 Her *magnum opus* (with husband Sidney) – *The Soviet Union: A New Civilisation?* – had recently been reissued by the Left Book Club pointedly, without the question mark.

16 *The Diaries of Beatrice Webb*, vol. IV, p. 441.

17 *Cadogan Diary*, p. 218.

18 HMSO, *Documents on German Foreign Policy*, series D, vol. VIII, no. 131.

19 Dutch-built and delivered in early 1939, the *Orzel* (*Eagle*) put in to Tallinn with an ailing captain. Pursued around the Baltic by the *Kriegsmarine* as well as the Red Baltic fleet, it was to finally escape, later doing sterling service.

20 *Documents on German Foreign Policy, op. cit.*, no. 130.

21 See A. Rei, *The Drama of the Baltic Peoples* (Stockholm, 1970) p. 260. This passage cited by van Dyke, *The Soviet Invasion of Finland*, ch. 1.

22 And all of which was at least still technically protected by an Anglo-French guarantee, as had been Poland.

23 In common, it seems, with many other German Foreign Service officers.

24 *Documents on German Foreign Policy, op. cit.*, no. 206.

25 As did the Finns; a hint of collusion is presented by the form of words used by von Blücher and the press release from the Finnish Foreign Ministry.

26 Letter to his sister-in-law, September 1939, cited by Screen, *The Finnish Years*, p. 130

27 *Ibid.*, p. 130. In fact, Hitler preferred to think in terms of 'Red Indians'.

28 Paasikivi was not only a financier and a lawyer, he was also a knowledgeable historian and no ostrich. His central philosophy was straightforward – Russia had to be dealt with. Some had considered him 'soft' on Russia – he was not, merely realistic.

29 Tanner, *The Winter War*, p. 22.

30 *Documents on German Foreign Policy*, D, VIII, no. 213.

31 Jakobson, *The Diplomacy of the Winter War*, p. 12.

32 Presumably, the slave camps would have to be relocated first – Karelia was dotted with them. Aside from those, there were very many trees – a commodity not exactly in short supply in Finland. But this territory would play a role later in the wider war.

33 When Paasikivi lost his temper he had been known to throw files, folders, paperweights, inkwells and even ashtrays at his interlocutors, but not, of course, in the Kremlin.

34 Jakobson *The Diplomacy of the Winter War*, pp. 117–8.

35 Obviously no coincidence.

36 Tanner, p. 30.

37 Many, indeed, had friends and relatives in the Finnish Officer Corps.

38 Ernest Wigforss, *Minnen*, vol. III, cited by Jakobson, *The Diplomacy of the Winter War*.

39 Paasikivi, even longer. He had received his higher education there (and Novgorod) in the 1890s.

40 The polite request to converse in the language of the interlocutor is a common Finnish courtesy, usually for historical reasons extended to Swedes.

The proposal made here, to speak a third language not Russian *could*, under certain circumstances, be considered rude.

41 Tanner, *op. cit.*, p. 45.

42 Tanner, *op. cit.*, pp. 45–6.

43 Tanner, *op. cit.*, pp. 47–8.

44 This was a rather untypical discourtesy to a fellow-traveller – as Hedin was. Perhaps the possibilities of potential disaster had an effect on Hitler's demeanour.

45 Sven Hedin, *Ohne Auftrag in Berlin* (Internationaler Universitätsverlag, 1950).

46 Hull's memoirs are almost embarrassingly self-serving on this matter and are therefore of only slight practical use to the student. A more robust analysis is presented by William L. Langer and S. Everett Gleason in *The Challenge to Isolation*.

47 This 'initiative' would get even more banal. It is interesting to contrast the role played by Franklin Roosevelt here, as against that played by Theodore in the Russo-Japanese War in 1905, in which he mediated, leading to the Treaty of Portsmouth. Soviet attitudes were perhaps influenced by this; it was not an argument from which they could now withdraw.

48 Gripenberg, *Finland and the Great Powers – Memoirs*, p. 79.

49 *Ibid.*, p. 80

50 *Ibid.*, p. 82.

51 Emphasis mine; Maisky was already on the defensive concerning, among other matters, Poland.

CHAPTER THREE
Questions of Command

1 van Dyke, *Soviet Invasion of Finland* p. 19.

2 It is interesting that whereas the 'intellectuals' of the Revolution were drawn extensively from the political class, the army command was not; to prosper in the Workers' and Peasants' Revolutionary Army it was only sensible to talk of a shoeless and unlettered childhood, whether true or not. Several who doctored their Tsarist era résumés to fit the mould paid a very heavy price. There were some notable exceptions (like Shaposhnikov and Vasilevski), however, more of whom we shall meet shortly.

3 A clear reference to Mannerheim.

4 In fact, in the period immediately after the execution of Tukhachevski, a resurgence of middle-class values and mores made itself felt in the upper reaches of the Red Army. Foreign languages were taught routinely, as well as social graces of a kind frowned upon by strict Bolshevism – ballroom dancing, for example.

5 Two types of officer suffered the most under the purges: the old Bolsheviks and the ex-Imperial cadres. By 1939, though, 50 per cent of the Officer Corps were Party members, a much greater proportion than the Red Army as a whole, which was seldom more than 20 per cent and in some cases as low as 4–5 per cent.

6 *The Vistula – The History of the 1920 Campaign* The issue revolved around the conduct of the campaign in Poland in 1920. Tukhachevski had been unwise enough to tell anyone who would listen that the conduct of the First Cavalry Army had in effect cost the Red Army the battle of Warsaw. Unhappily, the three senior men in that unit were Stalin, Voroshilov and Budenny.

7 See the profile of Voroshilov by General Dmitri Volkogonov in *Stalin's Generals* (ed. H. Shukman) and marvel.

8 Zek – from Zachlyuchennyi – prisoner, in this case a slave worker.

9 It lay, undiscovered and clearly unloved, lacking even an opus number, for over sixty years. See *Daily Telegraph*, 'Party piece uncovered', 6 September 2001.

10 van Dyke, *op cit.*, p. 20, cites G. L. Rozanov, *Stalin/Hitler* (Moscow, 1991) as the source for this.

11 At the same time another Swede, Birger Dahlerus, also a friend of Göring's, had been acting as a semi-official diplomatist between Berlin and London. The Scandinavian crisis rather served to switch his attention.

12 Tanner, *The Winter War*, p. 74. Mannerheim was not bluffing; he really believed it.

13 *Ibid.* p. 72.

14 The official paper of the Russian Navy.

15 Tanner, *op. cit.*, p. 79

16 See Gilbert, *Finest Hour*, pp. 99–100.

17 Estonia and Finland share much in historical and cultural terms, notably a similarity of language

18 Quoted in the *New York Times*, 18 November 1939.

19 A translation of the article can be found in Bror Laurla, *The Road to the Winter War*, (Finland, 1978).

20 Tanner, *op. cit.*, pp. 85–6.

21 Elliston, *Finland Fights*, p. 177.

22 The same day, a Red Army patrol had crossed the border at Petsamo and kidnapped three Finnish border guards.

23 Tanner, *op. cit.*, p. 87.

24 Mannerheim to Kallio, 27 November, 1939.

25 Meretskov, *Serving the People*, (Progress, 1991)

CHAPTER FOUR
The Assault on the Isthmus

1 Known to the Russians as Khotinen.

2 *The Soviet-Finnish Campaign, 1939–40*. The authors of this, W. P. and Zelda Coates, had 'form' as Soviet propagandists. The leaden and unpromising titles of their previous oeuvre – *The First Five Year Plan*, followed by a truly brain-numbing sequel *The Second Five Year Plan* – and so on, rather set the tone. To be fair, they were doing a job of work as agents of the Comintern, but the author of the foreword, Frank Owen, editor of the *Evening Standard* (he of *Guilty Men*), really should have known better. Examples of the work of this husband-and-wife team can still be found from time to time (this writer bought one at a Sussex village fête, of all places) and they are almost the perfect exemplar of the mare-eyed, fellow-travelling left at its most creatively risible.

3 Quite simply because by the time the book was published, the line was safely in Russian hands.

4 The 'million' bunker, near Summa, had cost just that; 1 million markka, about £5,000, in 1937

5 i.e. the concrete had no steel reinforcing bars, merely granite rubble to improve its density.

6 Elliston, *Finland Fights*, p. 142.

7 Typically, the First World War Russian version of the Maxim from the Imperial factory at Tula. These were of 7.92mm rifle calibre. Foreign weapons arrived in a bewildering variety of calibres. Similarly, the Finns were to employ grenades

from no less than seven different origins (with differing fuses) that were thus perilous to use.

8 Soon to be obsolete, given the rapid developments in tank design.

9 The Finnish tank park consisted of twenty-year-old Renault models, leavened by a few Carden-Vickers types most of which, for reasons of economy, were unarmed.

10 It is reasonable to suppose, indeed, it would be irresponsible *not* to suppose, that the terrified atmosphere generated by the savage purges had something to do with Kuusinen's boundless enthusiasm for this hopeless project.

11 See Goodrich, *A Study in Sisu*, pp. 52–3

12 Eventually, after the war, he did return to Finland, disavowed the cause and joined Tanner's Social Democrat Party; he later became a newspaper editor in the industrial city of Tampere.

13 *politichesky rukovotidel*, a political 'adviser' attached to the military.

14 Raymond L. Garthoff, *How Russia Makes War: Soviet Military Doctrine*, p. 257.

15 *Pravda*'s expression.

16 The Soviet T-26 was a near copy of a Vickers 6-ton tank of the early 1930s, and just as useless, but still terrifying to an inexperienced infantry-man.

17 i.e. Great Britain – never let it be said that it might have been Germany.

18 The translation is from Elliston, *op. cit.*, pp. 230 and 237

19 The Finns, justifiably, were and are rather proud of their paper industry. Many of these leaflets were put to more 'informal' use.

20 And his deputy, Mauri Rosenberg, another Finnish exile from 1918.

21 Screen, *Mannerheim*, vol. II, pp. 137–8.

22 Order of the Day No. 1, 1 December 1939.

23 This may have been an ill-reported sighting of a *Finnish* armoured car, but records (like memories) are vague.

24 See van Dyke, *Soviet Invasion of Finland*, ch. 2, n. 91.

25 Perhaps oddly, he was not executed, but given a harmless job in administration, where he proved just as incompetent.

CHAPTER FIVE
Responses

1 *Daily Mail*, 2 December 1939.

2 As a gentleman, that is; it was not considered 'proper' (and still isn't) for an officer of below field rank (major) to keep that title upon resignation or retirement.

3 John Colville, *Downing Street Diaries*, vol I.

4 *The Diaries of Beatrice Webb*, vol. IV, p. 441.

5 *Daily Telegraph* (from Copenhagen), 2 December 1939.

6 *The Times*, 2 December 1939.

7 Reuters bulletin, 3 December 1939.

8 *The Goebbels Diaries* (ed. F. Taylor), 1 December 1939, p. 58.

9 *Ibid.*, 6 December 1939, p. 61.

10 *Ciano's Diary*, (ed. M. Muggeridge) 2 December 1939, p. 179. The issue of 'discipline' would be fixed very shortly.

11 *Ibid.*, 4 December 1939. Curiously, the Italian police were absent!

12 The first instalment of thirty-five Fiat fighter aircraft and spares, crated in rail cars and shipped to Sweden.

13 In his *Memoirs*, Mannerheim refutes this entry of Ciano's with some vigour.

14 Some 10 per cent of the putative value of machine-tool sales to the USSR from Germany under the pact.

15 *Documents on German Foreign Policy*, Series D, Vol VIII, no. 446.

16 *Ibid.*, no. 447. German deliveries were made at the expense of standing orders from elsewhere, particularly Holland, which were unilaterally cancelled or 'slowed down'.

17 The Swedish military attaché in London and Göring's ex-brother-in-law.

18 Tanner, *The Winter War*, p. 160.

19 Hungarian (Magyar) is a distant linguistic relative of Finnish and Estonian.

20 The bulk of it was ammunition, but it included forty AA guns. The shipments were delivered via Germany to Norway.

21 *Memoirs*, p. 359

22 Technically, it was not war debt, but rather a scrupulous assumption of the standing obligations of the autonomous Grand Duchy (which had clearly been rather profligate) at independence.

23 Cited in Keith Feiling, *The Life of Neville Chamberlain*, p. 426.

24 One is unavoidably reminded of the encounter between two diplomatists, one German, one Belgian, at the Versailles conference: 'I wonder what history will say about this?' speculated the German. The Belgian replied coldly: 'I cannot say, but one thing will be clear – no one will ever say that Belgium invaded Germany.' The *Daily Worker* headline appeared in the US edition of 1 December .

25 Walter Citrine, Philip Noel-Baker et al.

26 And worse still, were using explosive bullets with which to do it.

27 André Géraud, (Pertinax), *Les Fossoyeurs*, Vol. I p. 176.

28 A community represented by his personal *bête noire*, Leon Blum, late of the Popular Front.

29 cf. UN Security Council and General Assembly.

30 See *The Finnish Blue-White Book*, p. 87.

31 Litvinov had not, of course, been talking about Spain on that occasion – rather he had been preparing the ground for 'activity' in the Ukraine where it was suspected, probably correctly, a Nationalist movement headed by Hetman Skoropadsky was receiving German support.

32 Germany would need at least 10 million tons of iron ore per annum, not the least reason being her commitments to the Soviet Union.

33 Weizsäcker had observed to Blücher, in a private note of 2 December, that 'disaster had descended upon your host country'.

34 *Documents on German Foreign Policy*, *op. cit.*, no. 426.

35 *Ibid.*, no. 429.

36 Text from Hull, *Memoirs*, vol. 1, p. 706.

37 Telegram from Steinhardt (Moscow) 1 December, 1939.

38 The loan was finally agreed for $10 million, but with the proviso that it could not be used to buy arms – Procopé cleverly bought food with it from America and sold the food to Britain in

exchange for armaments. Thus, the $10 million never left the country, all credit risk was avoided and Finland was forced to rely on weapons supplies from a country already at war and for whom supplies were short.

39 Langer & Gleason, *The Challenge to Isolation*, p. 337. Much of this went straight to Germany, of course.

40 Churchill Archive.

41 See Gilbert, *Finest Hour*, p. 102.

42 *Ibid.*, p. 103.

43 *Temps*, 9 December.

44 War Cabinet, 22 December 1939.

45 Gripenberg, *Memoirs*, p. 106.

46 *Ibid.*, p. 107. In fact, Halifax had been urging a constructive response from the Swedes and Norwegians since 7 December.

47 *Dokumenty vneshnei politiki S.S.S.R.*. (Moscow, 1958), tr. and cited by M. J. Carley, 1939.

48 The Soviet ambassador would pay fulsome tribute in his memoirs to Butler (a matter not necessarily found to be a particular boost to Butler's later political reputation, as it turned out).

49 The Leads are stretches of water between the Norwegian coast and the chain of offshore islands.

50 Mussolini is referring here to the Finns' sub-scribing to League Sanctions under Article 16 as a result of the Abyssinian crisis of 1935. He is erroneous in his assumption re: the general population.

51 *Documents on German Foreign Policy, op. cit.*, no. 504.

CHAPTER SIX
The Ordeal of Ninth Army

1 Quite by coincidence, Mannerheim himself had served with the Tsar's Ninth Army in Transylvania in 1916 – needless to say, this was an entirely different organization – the Red Army shared few designations with its Imperial predecessor.

2 One is unavoidably reminded of a similar situation sixty years previously, that of Lord Chelmsford in Natal, before Isandlwhana.

3 Siilasvuo, like the majority of Mannerheim's

officers of field rank and above, was a veteran of the First World War Jäger battalion.

4 JR = *Jalkaväki Rykmentti*.

5 Nor even uniforms; like much of the Finnish Army, they were dressed in the Cajander Model 1939 uniform – mufti, in fact.

6 More correctly, they fortified their position with felled trees; permafrost prevented the digging of anything but the most superficial trenches.

7 Major Nikolayev, a *politruk* attached to the 44th.

8 Akhmedov, *In and out of Stalin's G.R.U.*, p. 111.

9 This technique was simplicity itself: a path was scraped clear and then simply flooded. The resulting smooth surface was perfect for skiing soldiers to make rapid progress, towing their supplies with them on *puulka* sleds.

10 The timetable instructed the division to reach Oulu on 17 December.

11 It is even possible that these soldiers were lost; after the war, Russian commanders complained that their compasses did not work, a matter attributed to the presence of 'magnetic ores in the lakes', perhaps the most novel excuse for utter failure ever offered. See Chubaryan & Shukman, *Stalin and the Soviet-Finnish War*, p. 91.

12 The Red Army was not issued with camouflaged uniforms until the end of January.

13 It has been said, this writer suspects unfairly, that the major motivation for the dogged persist-ence of the Red Army soldiers lay in the blood-curdling threats offered in their indoctrination. Yet it is a Russian tradition...

14 It had been considered sensible by the Finns to use Soviet-calibre ammunition (7.92 mm in 1939) in the bulk of their infantry weapons; either that or international standard 'Parabellum' (9 mm. or short .38in.) rounds. In general, this is still Finnish policy.

15 The bulk of this material was dehydrated millet gruel and pork fat; little vodka was recovered, but many useful empty bottles. For the Muslim soldiers of the Red Army (of which there were naturally very many) this *haram* (forbidden) provender was hardly an appetizing prospect.

16 It is quite possible that Russian reinforcements were actually 'blocking' units, there to prevent retreat rather an assist in attack.

17 A Red Army colonel, Raeskii, had already suggested this policy of 'thorough combing' (*sploshnyi prochesyvanie*) on the Isthmus. It was rejected; not enough Red Army soldiers knew how to ski.

18 Akhmedov, *op. cit.*, p. 114.

19 It had not been the habit of the Red Army to stage exercises either at night or in temperatures below −15°. In Finland, the short winter days, with less than six hours of daylight, coincided with the lowest temperatures recorded since 1828.

20 The Moisin rifle was the basic long-arm of the Finnish Army, too. The important difference was really the lubricants used. The Finns used a combination of alcohol and glycerine.

21 Most famously the T-34.

22 The 44th, despite being a motorized division, had with it over 1,200 horses, for the use of both cavalry and transport.

23 Akhmedov, *op. cit.*, p. 113.

24 This is not to assume that the Finns were immune to frostbite and its attendant perils; far from it.

25 Throughout the whole war, the Finns were to take less than 6,000 prisoners, out of a total of 1.2 million Russians involved in battle. Many Red Army soldiers clearly preferred suicide rather than surrender – it had been made clear to them by *politruki* that their families would be at risk in the event that they capitulated. No accurate numbers exist for this; the 'extraordinary occurrences' files covered mutiny, self-injury, drunkenness, cowardice, desertion and insubordination, but not – perhaps sensibly – suicide.

26 Akhmedov, *op. cit.*, p. 120.

27 And presumably shot; there is certainly no record of him from February 1940 onwards.

28 Beria had replaced N. N. Ezhov as head of the NKVD in December 1938. Whereas Ezhov had been an alcoholic bisexual, Beria was merely a heterosexual paedophile. For reasons unassociated with this narrative, Ezhov was executed on 4 February 1940.

29 Akhmedov, *op. cit.*, p. 120.

30 The suspension of dual command by Timoshenko (see Chapter 11) had an *immediate* effect upon the willingness of commanders to state their concerns.

31 van Dyke, *Soviet Invasion of Finland*, p. 88.

32 There has in no case been discovered any surviving prisoner of war who returned to Russia, leading to the supposition that none in fact survived after repatriation in 1940. This is supported by later comments.

33 *News Chronicle*, January 1940.

34 See page 125.

35 *Finnish Meteorology Yearbook, 1940*, vols. I & II.

36 There is no recorded wind chill factor applying here; temperatures are measured statically.

37 By the 80th Air Regiment of the Ninth Army.

38 Until the summer of 1941.

39 Langdon-Davies, *Finland – The First Total War* p. 61.

40 Or, at least, it *looked* like a *coup d'état*; there had been an attempt to kidnap President Svinhufvud, which had failed, utterly.

CHAPTER SEVEN
In Ladoga-Karelia

1 Essentially, these were agricultural machines and, importantly, not armoured. Simply, a moving traffic jam.

2 Mannerheim, *Memoirs*, p. 334.

3 Chew, *The White Death*, p. 36, citing *Honour and Fatherland: The Russo-Finnish War, 1939–40*, by Tuompo and Karikoski (p. 222).

4 In 1935, Mannerheim himself had said derisively (and presciently): 'If a company of Russian soldiers could be dropped suddenly into the middle of one of our prosperous country towns, they would probably be too surprised to fight. They would set about eating instead.' See Forbes, *The Men I Knew*, p. 275.

5 But not for long; Shtern was executed by firing-squad in June 1941 for reasons unassociated with this narrative. He was later 'rehabilitated'.

6 Mannerheim, *op. cit.*, p. 337.

7 The 139th Division lost well over 4,000 dead just on the Ägläjärvi road, without factoring in the fighting on and around the lakes, let alone reconnaissance groups, many of which simply disappeared, never to be found, like the lost legions of Varus.

8 Khadzhen-Umar Dzionovich Mamsurov (1903–1968), then a regimental commander, Ninth Army.

9 Chubaryan & Shukman, *Stalin and the Soviet-Finnish War*, p. 236.

CHAPTER EIGHT
Counter-attacks

1 After the war, Stalin would invent a new, chilling term: artillery 'processing', reflecting the industrial imagery of war, which he clearly found so satisfying.

2 In this sense, the frequencies of the various radios were not harmonized.

3 Chubaryan & Shukman, *Stalin and the Soviet-Finnish War*, p. 259.

4 It was quickly realized that the Finnish anti-tank obstacles were insufficient for the task, being simply not large enough.

5 The full text of Yanov's account can be found at the National Archives in Kew, War Office 208/582. Carl van Dyke (*Soviet Invasion of Finland* p. 100, n. 145) points out that Yanov's abandonment of his tanks could constitute the breaking of his 'soldier's oath', a serious matter under fire. Mannerheim recalled: 'A Russian tank commander who deserted to us [perhaps Yanov] gave as his motive his fear of facing his superiors after his losses.' *Memoirs*, p. 343.

6 Mannerheim, *op.cit.*, p. 344.

7 Several of these letters bear no evidence of a military censor, which is perhaps surprising.

8 Mannerheim, *op.cit.*, p. 344.

9 Mannerheim, *op.cit.*, pp. 344–5.

10 All three journals 23 December 1939.

11 Chew, *The White Death*, p. 69.

12 But when they did, it was outside all Finnish experience.

13 See Goodrich, *Study in Siso*, p. 74.

CHAPTER NINE
Manoeuvres: The Gate of the Year

1 The text of the King's Christmas message was, as was customary, dispatched to the media globally. He was after all not only king; he was the king emperor and the constitutional ruler of the biggest empire the world had ever known: 'King of practically everything' as one commentator had it. The general response to the quotation he had used was quite extraordinary; cables flooded in requesting the authorship of this simple, trite message. It transpired that it had originated in 1908, by the hand of one Minnie Louise Haskins, an expatriate American lecturer at the LSE, by then retired, who became rather famous as a result.

2 *Daily Sketch*.

3 Although Mannerheim himself, it seems, followed the Orthodox Russian faith.

4 Meretskov, *Serving the People*, cited by van Dyke, *Soviet Invasion of Finland* ch. 3.

5 From their actions, we can only assume that this order went out to the Isthmus alone, for those elements of the Red Army who were in a fit state to attack proved themselves quite willing to do so, particularly at Kollaa.

6 And a decorated one.

7 Timoshenko would learn, in 1941, that militarily it was far from that.

8 According to a telegram received from Ambassador Schoenfeld in Washington on 8 January, the Finns acknowledged receiving German and Italian munitions via Sweden up to this date. They assumed it was Göring's doing. Langer & Gleason, *The Challenge to Isolation*, vol. I, p. 340.

9 And the day after Daladier had announced to a cheering Chamber of Deputies that France intended to help the Finns 'in no half hearted manner'.

10 See Horne, *To Lose a Battle*, p. 116.

11 *Ibid.*, p. 118.

12 *The Scum of the Earth*, cited by Horne, *ibid.*, p. 116.

13 *Ironside Diaries*, p. 186.

14 US Chief Counsel, *Nazi Conspiracy and Aggression*, Vol. VI, p. 981.

15 As opposed to a 'useful idiot', although not all would agree.

16 The next British ambassador to Moscow would be Stafford Cripps, but not until July 1940. Accordingly, for the rest of this conflict, neither Britain nor France had diplomatic representation in Moscow.

17 Kollontay had also been an advocate of 'free love' and went ahead to demonstrate *exactly* what she meant by that. The prudish Lenin did *not* approve, although Leon Trotsky might well have done.

18 *Documents on German Foreign Policy*, Series D, Vol. VIII, no. 521, January 10 1940.

19 W. P. & Zelda Coates, *The Soviet-Finnish Campaign*, pp. 137–8. It is astonishing that this book was even published in Britain – but the Soviet Union was in the war by then.

20 *Cripps Diary*, 17 January 1940. See Clarke, *The Cripps Version*, p. 157 and Cooke, *The Life of Stafford Cripps*, pp. 258–9.

21 Clarke, *ibid.*, p. 158.

22 Tanner, *The Winter War*, p. 124.

23 *ibid.*, p. 125.

CHAPTER TEN

A Hare-brained Scheme

1 Ex-CIGS, now commander of the BEF in France.

2 *Cadogan Diaries* (ed. D. Dilks), p. 241: 'H [Halifax] told me Hore-Belisha must be got out of War Office.'

3 *Ironside Diaries*, p. 192.

4 *Ibid.*, p. 193.

5 *Channon Diaries* (ed. R. James), 5 January 1940.

6 Because of Hore-Belisha's Jewish ancestry, he was routinely called by this sobriquet in Whitehall.

7 Although Ironside does not appear to have been involved in the cabal.

8 The *Thomas Walton*, the *Deptford* (both carrying Swedish ore for Britain) and the Greek vessel *Garaufalia*, were all sunk 11–13 December 1939 by U-boats within the territorial waters of Norway.

9 *Soviet Documents on Foreign Policy*, (ed. J. Degras), pp. 416–20.

10 *Documents on German Foreign Policy*, Vol. VIII, Series D, n. to 503. (Emphasis mine).

11 *Documents on German Foreign Policy*, D, VIII, No. 515.

12 W. S. Churchill, *The Second World War*, vol. I, p. 438.

13 *Fall Gelb*, Directives No. 6/7/8, 9 October – 20 November 1939.

14 He would commit suicide shortly afterwards.

15 Not only in the West – '*this was the time to settle the Leningrad problem; it was the time when other countries were busy elsewhere..*' Stalin (after the event) 17 April 1940. Chubaryan & Shukman, *Stalin and the Soviet-Finnish War*, p. 264.

16 See H. R. Trevor-Roper, *Hitler's War Directives*. Also *Halder Diary* (eds. Burdick & Jacobsen), p. 90.

17 Appointed British military attaché in Helsinki.

18 A similar price to the two most expensive single fortifications on the Mannerheim Line, and at twice the price that the British government paid for them. However, familiarization and training was also included.

19 From Harold Macmillan, who was pitiless in his *critique* of Chamberlain's policy.

20 Feiling, *The Life of Neville Chamberlain*, p. 436.

21 The *hakaristi* – hooked cross – motif, the swastika, was originally a family emblem of the von Rosen family, who donated some aircraft decorated with it to the Finns in 1918. It was thus adopted as a Finnish emblem – it is a not uncommon Nordic symbol (as well as an oft-found Hindu one). The Nazis, who adopted it in 1920, obviously preferred the northern association.

22 Interestingly, they were described as 'English Spitfires' by Corps Commander Ptukhin, head of the North Western Front Air Arm, 1940. See Chubaryan & Shukman, *op.cit.*, p.125.

23 Charmley, *Churchill: The End of Glory*, p. 380; Gripenberg, *Finland and the Great Powers*, p. 112; printed record – Churchill archive.

24 Gilbert, *Finest Hour*.

25 Halifax had included with his note a digest of purely *negative* responses, collated by E. H. Carr.

26 *The Goebbels Diaries*, 24 January 1940, p. 102.

27 *Documents on German Foreign Policy*, Series D, vol. VIII, no. 565.

28 Günther would remain in office until 1945, Koht until 1941, i.e. well after the German occupation.

29 See Dalton, *The Fateful Years*, pp. 292–7.

CHAPTER ELEVEN
The Red Army Reforms Itself

1 A serious uprising (almost a third revolution) in February/March 1921 – partly in the wake of the Red Army's failure in Poland, partly as a result of food shortages, and suppressed with great (if costly) efficiency by Tukhachevski. The fate of the Russian sailors who were captured is uncertain, but most were probably put to death.

2 There are several examples of Soviet citizens bravely expressing reluctance to serve in the Red Army given its operations outside Soviet territory.

3 Despite Zhukov's startling success against the Japanese.

4 Schulenburg had been in post since 1934.

5 The Kronstadt rebellion.

6 Propaganda workers, more accurately.

7 But little praise for anyone from the post-Napoleonic era – particularly the Crimean or Great Wars.

8 The linguistic difficulties which dogged certain Red Army units cannot be overstated. The lack of commanders who could speak the language of their own soldiers was marked, and remarked upon after the war. See Chubaryan & Shukman, *Stalin and the Soviet-Finnish War*, p. 93.

9 See van Dyke, *Soviet Invasion of Finland*, ch. 3, n. 99 in which Tërkin is described as a "routine personality" devoid of political, spiritual and intellectual development'. The adventures of Vasia were to last, significantly, until 1945.

10 *Pasha* was at first criticized, later 'suppressed' by the authorities.

11 *Daily Sketch*, 22 December.

12 Owned by the Cadbury family, noted Quakers, who had helped support the dispatch of a 56-strong ambulance unit to Finland, including a family member, Brandon Cadbury.

13 Beaverbrook and Hore-Belisha were close friends; his papers were highly critical over Hore-Belisha's sacking.

14 A habit which continued until the 1970s; this war did Jean Sibelius a great deal of good in terms of reputation; the intermezzo passage of the Karelia Suite still having huge resonance today.

15 And, at the time of writing this (2005), Iraq, not altogether for different reasons.

16 French Foreign Legion base in north Africa.

17 Anglo-French policy during the Spanish Civil War had been one of non-intervention, indeed an 'NI' cap badge had been minted. This would be inverted now, to read 'IN' for 'International'.

18 Gripenberg, *Memoirs* p. 100. The news of this unsurprisingly appeared in the *Daily Express* shortly afterwards.

19 *Hansard*, 6 February 1940.

20 Pritt would 'turn a few bob' with a book, *Must the War Spread?*, which came out shortly after this. Like the Coates' duo's effort (see ch. 4, n. 2) it was one of a series, the previous turgid effort being called *Light on Moscow*. This writer read both as background for the present work and felt in need of a bath afterwards.

21 The Brigades were organized by the Communist parties of Europe and the Soviet Union.

22 He would commit suicide in 1943 – in all ways, then, an Ernest Hemingway figure.

23 Gripenberg, *op. cit.*, p. 102. Emphasis mine.

24 In the context of Red Army casualties, L. Z. Mekhlis is reported to have remarked in December: 'They can't kill them all!' (See Chew, *The White Death* p. 63.)

25 See Solov'ev, *My Nine Lives in the Red Army*, pp. 27–9.

26 van Dyke, *op. cit.*, ch. 3, n. 16.

27 There is some thought that Göring, under his own authority, had instructed that German anti-tank weapons be shipped back to Sweden in order to be supplied to the Finns. As late as 8 January 1940 Finnish officials were admitting to US diplomatists that this was the case, despite vehement denials by Ribbentrop to Molotov in mid-December 1939 that this was *not* the case. It is most likely that Ribbentrop, together with the Führer, was simply ignorant of the facts, or chose to be.

28 Unhappily for the Finns, the large numbers of tanks and armoured vehicles captured at Suomussalmi and elsewhere were, for various reasons, unavailable for use, the main reason being a shortage of trained tank crews as well as the general condition of the vehicles, which were assessed as 'junk'.

29 The demoted Commander Meretskov's Seventh Army headquarters, in front of Summa.

30 It seems likely that these machines were German Focke-Wulf 266 types.

31 It has been estimated that up to 20 per cent of Finnish medium to heavy calibre ordnance failed to explode. This is possibly due to the age of the hardware – some of it was more than seventy years old – as old (if not older) as the Marshal.

32 These latter were anti-tank weapons, but used for their muzzle velocity against blockhouses and bunkers.

CHAPTER TWELVE
Endgame: Red Storm

1 June, 1916. In preparing for the assault on the Isthmus Timoshenko used the same arithmetical formulae regarding the strength of attacking forces (3:1 against defenders) as the Tsarist general had. Mannerheim would have been similarly familiar with them.

2 The purge culture would not, in fact, disappear until Stalin did in 1953.

3 A 10-mile front, much of which was 'real' ground as opposed to frozen water, which had already proved itself unreliable and vulnerable to Finn artillery.

4 See OKH report, 31 December 1939.

5 *Ironside Diaries*, p. 215.

6 Gripenberg, *Memoirs* p. 117 This force would have amounted to at least 50,000 men.

7 Ironside, *op. cit.*, p. 216.

8 After the war, Mannerheim was to voice the opinion (unsupported by any particular evidence) that German advisers must have coordinated the coming Russian attack, as the tactics of the Red Army were now obviously lifted straight from the Wehrmacht drill book, which he had also read. There can be little doubt that Red Army tactics at the point of delivery were most un-Soviet,

demanding as they did a high degree of personal initiative from all, but particularly on the part of junior officers and even NCOs – unheard of previously.

9 One Red Army commander testified after the war that over 12,000 lb of explosive was required to destroy the heavist Finnish bunkers. This is clearly an exaggeration, or the result of poor training.

10 KV1 – Klimenti Voroshilov type 1. This type (and its KV2 successor) would see service until the end of the Second World War; it would cause problems for the Wehrmacht, too; only an 88 mm cannon could deal with it reliably, and then only with some effort. The Finns had none – yet. Until the advent of the Tiger, the KV was invulnerable. Odd, then, that the appearance of these models on the Eastern Front in 1941 was such a shock to the Wehrmacht – they had already seen service in Finland, although the T-34 did not.

11 Of 75 mm calibre, and thus perfect for the task in hand.

12 See Langer & Gleason, *The Challenge to Isolation*, pp. 338–9.

13 *Ibid.*, p. 339.

14 Ironside, *op. cit.*, p. 217. The guns would be sent, in fact, arriving after the end of the war – but only after prolonged haggling.

15 Langer & Gleason, *op. cit.*, p. 14

16 It will not be forgotten that it was only Hitler's declaration of war on the United States at the end of 1941 which prompted American involvement in the Second World War. Policy prior to that was, unarguably, to bleed Britain.

17 J. L. Harper, *American Visions of Europe – Franklin D. Roosevelt, George F. Kennan and Dean G. Acheson*, 1996, cited by Robert Kagan, *Paradise and Power*, p. 70.

18 White wasn't anywhere near it, of course.

19 Interestingly, when the play was filmed, the theatre of war was switched to Hungary in 1956 – Sherwood himself died in 1955, and unavoidably, some of the impact was lost.

20 At this very point. By way of comparison, the Red Army assault on the Isthmus contained within it approximately four times the artillery assets as later deployed by General Montgomery at El Alamein.

21 Arkady Ermakov (1899–1957) served later as deputy commander of the Bryansk Front during *Barbarossa*. Filipp Alabusher (1893–1941), later commander of the 87th Rifle Division, was killed in action in the opening phase of *Barbarossa*.

22 100 grammes per man – a decent slug.

23 Chew, *The White Death*, p. 152.

24 Named for its cost – Lieutenant Poppius was the commander of the other one.

25 The 123rd was even the recipient of a long ode, written by the journalist Tvardovsky (he of *Vasia Tërkin*). It is worthy of William McGonagall (or even Kuusinen) and far too tedious a work with which to trouble the present reader.

26 An interesting contrast is observable between Norwegian public and private attitudes. When the German Naval attaché in Oslo, Schreiber, interviewing the Norwegian Admiral Diesen, demanded to know why he had exhibited such a 'weak attitude' in dealing with the *Cossack*, 'he replied only by shrugging his shoulders'. Koht, true to form, issued a violent protest. *Documents On German Foreign Policy*, Series D, vol. VIII, no. 618.

27 Tukhachevski's assault on Kronstadt in 1921 had been carried out in similar conditions.

28 The Russians had noted that the Finns invariably whitewashed captured equipment, but inexplicably failed to do this themselves.

29 On 6 January, for example, two Finnish Fokker D21 fighters had destroyed all seven of a flight of DB3 bombers – in five minutes.

30 See Jukka L. Mäkelä, *Suomi taisteli: Sotiemme suurlukemisto* (W. Süderstrom, 1977), pp. 146–151. Translated by S. Korhonen (with thanks).

31 Ironside, *op. cit.*, p. 216.

32 Not the least reason being, one imagines, that they felt that the army would be needed – when the Allies arrived. But, as has been noted, 8,000 volunteers did go to Finland.

33 *Cadogan Diary* (ed. D. Dilks), p. 255.

34 Tanner, *The Winter War*, p. 177. Quite what gave Vereker the idea that anyone would *believe* this is unclear.

35 *Chasseur* equivalent to Jäger, or light infantry.

36 Later Field Marshal, the Viscount Alanbrooke.

37 Alanbrooke Diary, 8 February 1940, see Bryant, *The Turn of the Tide*, p. 76.

38 Brooke to Dill, 11 February 1940, cited by Bryant, *The Turn of the Tide*, p. 77.

39 *Documents on German Policy*, Series D, vol. VIII, no. 654.

40 Case Weser Exercise, Directive 10A, 1 March 1940

41 The Marshal did not like Wallenius *at all*; in his *Memoirs* he does not mention him even in passing, which might be quite understandable but rather tends to discount the success which this 'difficult' general had enjoyed in the far north. His crime, in Mannerheim's eyes, was simple lack of grace under pressure.

42 By a circuitous route. Tanner stated in his account that Blücher's communications were, naturally, extensively bugged.

43 *Documents on German Foreign Policy*, *op. cit.*, no. 628.

44 He remained in post until the end of the war.

45 *Documents on German Foreign Policy*, *op. cit.*, no. 650.

46 Hitler fobbed him off with concerns re: Göring's health precluding him from being consulted, never mind that when the *Weserübung* plan broke cover, Göring was fit enough and working hard to entertain the charmless American envoy Sumner Welles at Carinhall.

47 See Leonard Mosley, *The Reich Marshal*, ch. 18, for insights on these and other matters.

48 *Ibid.*, p. 301.

49 Just over a month later, Stalin himself recalled the moment in rather earthier terms: 'Either you, Messrs. Finnish bourgeois, make concessions, or we will impose a government under Kuusinen on you which will disembowel you...'. Chubaryan & Shukman, *Stalin and the Soviet-Finnish War*, p. 266.

50 Molotov: 'Why stop the fighting if one cannot rule out the possibility of having to resume it over a difference?' See van Dyke, *Soviet Invasion of Finland*, p. 175.

51 See n. 14, ch 9, German General Staff Report on Red Army.

52 *Documents on German Foreign Policy, op. cit.,* no. 663.

53 As opposed to c. 750–800 men, i.e. two-thirds losses.

54 Jakobson, *The Diplomacy of the Winter War,* p. 251.

55 Mannerheim, *Memoirs*, p. 387.

56 French Ambassador to the Court of St James.

57 Ironside, *op. cit.*, p. 226.

58 It did, too; less than a year later the poor man had a stroke, collapsing in Mannerheim's arms.

59 Ironside, *op. cit.*, p. 227.

60 Kennedy, *The Business of War,* p. 49.

CHAPTER THIRTEEN
Outcomes

1 Tr. By Joseph Chitty, 1834, p. 445.

2 He was presumably philosophical; the *Suite on Finnish themes* was never listed in his official oeuvre.

3 Gripenberg, *Memoirs*, p. 145. In fact, despite this lapse, Gripenberg was rather kind about Halifax in his memoirs.

4 A. Géraud (Pertinax), *Les Fossoyeurs*, vol. I, p. 197.

5 *Hansard*, 19 March 1940.

6 *Hansard*, 19 March 1940.

7 As indeed had Air Marshal Sir Cyril Newall – using that exact phrase on 11 March.

Select Bibliography

Akhmedov, I., *In and Out of Stalin's G.R.U.* (Arms and Armour Press, 1984)

Allen, S., *Comrades And Citizens* (Left Book Club & Victor Gollancz, 1938)

Amery, L., *My Political Life* (Hutchinson, 1953)

Applebaum, A., *GULAG* (Allen Lane, 2003)

Beckett, F., *Enemy Within: The Rise and Fall of the British Communist Party* (Murray, 1995)

Beloff, M., *The Foreign Policy of the Soviet Union*, vols. I & II (Oxford University Press, 1947)

Bialer, S., ed., *Stalin and His Generals* (Souvenir Press, 1970)

Bonnet, G., *Quai d'Orsay* (Anthony Gibbs & Philips, 1965)

Borenius, T., *Field Marshal Mannerheim* (Hutchinson, 1940)

Bosworth, R., *Mussolini* (Hodder, 2002)

Brome, V., *The International Brigades* (Heinemann, 1965)

Brooke, J., *The Volunteers* (Justin Brooke, 1990)

Bryant, A., *The Turn of the Tide* (Collins, 1956)

Bullock, A., *Hitler & Stalin: Parallel Lives* (HarperCollins, 1991)

Burckhardt, C., *Meine Danziger Mission* (Munich, 1960)

Burdick, C. & Jacobsen, H-A., *The Halder War Diary 1939–1942* (Greenhill Books, 1988)

Butler, J., *Grand Strategy*, vol. II (HMSO, 1957)

Calder, A., *Myth of the Blitz* (Jonathan Cape, 1991)

Carley, M., *1939* (House of Stratus, 2000)

Carton de Wiart, A., *Happy Odyssey* (Jonathan Cape, 1950)

'Cato' (Foot, M., Owen, F. & Howard, P.), *Guilty Men* (Left Book Club & Victor Gollancz, 1940)

Charmley, J., *Churchill: The End of Glory* (Hodder & Stoughton, 1993)

Chew, A., *The White Death* (Michigan State University Press, 1971)

Chubaryan, A. & Shukman, H., *Stalin and the Soviet-Finnish War* (Frank Cass, 2002)

Churchill, W., *The Second World War*, vol. I, *The Gathering Storm* (Cassell, 1948)

Churchill, W., *The Second World War*, vol. II, *Their Finest Hour* (Cassell, 1949)

Citrine, W., *My Finnish Diary* (Penguin, 1940)

Clark, A., *Barbarossa* (Weidenfeld & Nicolson, 1965)

Clark, A., *The Tories* (Weidenfeld & Nicolson, 1999)

Clark, D., *Three Days to Catastrophe* (Hammond & Hammond, 1966)

Clarke, P., *The Cripps Version* (Allen Lane, 2002)

Clausewitz, C., *Vom Kreig* (various publishers, 1834)

Coates, W. P. & Z., *The Soviet-Finnish Campaign* (Eldon Press, 1941)

Colville, J., *The Fringes of Power – Downing Street Diaries* (Hodder & Stoughton, 1985)

Conquest, R., *The Great Terror* (Macmillan, 1968)

Conquest, R., *Stalin: Breaker of Nations* (Viking, 1991)

Cooke, C., *The Life of Richard Stafford Cripps* (Hodder & Stoughton, 1957)

Cox, G., *The Red Army Moves* (Victor Gollancz, 1941)

Crankshaw, E., *Krushchev* (Collins, 1966)

Dahlerus, B., *De Letzte Versuch* (Nymphenburger, Munich, 1948)

Dalton, H., *The Fateful Years* 1931–45 (Muller, 1957)

Degras, J., ed., *Soviet Documents on Foreign Policy*, vol. III (Oxford University Press, 1953)

Dilks, D., ed., *The Diaries of Sir Alexander Cadogan* 1938–1945 (Cassell, 1971)

Djilas, M., *Conversations with Stalin* (Harcourt Brace, 1962)

Drax, R., *Mission to Moscow* (Wareham, 1966)

Earle, E., ed., *Makers of Modern Strategy* (Princeton University Press, 1941)

Elliston, H., *Finland Fights* (Harrap, 1940)

Engle E. & Paananen, L., *The Winter War* (Sidgwick & Jackson, 1973)

Erickson, J., *The Soviet High Command* (Macmillan, 1962)

Erickson, J., *The Road to Stalingrad* (Weidenfeld & Nicolson, 1975)

Erickson, J. & Dilks, D., eds., *Barbarossa: The Axis and the Allies* (Edinburgh University Press, 1994)

Estorick, E., *Stafford Cripps* (Heinemann, 1949)

Feiling, K., *The Life of Neville Chamberlain* (Macmillan, 1946)

Figes, O., *A People's Tragedy* (Jonathan Cape, 1996)

Forbes, R., *These Men I Knew* (The Right Book Club, 1940)

Fraser, D., *And We Shall Shock Them* (Hodder & Stoughton, 1983)

Fuller, J., *The Conduct of War, 1789–1961* (Eyre & Spottiswoode, 1961)

Gamelin, M., *Servir* (Libraire Plon, Paris, 1947)

Garthoff, R., *How Russia Makes War: Soviet Military Doctrine* (Rand Corporation, 1953)

Garthoff, R., *Soviet Military Policy* (Faber, 1966)

Géraud, A., (Pertinax), *Les Fossoyeurs*, vol. I (Maison Française, NY, 1943)

Gilbert, M., *Finest Hour* (Heinemann, 1983)

Glantz, D., *The Siege of Leningrad* (Spellmount, 2002)

Goodrich, A., *A Study in Sisu* (Ballantyne, 1960)

Gorodetsky, G., *Grand Delusion* (Yale University Press, 1999)

Graves, R. & Hodges, A., *The Long Week-End* (Faber & Faber, 1941)

Griffith, S., ed., *Sun Tzu: The Art of War* (Clarendon, 1963)

Gripenberg, G., *Finland and the Great Powers – Memoirs* (University of Nebraska Press, 1965)

Halifax, Earl of, *Fullness of Days* (Collins, 1957)

Hansard, *Parliamentary Debates*, 1939–40 (HMSO, 1939–40)

Hitler, A., *Mein Kampf*, tr. J. Murphy (Hurst & Blackett, 1939)

HMSO, *Documents on German Foreign Policy*, series D (HMSO, 1956)

Holroyd, M., *Bernard Shaw*, vol. III (Random House, 1991)

Horne, A., *To Lose a Battle: France 1940* (Macmillan, 1969)

Hosking, G., *A History of the Soviet Union* (HarperCollins, 1992)

Howard, M., *War And The Liberal Conscience* (Maurice Temple Smith, 1978)

Hull, C., *Memoirs* (Hodder & Stoughton, 1948)

Ironside, E., *Time Unguarded – The Ironside Diaries* (David McKay, 1962)

Ismay, Lord, *The Memoirs of Lord Ismay* (Heinemann, 1960)

Jakobson, M., *The Diplomacy of the Winter War* (Harvard University Press, 1961)

Jakobson, M., *Finland Survived* (Otava, 1964)

James, R., ed., *Chips: The Diaries of Sir Henry Channon* (Weidenfeld & Nicolson, 1967)

Kagan, R., *Paradise & Power* (Alfred Knopf, 2003)

Kennedy, J., *The Business of War* (Hutchinson, 1957)

Kershaw, I., *Hitler 1936–1945: Nemesis* (Allen Lane, 2000)

Koestler, A., *The Scum of the Earth* (Left Book Club and Victor Gollancz, 1941)

Krivosheev, G., *Soviet Casualties and Combat Losses in the Twentieth Century* (Greenhill Books, 1997)

Krosby, H., *Finland, Germany and the Soviet Union, 1940–1941* (University of Wisconsin Press, 1968)

Krushchev, N., *Krushchev Remembers* (André Deutsch, 1971)*

Langdon-Davies, J., *Finland – The First Total War* (Routledge, 1940)

Langer, W. & Gleason, E., *The Challenge to Isolation*, vols. I & II (Harper & Row, 1952)

Leonard, R., *Clausewitz: A Short Guide* (Weidenfeld & Nicolson, 1966)

Lundin, C., *Finland in the Second World War* (Bloomington, 1957)

Luukkanen, E., *Fighter Over Finland* (Macdonald, 1963)

Luukkonen, F. & Viherjuuri, H., *Lotta-Svärd: Kuvateos – Bildwerk* (Otava, 1937)

Macleod, I., *Neville Chamberlain* (Muller, 1961)

Maisky, I., *Memoirs of a Soviet Ambassador: The War 1939–43* (Hutchinson, 1967)

Mann, C. & Jörgensen, C., *Hitler's Arctic War* (Ian Allen, 2002)

Mannerheim, Baron, *The Memoirs of Marshal Mannerheim* (Cassell, 1953)

Meretskov, K., *Serving the People* (Progress, Moscow 1971)

Ministry of Foreign Affairs of Finland, *The Finnish Blue-White Book* (Lippincott, 1940)

Minney, R. J., ed., *The Private Papers of Hore-Belisha* (Collins, 1960)

Mosely, L., *The Reich Marshal* (Weidenfeld & Nicolson, 1974)

Muggeridge, M., ed., *Ciano's Diary: 1939–1943* (Heinemann, 1947)

Muggeridge, M., ed., *Ciano's Diplomatic Papers* (Odhams, 1948)

Namier, L., *Diplomatic Prelude* (Macmillan, 1948)

O'Ballance, E., *The Red Army* (Faber & Faber, 1964)

Pritt, D., *Light on Moscow* (Penguin, 1939)

Pritt, D., *Must the War Spread?* (Penguin, 1940)

Ries, T., *Cold Will: The Defence of Finland* (Brassey, 1988)

Rintala, M., *Three Generations: The Extreme Right Wing in Finnish Politics* (Indiana University Press 1962)

Rintala, M., *Four Finns* (University of California Press, 1969)

Roberts, A., *The Holy Fox* (Weidenfeld & Nicolson, 1991)

Schapiro, L., *The Communist Party of the Soviet Union* (Eyre & Spottiswoode, 1960)

Screen, J., *Mannerheim: The Years of Preparation* (Hurst, 1970)

Screen, J., *Mannerheim: The Finnish Years* (Hurst, 2000)

Sebag-Montefiore, S., *Stalin: The Court of the Red Tsar* (Weidenfeld & Nicolson, 2003)

Serge, V., *Year One of the Russian Revolution*, tr. Peter Sedgwick (Allen Lane, 1972)

*Note that there has been some doubt expressed as to the veracity, even the authorship, of this book.

Sherwood, R., *The White House Papers of Harry Hopkins* (Eyre & Spottiswoode, 1948)

Shirer, W., *Berlin Diary* (Hamish Hamilton, 1941)

Shirer, W., *The Rise and Fall of the Third Reich* (Secker & Warburg, 1961)

Shtemenko, S., *The Soviet General Staff at War* (Progress, Moscow, 1970)

Shukman, H., ed., *Stalin's Generals* (Weidenfeld & Nicolson, 1993)

Solov'ev, M., *My Nine Lives in the Red Army* (David McKay, 1955)

Sontag, R. & Beddie, J., *Nazi-Soviet Relations* (US Department of State, 1948)

Spears, E., *Assignment to Catastrophe* (Heinemann, 1956)

Stewart, G., *Burying Caesar* (Weidenfeld & Nicolson, 1999)

Tanner, V., *The Winter War* (Stanford University Press, 1957)

Taylor, A., *The Origins of the Second World War* (Hamish Hamilton, 1963)

Taylor, F., ed., *The Goebbels Diaries* (Putnam, 1983)

Thompson, L., *1940* (Collins, 1966)

Toland, J., *Hitler* (Doubleday, 1976)

Trevor-Roper, H., *Hitler's War Directives, 1939–1945* (Sidgwick & Jackson, 1964)

Trotter, W., *A Frozen Hell* (Algonquin Books, 1991)

Upton, A., *Finland in Crisis 1940–1941: A Study in Small Power Politics* (Faber, 1964)

Upton, A., *Finland 1939–1940* (Davis-Poynter, 1974)

US Chief Counsel, Nuremburg Trials, ed., *Nazi Conspiracy and Aggression* (1946)

van Dyke, C., *The Soviet Invasion Of Finland, 1939–40* (Frank Cass, 1997)

Volkogonov, D., *Stalin: Triumph and Tragedy* (Weidenfeld & Nicolson, 1991)

von Weizsäcker, Baron E., *Memoirs* (Gollancz, 1951)

Warner, O., *Marshal Mannerheim and the Finns* (Weidenfeld & Nicolson, 1967)

Webb, B., *The Diaries of Beatrice Webb*, vol. IV (Virago & LSE, 1985)

Werner, M., *The Military Strength of the Powers* (Left Book Club, 1939)

Woodward, L., *British Foreign Policy in the Second World War* (HMSO, 1962)

Wuorinen, J., ed., *Finland in World War II: 1939–44* (Ronald Press, NY, 1948)

Index